NASA Monographs in Systems
and Software Engineering

The *NASA Monographs in Systems and Software Engineering* series addresses cutting-edge and groundbreaking research in the fields of systems and software engineering. This includes in-depth descriptions of technologies currently being applied, as well as research areas of likely applicability to future NASA missions. Emphasis is placed on relevance to NASA missions and projects.

Also in this series:

Christopher A. Rouff, Michael Hinchey, James Rash, Walter Truszkowski and Diana Gordon-Spears (Eds)
Agent Technology from a Formal Perspective
1-85233-947-0

K.K. Breitman, M.A. Casanova and
W. Truszkowski

Semantic Web: Concepts, Technologies and Applications

 Springer

Karin Koogan Breitman, MSc, DSc
Marco Antonio Casanova, PhD
Departamento de Informática, Pontifícia Universidade Católica do Rio de Janeiro, Brazil

Walter Truszkowski, MA, BA
NASA Goddard Space Flight Center, USA

Series Editor
Professor Michael Hinchey

British Library Cataloguing in Publication Data
A catalogue record for this book is available from the British Library

Library of Congress Control Number: 2006932966

NASA Monographs in Systems and Software Engineering ISSN 1860-0131
ISBN-10: 1-84628-581-X   e-ISBN: 978-1-84628-710-7
ISBN-13: 978-1-84628-581-3

Printed on acid-free paper

9 8 7 6 5 4 3 2 1

Springer Science+Business Media, LLC
springer.com

Preface

As the volume of Web resources grows exponentially, researchers from industry, government, and academia are now exploring the possibility of creating a Semantic Web in which meaning is made explicit, allowing machines to process and integrate Web resources intelligently. How will this Web of the future be effectively built? No one really knows. Although guesses vary from author to author, some themes are recurrent, most of which are covered in this book. In general, emerging technologies will allow semantics to be added to existing Web resources, so as to make the Semantic Web vision come true.

This book provides a succinct account of this new Web, its principles, concepts, and related tools. Its main contribution lies in the ability to demonstrate how Semantic Web technologies may be integrated and realized in several application domains.

Organization of the Book

The text is divided into four parts. Part I begins with an educated forecast for the future of the current Web. This sets the foundation for the rest of the book. Chapter 1 provides a well-paced introduction to the Semantic Web, from motivations to requirements and guidelines on how to realize this concept.

Part II introduces the fundamental building blocks one should master to grasp the full meaning of the Semantic Web. Chapter 2 summarizes the various uses of the term ontology in computer science. Chapter 3 covers knowledge representation in description logic and provides the background for a better understanding of ontology description languages and tools. Chapters 4 and 5 introduce the Resource Description Framework (RDF), the RDF Vocabulary Description Language 1.0:

RDF Schema, and the Web Ontology Language (OWL), the knowledge representation languages proposed as standards for the Semantic Web. Chapter 4 also contains a very brief introduction to some essential XML concepts. Chapter 6 summarizes four rule languages, Datalog, the Rule Markup Language (RuleML), the Semantic Web Rule Language (SWRL) and TRIPLE, designed to manipulate knowledge bases. Chapter 7 provides a brief description of Web services and introduces OWL-S, a service upper ontology for Web services.

Part III focuses on emerging technologies that provide the necessary application development infrastructure and guidelines to develop Semantic Web applications. Chapter 8 surveys several ontology development methods, addressing their background and applicability. Chapter 9 discusses metadata standards, upper ontologies, and ontology libraries that are relevant to the indexing of resources in the Semantic Web, including the Dublin Core, the Warwick Framework, the Suggested Upper Merged Ontology (SUMO), the Knowledge Representation (KR) ontology, CYC, and WordNet. Chapter 10 covers a small selection of Semantic Web tools, with no intention of producing a complete survey.

Part IV illustrates how Semantic Web technologies, discussed throughout the book, can be consistently applied to four distinct application domains. Chapter 11 discusses software agents in the context of information technology systems and the role that ontologies play in their construction. Chapter 12 exemplifies the use of Semantic Web technologies in computing applications called semantic desktops, which enhance personal information management, software application usage, and collaboration. Chapter 13 reviews standardization efforts that facilitate the development of applications devoted to the cataloguing and dissemination of data about cultural collections. It also describes an application that combines a metadata schema with controlled vocabularies to create semantic annotations for still images of works of art. This profitable combination—metadata schemas, controlled vocabularies, and standardization efforts—is repeated in the next chapter in the context of geospatial applications, setting a pattern for other application areas. Chapter 14 then overviews the technologies that facilitate the development of the Geospatial Semantic Web, emphasizing the role of standard proposals. Each technology is first discussed from a broad perspective and then illustrated with implemented applications.

Possible Uses for the Book

This book is intended as a reference text on the Semantic Web for software engineers, database and information technology students, academics, and practitioners. It differs from other books on the topic because, rather than presenting the Semantic Web as a quilt of disconnected topics and examples, it provides a coherent body of concepts and technologies. The book reflects the authors' experience in research, graduate and undergraduate teaching, corporate training, and industry and government projects using Semantic Web technologies.

The text may be used as the main reference for an upper-level undergraduate course or an entry-level graduate course. At the graduate level, the text may be covered at a faster pace and complemented with additional material touching, for example, on description logic, ontology tools, or different application areas, as suggested at the end of each chapter. The second format was tested in several one-semester offerings at the Department of Informatics of the Pontifical Catholic University of Rio de Janeiro, during 2003–2006. Portions of the text were also the subject of conference tutorials and short courses given by the authors.

Acknowledgments

The authors wish to thank Beverley Ford, Helen Desmond, Lesley Poliner, and Frank Ganz, from Springer, for their support throughout the preparation of the manuscript. The authors wish to extend their thanks to Michael G. Hinchey, editor of the *NASA Monograph on Software*, who gave them the opportunity to include this text in the series. Finally, the authors wish to thank Alice A. Casanova for her support in producing the final manuscript.

Karin K. Breitman
Marco A. Casanova
Walter Truszkowski

September 2006

Contents

Part II — Concepts

Chapter 2 — Ontology in Computer Science

Chapter 3 — Knowledge Representation in Description Logic

Chapter 4 — RDF and RDF Schema

Chapter 5 — OWL

Chapter 6 — Rule Languages

Chapter 7 — Semantic Web Services

Part III — Technologies

Chapter 8 — Methods for Ontology Development

Chapter 9 — Ontology Sources

Chapter 10 — Semantic Web Software Tools

Part IV — Applications

Chapter 11 — Software Agents

Chapter 12 — Semantic Desktop

Chapter 13 — Ontology Applications in Art

Chapter 14 — Geospatial Semantic Web

Part I — Introduction

1

The Future of the Internet

1.1 Introduction

In the beginning of the Internet days, software programmers developed all Web pages. Today, the Web provides perhaps the simplest way to share information, and literally everyone writes Web pages, with the help of authoring tools, and a large number of organizations disseminate data coded in Web pages. The *Hypertext Markup Language* (HTML) is typically the language used to code information about renderization (font size, color, position on screen, etc.) and hyperlinks to other Web pages or resources on the Web (multimedia files, text, e-mail addresses, etc.).

The net result is that the Web keeps growing at an astounding pace, now having over eight billion Web pages. However, most Web pages are still designed for human consumption and cannot be processed by machines. Computers are used only to display the information, that is, to decode the color schema, headers, and links encoded in Web pages.

Furthermore, Web search engines, the most popular tools to help retrieve Web pages, do not offer support to interpret the results. For that, human intervention is still required. This situation is progressively getting worse as the size of search results is becoming too large. Most users only browse through the top results, discarding the remaining ones. Some search engines are resorting to artifice to help control the situation, such as indexing the search result, or limiting the search space to a relevant subset of the Web (such as in Google Scholar).

The conclusion is that the size of search results is often just too big for humans to interpret, and finding relevant information on the Web is not as easy as we would desire.

1.2 The Syntactic Web

Today's Web may be defined as the *Syntactic Web*, where information presentation is carried out by computers, and the interpretation and identification of relevant information is delegated to human beings. Of course, the interpretation process is very demanding and requires great effort to evaluate, classify, and select relevant information. Because the volume of available digital data is growing at an exponential rate, it is becoming virtually impossible for human beings to manage the complexity and volume of the available information. This phenomenon, often referred to as *information overload*, poses a serious threat to the very usefulness of today's Web. The question is: Why can't computers do this job for us?

One of the reasons resides in the fact that Web pages do not contain information about themselves, that is, about their contents and the subjects to which they refer. We can make an analogy with a library where books, instead of being organized by subject, are randomly displayed. Every time we wanted to borrow a book, we would have to search for it based on title and related words. Imagine that we wanted to learn about the TCP/IP protocol. We would have to look for a book about networks. If we only used "network" as a keyword, we would retrieve computer science books, as well as books about telephone and electrical networks. We would then be responsible for filtering and selecting those books that are of genuine interest. This is precisely the situation we are dealing with in the Syntactic Web of today.

Web search engines do help identify relevant Web pages, but they suffer from the following limitations.

- Search results might contain a large number of entries, but they might have low recall precision. For example, a search for Web pages where "TCP/IP" and "protocol" occur might return all relevant Web pages, but the result would be of very little use if the user had to sift through 39,857 Web pages of little interest.

- Search results are sensitive to the vocabulary used. Indeed, users frequently formulate their search in a vocabulary different from that which the relevant Web pages adopt. In the TCP/IP example, the relevant Web pages might use "standard", instead of "protocol"; hence, these Web pages would not be the best match for a search using the keywords "TCP/IP" and "protocol".

- Search results appear as a list of references to individual Web pages. However, it is often the case that, among the Web pages listed in the search result, there are many entries that belong to the same Web site. Conversely, if the relevant information is scattered in more than one entry, it is difficult to determine the complete set of relevant entries.

The conclusion is that the Web has evolved as a medium for information exchange among people, rather than machines. As a consequence, the semantic content, that is, the meaning of the information in a Web page, is coded in a way that is accessible to human beings alone. Figures 1.1 and 1.2 illustrate the difference between how humans and computers perceive a Web page, dramatizing why we urgently need to add more semantics to the Web pages so they can be processed by machines as well as humans.

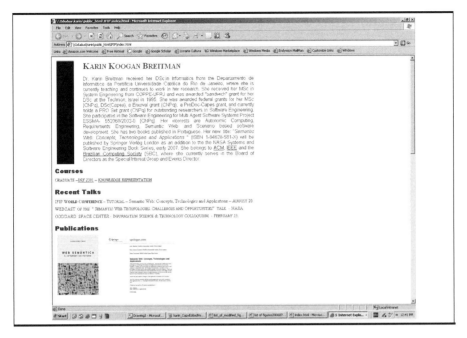

Fig. 1.1 How humans see a Web page.

Fig. 1.2 How computers see the same Web page.

1.3 The Semantic Web

In 2001, Berners-Lee, Hendler, and Lassila published a revolutionary article in the magazine *Scientific American*, entitled "The Semantic Web: A New Form of Web Content That Is Meaningful to Computers Will Unleash a Revolution of New Possibilities" (Berners-Lee et al. 2001). In this article, the authors describe future scenarios in which the Semantic Web will have a fundamental role in the day-to-day life of individuals.

In one of the scenarios, Lucy needs to schedule a series of medical consultations for her mother. A series of restrictions applies to this scenario: Lucy's tight schedule, geographical location constraints, doctor's qualifications, and adherence to their Social Security plan. To help Lucy find a solution, there is a software agent, capable of negotiating among different parties: the doctor, Lucy's agenda and medical services directory, among others. The point is that, although each party codes its information in a different way, because of a semantic layer, they are able to interact and exchange data in a meaningful way. The enabling technology that will bring this scenario forward is what the authors called the Semantic Web.

The authors emphasized the important point that most of the actions described in the scenarios can be achieved in the Syntactic Web of today, but not without considerable effort and many comes-and-goes between different Web sites. The promise of the Semantic Web is that it will unburden users from cumbersome and time-consuming tasks.

1.4 How the Semantic Web Will Work

In order to organize Web content, artificial intelligence researchers proposed a series of conceptual models. The central idea is to categorize information in a standard way, facilitating its access. This idea is similar to the solution used to classify living beings. Biologists use a well-defined taxonomy, the Linnaean taxonomy, adopted and shared by most of the scientific community worldwide. Likewise, computer scientists are looking for a similar model to help structure Web content.

On the other hand, it is believed that the huge success of the Web is due to the freedom it provides. In the same environment, we can find very sophisticated Web sites, designed by specialists, and personal Web pages, created by individuals with little or no computer expertise. There is no censorship to the quality of the information in a Web page either; it virtually depends on the Web page owner's discretion. In the Web, scholarly papers cohabit peacefully with vendors' Web sites and personal blogs. In this scenario, anarchical at best, it is very hard to imagine that a single organization model could prevail.

Similarly to the Syntactical Web, the Semantic Web should be as decentralized as possible, asserts Berners-Lee (Berners-Lee et al. 2001). However, the fact that there should be no central control requires many compromises, the most important being to give up the consistency ideal. Hendler, from the University of Maryland and one of the founding fathers of the Semantic Web, believes that, in the future, instead of a single information organization model, we will have a series of parallel

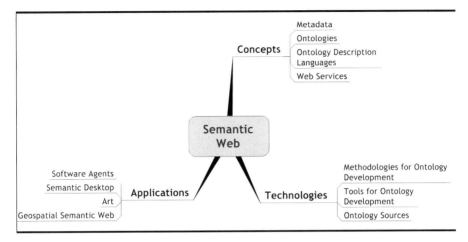

Fig. 1.3 Themes related to the Semantic Web.

models (Hendler 2001). Hendler's prediction is that every business, enterprise, university, and organization on the Web of the future will have its own organizational model or ontology.

How will this "Web of the Future" be effectively built, no one really knows. Although guesses vary from author to author, some themes are recurrent in most discussions. We illustrate the most important ones in Fig. 1.3 and discuss them separately in the remainder of this section.

Metadata

Metadata are data about data. They serve to index Web pages and Web sites in the Semantic Web, allowing other computers to acknowledge what the Web page is about.

Knowledge organization dates back from antiquity. The Greek philosopher Aristotle provided the first known solution with his category system. He proposed that all knowledge should be structured in categories, organized under supertypes (genus) and subtypes (species). In Table 1.1, we illustrate the categories proposed by Aristotle.

Traditional use of metadata was often limited to a relatively few participating institutions, such as libraries and museums. The use of metadata was mostly restricted to the cataloguing of specific collections, such as works of art, which typically consisted of a limited, thus enumerable, number of physical objects. The use of metadata in the context of the Semantic Web is somewhat similar, except for the fact that the number of institutions and the number of objects—Web pages—are orders of magnitude larger, and here lies the problem. Indeed, in the Semantic Web, we want to catalogue an enormous number of resources, mostly virtual, distributed all over the world, coded in different languages, by different groups.

Table 1.1 Categories with examples.

Category	Example
Substance	Cat.
Quality	The cat is black.
Quantity	The cat is one foot long.
Relationship	The cat is half the size of a cocker spaniel.
Where	The cat is at home.
When	The cat came back last night.
Position	The cat is sitting.
Possession	The cat has a toy.
Action	The cat is jumping.
Emotion	The cat likes milk.

In Chapter 9, we discuss the use of metadata and introduce the most relevant metadata schemes used in the context of the Semantic Web.

Ontologies

The word ontology comes from the Greek *ontos* (being) + *logos* (word). It was introduced in philosophy in the nineteenth century by German philosophers to distinguish the study of being as such from the study of various kinds of beings in the natural sciences. As a philosophical discipline:

The subject of Ontology is the study of the categories of things that exist or may exist in some domain. The product of such a study, called an ontology, is a catalogue of the types of things that are assumed to exist in a domain of interest D from the perspective of a person who uses a language L for the purpose of talking about D. The types in the ontology represent the predicates, word senses, or concept and relation types of the language L when used to discuss topics in the domain D.

(Sowa 1997)

In computer science, ontologies were adopted in artificial intelligence to facilitate knowledge sharing and reuse (Fensel 2001; Davies et al. 2003). Today, their use is becoming widespread in areas such as intelligent information integration, cooperative information systems, agent-based software engineering and electronic commerce. Ontology is defined in Guarino (1998) as "an artifact, constituted by a specific vocabulary used to describe a certain reality, plus a set of explicit assumptions regarding the intended meaning of the vocabulary." Ontologies are conceptual models that capture and make explicit the vocabulary used in semantic applications, thereby guaranteeing communication free of ambiguities. They will be the *lingua franca* of the Semantic Web.

In Chapter 2, we discuss ontologies, their origins, formalisms, types, and basic elements and, in Chapter 9, we present upper-level and domain ontologies, and list ontology libraries.

Formal Systems

Formal systems provide the ability to deduce new sentences from existing sentences using specific inference rules. This ability, referred to as logical inference, is an essential component of a Semantic Web ontology formalism.

To ensure effective information sharing among software agents, ontologies will need to be expressive enough to establish a common terminology that guarantees consistent interpretation. Because first-order logic is known to be intractable, the Semantic Web community has been exploring the possibilities of adopting description logic as the paradigm formal system. Briefly, description logic models the application domain by defining the relevant concepts of the domain and then using these concepts to specify properties of objects and individuals occurring in the domain.

In Chapter 3, we provide a concise introduction to description logic.

Ontology Description Languages

Ontology description languages are specifically designed to define ontologies. They recently received considerable attention, boosted by the emergence of the Semantic Web. This new breed of ontology description languages is sometimes called lightweight ontology languages, Web-based ontology languages, or markup ontology languages.

The Resource Description Framework (RDF) is a general-purpose language for representing information about resources in the Web and, to some extent, a lightweight ontology language. The lack of expressiveness of RDF was partly eased with the introduction of the RDF Vocabulary Description Language 1.0: RDF Schema (RDF Schema or RDF-S), which offers primitives to model hierarchies of classes and properties. The Ontology Inference Layer (Oil) is the result of the On-To-Knowledge Project, and has a formal semantics based on description logic. At about the same time Oil was developed, the Defense Advanced Research Projects Agency (DARPA) sponsored the DARPA Agent Markup Language (DAML) Program. These two languages were amalgamated into a single language, DAML+Oil. A reformatted version of DAML+Oil served as a starting point for the Web Ontology Language (OWL).

In Chapters 4, 5, and 6, we review RDF, OWL, and rule languages recently proposed for the Semantic Web.

Web Services

In the Semantic Web vision, the services provided by the Web of the future will be greatly extended and improved, if semantics is added to the present Web resources. Computers will be able to make doctor appointments, synchronized with our agenda, find new suppliers for products we consume, and make traveling arrangements, among many other tasks.

In Chapter 7, we discuss the possibilities of semantic Web services, including OWL-S, an upper ontology to describe services.

Methodologies and Tools for Ontology Development

According to Jim Hendler, in the near future, most Web sites of interest will sport their own ontology (Hendler 2001). Therefore, the Web will be, quoting Hendler, a composition of a "great number of small ontological components consisting largely of pointers to each other."

Tracing a parallel to the history of the Web itself, Hendler assumes that ontology creation will be conducted in the same, nearly anarchic and decentralized fashion as the more than eight billion Web pages have been created. The result will be a great variety of lightweight ontologies, created and maintained by independent parties.

His predictions seem to be true, as the number of tools for ontology edition, visualization, and verification grows. The best examples are the Protégé and OilEd tools, which sprung from large cooperation projects, involving many universities and different countries. With the increasing number of available books and online tutorials, crafting an ontology today is possibly no harder than creating a Web page was ten years ago. Our experience with ontologies has demonstrated that ontology development is not particularly challenging, compared to building other conceptual models used in our software engineering practice.

Evidently, the quality of the resulting ontology depends on the ability of the person engaged in the modeling, which is also true for most conceptual models. Indeed, the number of "lightweight" ontologies, that is, developed by independent groups and organizations rather than by knowledge engineers, is rapidly growing as can be verified by visiting some of the public ontology repositories, such as the DAML repository (URL: http://www.daml.org).

In Chapter 8, we discuss ontology development methodologies and, in Chapter 10, we put forward a discussion on what ontology development tools are presently available. With the help of examples, we discuss and explore the necessary building blocks, so that readers will be able to create their own Semantic Web ontologies.

Applications of Semantic Web Technologies

Applications for the concepts and technologies discussed in this book are by no means limited to indexing Web pages. Other areas provide excellent challenges and opportunities for such technologies, as discussed in the last part of the book.

For example, consider software agents, defined as autonomous software applications that act for the benefit of their users. According to Antoniou and Harmelen (2004), a personal agent in the Semantic Web will be responsible for understanding the desired tasks and user preferences, searching for information on available resources, communicating with other software agents, and comparing information so as to provide adequate answers to its users. Of course software agents will not be a substitute for people, who will ultimately be responsible for making the important decisions. To accomplish their tasks, software agents will make heavy use of metadata and ontologies in general.

Semantic desktop applications provide a second example from the area of software engineering. Such applications use ontologies to integrate desktop applications and the Web, facilitating personal information management, information distribution, and collaboration on the Web, beyond the mere sending of e-mails.

As a third example, now from a different area, we point out that cataloguing our cultural heritage has been a major activity of museums and other cultural institutions throughout the world. Today, almost all major museums make their collections available over the Web, often with remarkable quality, such as the Hermitage Museum Web site. In parallel, many organizations have been working toward the development of metadata standards and controlled thesauri for describing cultural objects that facilitate their dissemination over the Web. Such efforts therefore contribute to and benefit from Semantic Web technologies.

A similar phenomenon occurs in the geospatial application area. We observe that the large volume of geospatial data available on the Web opens up unprecedented opportunities for data access and data interchange, facilitating the design of new geospatial applications and the redesign of traditional ones. A convenient way to provide access to geospatial data over the Web is to implement Web services that encapsulate the data sources and that adopt Semantic Web technologies. This evolution includes the development and encoding of formal geospatial ontologies, which leverage existing standards. The result is called the Geospatial Semantic Web.

We discuss software agents and semantic desktop applications in Chapters 11 and 12, respectively. In Chapter 13, we address standardization efforts that combine metadata and controlled vocabularies to describe works of art. Finally, in Chapter 14, we overview technologies that facilitate the development of the Geospatial Semantic Web.

1.5 What the Semantic Web Is Not

The Semantic Web Is Not Artificial Intelligence

The concept of machine-processable documents does not imply some sort of magic artificial intelligence (AI) that makes computers understand what humans mean. The concept means that computers will have enough semantics to allow them to solve well-defined problems through the sequential processing of operations. Instead of having computers that "understand" people's language, we argue in favor of going the extra mile to make representations that are passive to automatic processing (that is, ontologies as opposed to free text files).

It is true that most techniques that are currently used in the Semantic Web did come from research in AI. Given a history of unsuccessful AI projects, it is reasonable to suppose that the Semantic Web may be fated for the same destiny. According to Antoniou and Harmelen (2004), this supposition is completely unfounded. The realization of the Semantic Web potential does not depend on some sort of computational intelligence, as promised by some AI researchers (and most science fiction writers) some thirty years ago.

In the specific case of the Semantic Web, partial solutions are acceptable. It may be the case that a software agent does not come even close to conclusions a human being may be capable of, but still this software agent may contribute to building a better Web than that which we have today. Antoniou and Harmelen (2004) summarize this concept as follows: "If the ultimate goal of AI is to build an intelligent agent exhibiting human-level intelligence (and higher), the goal of the Semantic Web is to assist human users in their day to day online activities."

The Semantic Web Is Not a Separate Web

The Semantic Web is not a separate Web, but rather an extension of the current Syntactic Web. In this new Web, information will have well-defined meaning as a result of the use of semantic markup languages. Such languages, essentially ontology description languages, will be added to existing Web pages, in an architecture called *The Semantic Web Wedding Cake Architecture* by Berners-Lee et al. (2001).

In Chapter 2, we explain this architecture in more detail.

The Semantic Web Will Not Demand the Use of Complex Expressions

Although the Semantic Web language standard, OWL, supports very sophisticated constructs, it will not be mandatory that every Semantic Web application shows this level of complexity. It is believed by the World Wide Web Consortium (W3C) that, for most Semantic Web Applications, the lighter species of OWL will be sufficient. Most applications that generate RDF markup will, in practice, be limited to simplified expressions, such as access control, privacy settings, and search criteria.

The Semantic Web Is Not a Rerun of a Failed Experiment

Another common question is the relationship between the Semantic Web and knowledge representation systems. Hasn't it all been tried before with the KIF (Knowledge Interchange Format) and CYC projects? The answer is not very direct as the goals of the two initiatives are different.

The goal of the knowledge representation community is to create canonical representations, that is, unique models that are to be used as reference, standards with which applications must comply. That is the case with large projects, such as CYC and SUMO, discussed in Chapter 9. The Semantic Web, on the other hand, is seeking the integration of different models. Such models, known as domain ontologies and predicted to proliferate in the near future, will be developed and maintained by independent parties, according to Hendler (2001). Of course, the experience gained in the construction of large knowledge representations, such as CYC, will be taken into consideration in the path to the Semantic Web (Hendler 2001).

1.6 What Will Be the Side Effects of the Semantic Web

We centered the discussion so far on the potential benefits of the Semantic Web, where computers will be able to understand the information available on the Web and take over tasks that users have been doing manually. Evidently, the goal of the Semantic Web is to create a Web that is more adequate for the users' needs. Emerging technologies will allow semantics to be added to existing Web pages and applications so as to make the Semantic Web vision come true.

Perhaps the most pervading benefit of the Semantic Web might come as a collateral effect of creating truly global knowledge representations. To this day, every area of human endeavor has been using proprietary conceptual models that are believed to best represent the specific knowledge permeating the area. We have, for example, architectural plants, circuit designs, cartographic maps, artistic casts, object-oriented models, economy planning spreadsheets, and a myriad of other specific models. Specific conceptual models facilitate the coordination and communication among specialized communities. However, they make communication across different communities (or cultures) difficult. Even in the same field, we may find communities that use completely different conceptual models. This argues in favor of the adoption of ontologies, in the computer science sense.

The coordination of different communities (or subcultures), according to Berners-Lee, is "painfully slow and requires a lot of communication." Of course, the use of a common language, a *lingua franca*, is essential to the process. Perhaps, in the context of the Semantic Web, such a language will emerge (Berners-Lee 2001).

Recommended Reading

The primary reference on the Semantic Web is the Tim Berners-Lee, Ora Lassila, and James Hendler *Scientific American* paper. A visit to W3C Semantic Web, CO-ODE and OnToKnowledge Web sites is also recommended for an overview on the subject. We also recommend Vannevar Bush classic 1945 article, "As We May Think."

References

Antoniou, G.; Harmelen, F.V (2004) *A Semantic Web Primer.* MIT Press, Cambridge, Massachusetts, USA.

Berners-Lee, T.; Lassila, O.; Hendler, J. (2001) The Semantic Web: A new form of Web content that is meaningful to computers will unleash a revolution of new possibilities. *Scientific American*, 284(5), pp. 34–43. Available at:
http://www.scientificamerican.com/2001/0501issue/0501berners-lee.html.

Bush, V. (1945) As we may think. *Atlantic Monthly*, Vol. 176, No. 1, pp. 101–108.

Davies, J.; Fensel, D.; Harmelen, F.V. (Eds) (2003) *Towards the Semantic Web: Ontology Driven Knowledge Management.* John Wiley & Sons, New York.

Fensel, D. (2001) Ontologies: A Silver Bullet for Knowledge Management and Electronic Commerce. Springer, New York, USA.

Guarino, N. (1998) Formal ontology and information systems. In: *Proceedings of the First International Conference on Formal Ontologies in Information Systems, FOIS'98*, Trento, Italy, pp. 3–15.

Gurarino, N.; Welty, C. (2002) Evaluating ontological decisions with ontoclean– *Communications of the ACM*, Vol. 45, No. 2, February 2002, pp.61–65.

Hendler, J. (2001) Agents and the Semantic Web. *IEEE Intelligent Systems*, March/April 2001, pp. 30–37.

Sowa, J.F. (1997) Principles of Ontology. Available at: http://www-ksl.stanford.edu/onto-std/mailarchive/0136.html.

Sowa, J.F. (1999) Knowledge Representation: Logical, Philosophical and Computational Foundations. Brooks/Cole, Pacific Grove, CA, USA.

Web sites

W3C Semantic Web: http://www.w3.org/2001/sw/
CO-ODE: http://www.co-ode.org/
OnToKnowledge Project: www.ontoknowledge.org/

Part II — Concepts

2

Ontology in Computer Science

2.1 Defining the Term Ontology

The word ontology comes from the Greek *ontos* (being) + *logos* (word). The Merriam Webster online dictionary defines the term ontology as:

1. *A branch of metaphysics concerned with the nature and relations of being.*
2. *A particular theory about the nature of being or the kinds of existents.*

The term ontology was introduced in philosophy, in the nineteenth century, by the German philosopher Rudolf Gockel, in his *Lexicon Philosophicum*, to distinguish the study of "being" from the study of various kinds of beings in the natural sciences. As a philosophical discipline, ontology building is concerned with providing category systems that account for a certain vision of the world.

The first known category system was proposed by Aristotle. In his system, a category is used to classify anything that can be said about anything. In the third century BC, Porphyry, a Greek philosopher, commented on Aristotle's structure and organized the proposed categories in a tree diagram. This structure, known as the Tree of Porphyry, is illustrated in Fig. 2.1.

The definition of ontology most frequently quoted in the Semantic Web literature is Gruber's: "An ontology is a formal, explicit specification of a shared conceptualization" (Gruber 1993). Here, conceptualization stands for an abstract model; *explicit* means that the elements must be clearly defined; and *formal* indicates that the specification should be machine processable. Going further, in Gruber's view, an ontology is the representation of the knowledge of a domain, where a set of objects and their relationships is described by a vocabulary.

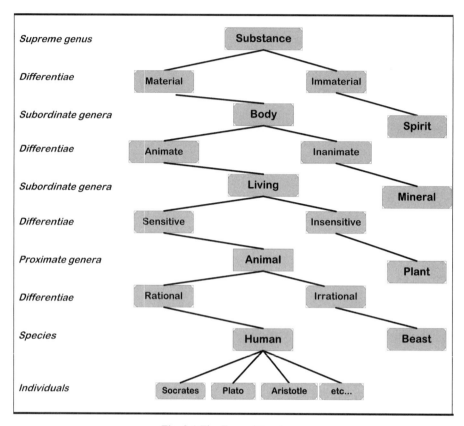

Fig. 2.1 The Tree of Porphyry.

According to Sowa (2004), ontology is "the study of categories of things that exist or may exist in some domain. The product of such study, called an ontology, is a catalogue of types of things that are assumed to exist in a domain of interest **D** from the perspective of a person who uses a language **L** for the purpose of talking about **D**."

There is, however, no universal definition for ontology. One of the reasons is the large spectrum of possible uses for ontologies. Gruninger and Lee (2002) relate, among others, using ontologies for communication between humans and implemented computational systems, for computational inference, and for the reuse and organization of knowledge.

Guarino el al. (1994) collected and published a list of definitions for the term ontology that occur in the literature:

1. Ontology is a philosophy discipline.
2. Ontology is an informal conceptualization of a system.
3. Ontology is a formal semantic description.
4. Ontology is a specification of a conceptualization.

5. Ontology is the representation of a conceptual system using some logic theory.
6. Ontology is a vocabulary used by some logic theory.
7. Ontology represents the specification metalevel of some logic theory.

Ontologies have been used in different areas of computer science, such as artificial intelligence, knowledge representation, natural language processing, Semantic Web, and software engineering, among others. Therefore, it is only reasonable to suppose that there might be some divergence among its multiple definitions. Uschold and Jasper (1999) indicate that, although an ontology may assume different formats, it typically includes a vocabulary of terms, a specification of their meaning, and an indication of how the terms are interrelated.

A more succinct definition comes from the W3C consortium: "Ontology is a term borrowed from philosophy that refers to the science of describing the kinds of entities in the world and how they are related" (McGuinness and Harmelen 2004). This organization also suggests that ontologies should provide descriptions for the following elements.

- Classes (or "Things") in the various domains of interest
- Relationships among those "Things"
- Properties (or attributes) that "Things" should possess

Maedche (2002) proposed that an ontology should be described by a five-tuple $O = \{C, R, CH, rel, OA\}$, where:

- C and R are two disjoint sets, called the set of *concepts* and the set of *relations*, respectively
- $CH \subseteq C \times C$ is a *concept hierarchy* or *taxonomy*, where $CH(C_1,C_2)$ indicates that C_1 is a *subconcept* of C_2
- $rel: R \rightarrow C \times C$ is a function that relates the concepts nontaxonomically
- OA is a set of *ontology axioms*, expressed in an appropriate logical language

According to the author, most existing ontology representation languages are consistent with this definition, including RDF, RDF Schema, and OWL, discussed in Chapters 4 and 5.

Independently of the definition adopted, it is important to understand that ontologies are being used to describe a great variety of models. The spectrum goes from simple taxonomies, such as that of the Open Directory Project (ODP 2006), to very sophisticated models, written in variants of first-order logic.

In the next section, we discuss different classification schemas proposed to categorize ontologies.

2.2 Differences Among Taxonomies, Thesauri, and Ontologies

2.2.1 Taxonomies Versus Ontologies

This and the next sections discuss the distinction between the concepts of taxonomy, thesaurus and ontology. The Merriam Webster dictionary defines the term taxonomy as:

1. *The study of the general principles of scientific classification: SYSTEMATICS.*
2. *CLASSIFICATION; especially: orderly classification of plants and animals according to their presumed natural relationships.*

Daconta et al. (2003) define a taxonomy artifact in the context of information technology as: "The classification of information entities in the form of a hierarchy, according to the presumed relationships of the real-world entities that they represent."

A taxonomy classifies terms hierarchically, using the father-son (generalization, is-a, or type-of) relationship. Indeed, taxonomies allow only the father-son relationship, ruling out other relationships, such as part-of, cause-effect, association, and localization. Furthermore, taxonomies do not permit defining attributes for terms. Hence, one must resort to ontologies if any of these features are required.

One of the classical examples is the classification of the human species in the Linnaean living being taxonomy, illustrated in Fig. 2.2. Note that all terms present in the taxonomy are related by the generalization relationship, that is, Mammalia is a type of Vertebrata, who in turn is a type of Chordata, who in turn is a type of Animalia. The Linnaean taxonomy would be classified as an informal is-a hierarchy, in the categorization discussed in Section 2.3.1.

Kingdom: Animalia
Filo: Chordata
Subfilo: Vertebrata
Class: Mammalia
Subclass: Theria
Order: Primata
Suborder: Anthropoidea
Family: Hominidae
Genera: Homo
Species: Sapiens

Fig. 2.2 Linnaean taxonomy of the living beings — human classification.

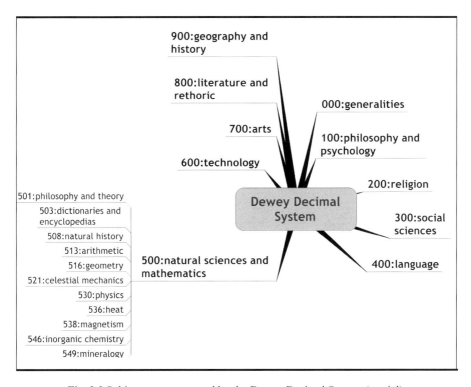

Fig. 2.3 Subject taxonomy used by the Dewey Decimal System (partial).

Another well-known example of a taxonomy is the Dewey Decimal System of subject classification, largely used by libraries to catalogue their collections. We illustrate some of the natural sciences and mathematics categories of the Dewey Decimal System in Fig. 2.3.

A third example of a taxonomy is a directory structure in a personal computer. As discussed before, in a taxonomy, items are arranged according to a generalization-specialization relationship. In the case of directories, this relationship is expressed by the "directory/subdirectory" pair. The semantics associated with this relationship is very weak, in the sense that we can store in a directory any information item we judge to be a subclassification of the directory item. The classification depends on the user's discretion and common sense to decide the level of formality that should be imposed on the items to be classified. In the example illustrated in Fig. 2.4, we have a directory named Ontology that has a subdirectory Languages (highlighted), which in turn has the following subdirectories: RDF, Oil, DAML, OWL, Protege_3_1, and OilEd. Strictly speaking, the last two subdirectories, Protege_3_1 and OilEd, are not languages, but ontology editing tools. By affinity, they were included under the directory Languages. This representation would be classified as an informal is-a hierarchy, according to Section 2.3.1.

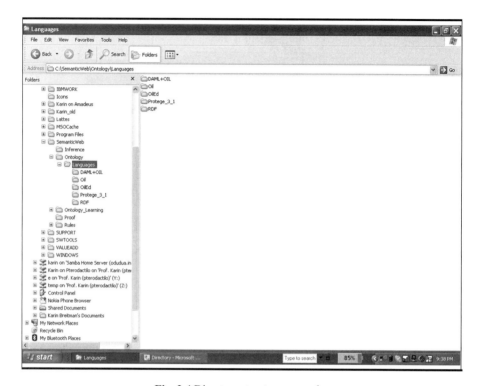

Fig. 2.4 Directory structure example.

2.2.2 Thesauri Versus Ontologies

A thesaurus contains a set of relationships among concepts, organized in a taxonomic way. The taxonomy underlying a thesaurus may have either weak or strong semantics. We may understand a thesaurus as a taxonomy together with a set of semantic relationships, such as equivalence, inverse, and association, that hold among the concepts. Thesauri may be adopted, for example, to guarantee consistency across multiple databases, which facilitates indexing and retrieval.

The ANSI/NISO Monolingual Thesaurus Standard defines *thesaurus* as:

a controlled vocabulary arranged in a known order and structured so that equivalence, homographic, hierarchical, and associative relationships among terms are displayed clearly and identified by standardized relationship indicators that are employed reciprocally. The primary purposes of a thesaurus are:
(a) to facilitate retrieval of documents and
(b) to achieve consistency in the indexing of written or otherwise recorded documents and other items, mainly for postcoordinate information storage and retrieval systems.

Table 2.1 Relationships in the UNESCO Thesauri (2005).

Type of Relationship	Description	Prefix
Hierarchical	Link terms to other terms expressing more general and more specific concepts. Hierarchically related terms are grouped under general subdivisions (known as microthesauri), grouped into the areas of knowledge covered by the *Thesaurus.*	BT (Broader Than) NT (Narrower Than) MT (MicroThesauri)
Associative	Link terms to other terms expressing more general and more specific concepts.	RT (Related Term)
Equivalence	Link nonpreferred terms to synonyms or quasi-synonyms which act as "preferred" terms.	UF (used-for, or nonpreferred term)

A thesaurus can be used to guarantee that concepts are described consistently to enable users to refine searches and locate the information they need. To facilitate this task, thesauri use additional relationships to help organize information. Table 2.1 details and exemplifies some of these relationships.

Note that, in a thesaurus, the set of allowed relationships that can hold between the concepts is finite and well-defined. The notion of a (binary) relationship between concepts is very useful when constructing vocabularies, but it is not sufficient to model other aspects of the real world. It is sometimes necessary to relate concepts using partonomy (part-of), member-group, stage-process, place-region, material-object, cause-effect, among many other types of relationships. If relationships other than those thesauri support are required, one must resort to more general ontologies.

WordNet is perhaps the most popular thesaurus in use today. WordNet is a lexical database for the English language, with over 42,000 terms. It can be used interactively online (URL: http://www.cogsci.princeton.edu/~wn/). WordNet was developed by cognition experts, adopting psycholinguistic theories of human lexical memory.

In WordNet, every word is associated with one or more definitions, also called senses. In natural language, words can have different senses, as exemplified in Table 2.1 for the word "tank". This phenomenon, called polysemy, is considered one of the most serious sources of difficulties that natural language processing software must face.

Figure 2.5 illustrates how to search WordNet for the term "tank", and Fig. 2.6 lists the result obtained. Note that, in addition to the definition, WordNet provides information about:

- Synonyms: nodes that possess the same meaning as the term in question.

- Hypernyms: nodes that maintain father-of or superclass relationships to the node in question. In other words, terms that have a broader meaning than the term in question.

- Hyponyms: nodes that maintain son-of or subclass relationships to the node in question. In other words, terms that have a narrower meaning than the term in question.

To conclude, in this and the previous sections, we compared ontologies to thesauri and taxonomies. According to Noy and McGuinness (2001), there are three properties that an ontology must possess to differentiate it from taxonomies and thesauri, which are:

- *Strict subconcept hierarchy:* every instance of a class must be an instance of its father (i.e., formal is-a hierarchy). The organization of terms must follow the generalization relationship. The spinal cord of this structure is a tree of concepts, all organized using the generalization (type-of) relationship.

- *Ambiguity-free interpretation of meanings and relationships:* users may define properties, whose values may be restricted to certain domains. More sophisticated ontologies may contain more expressive relationships, such as disjunction and part-of.

- *The use of a controlled, finite, but extensible vocabulary.*

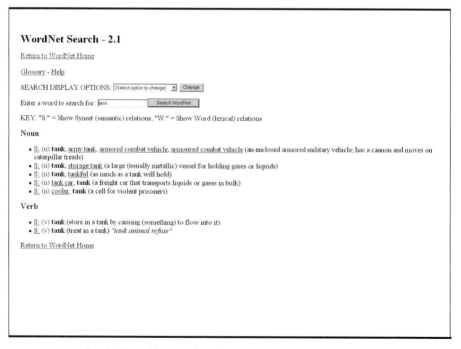

Fig. 2.5 Searching WordNet for the term "tank" (© WordNet).

```
Results for "Synonyms, ordered by estimated frequency" search of noun
"tank"


Display synonyms and immediate hypernyms of synsets
containing the search string.
Synsets are ordered by frequency of occurrence.

Hypernym is the generic term used to designate a whole class
of specific instances.
Y is a hypernym of X if X is a (kind of) Y.

Hypernym synsets are preceded by "=>".

5 senses of tank

Sense 1
tank, army tank, armored combat vehicle, armoured combat vehicle --
 (an enclosed armored military vehicle; has a cannon and moves on cate
rpillar treads)
        => military vehicle -- (vehicle used by the armed forces)
        => armored vehicle, armoured vehicle --
 (a vehicle that is protected by armor plate)
        => tracked vehicle -- (a self-
propelled vehicle that moves on tracks)

Sense 2
tank, storage tank --
 (a large (usually metallic) vessel for holding gases or liquids)
        => vessel --
 (an object used as a container (especially for liquids))

Sense 3
tank, tankful -- (as much as a tank will hold)
        => containerful -- (the quantity that a container will hold)

Sense 4
tank car, tank --
 (a freight car that transports liquids or gases in bulk)
        => freight car -- (a railway car that carries freight)

Sense 5
cooler, tank -- (a cell for violent prisoners)
        => cell, jail cell, prison cell --
(a room where a prisoner is kept)
```

Fig. 2.6 Result of searching WordNet for the term "tank" (© WordNet).

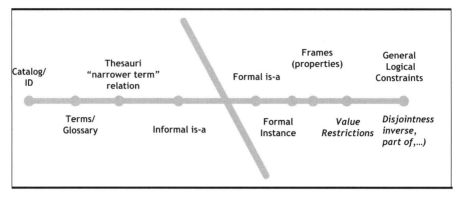

Fig. 2.7 McGuiness Ontology Spectrum Classification (McGuinness 2003).

2.3 Classifying Ontologies

2.3.1 Classifying Ontologies According to a Semantic Spectrum

Different classifications for ontologies have been proposed in the literature. McGuinness (2003) proposed a classification based on the internal structure and contents of the ontologies. The classification, illustrated in Fig. 2.7, follows a line where ontologies range from lightweight to heavyweight, depending on the complexity and sophistication of the elements they contain.

The spectrum ranges from informal catalogues of terms to sophisticated ontologies, which vary on the level of formalization and expressiveness, as follows.

- *Controlled vocabularies* are finite lists of terms. An example is the North American Industry Classification System (NAICS), which lists services and products offered in different areas, such as agriculture, finance, and wholesale.

- *Glossaries* are lists of terms whose meaning is described in natural language. The format of a glossary is similar to that of a dictionary, where terms are organized in alphabetical order, followed by their definitions. An example is the Multilingual Glossary of Internet Terminology (NetGlos), which covers terminology related to the Internet.

- *Thesauri* are lists of terms and definitions that standardize words for indexing purposes. Besides definitions, a thesaurus also provides relationships between the terms: the hierarchical, associative, or equivalence (synonymous) relationships. There are many thesauri available online. An example is the IEEE Web Thesaurus Keywords, which contains a vocabulary associated with the electric and electronic engineering disciplines.

- *Informal is-a hierarchies* are hierarchies that use generalization (type-of) relationships in an informal way. In this kind of hierarchy, related concepts can be aggregated into a category, even if they do not respect the generalization relationship. For example, "car rental" and "hotel", strictly speaking, are not "types-of-travel", but they could appear under "travel", in an informal is-a hierarchy. An example is Yahoo's hierarchy of subjects.

- *Formal is-a hierarchies* are hierarchies that fully respect the generalization relationship. An example is the Linnaean living being taxonomy, illustrated in Section 2.2.1.

- *Frames* are models that include classes and properties after the frame representation, first proposed in Minsky (1975). The primitives of the frame model are *classes*, or *frames*, that have *properties*, *slots,* or *attributes*. Slots do not have global scope, but they apply only to the classes for which they were defined. Each frame provides the context for modeling some aspect of the domain. Several refinements and extensions have been proposed to the frame model. Frames are largely used in modeling knowledge bases.

- *Ontologies that express value restrictions* are ontologies that provide constructs to restrict the values their class properties can assume.

- *Ontologies that express logical restrictions* are ontologies that allow first-order logic restrictions to be expressed.

2.3.2 Classifying Ontologies According to Their Generality

Guarino (1998) proposes a classification based on the generality of the ontology, as follows.

- *Upper Level Ontologies* describe generic concepts, such as space, time, and events. These ontologies are, in principle, domain independent and can be reused to construct new ontologies.

- *Domain Ontologies* describe the vocabulary pertaining to a given domain, by specializing the concepts provided by the upper-level ontology.

- *Task Ontologies* describe the vocabulary required to perform generic tasks or activities, again by specializing the concepts provided by the upper-level ontology.

- *Application Ontologies* describe the vocabulary of a specific application, whose concepts correspond, in general, to the roles performed by entities in a given domain while performing some task or activity.

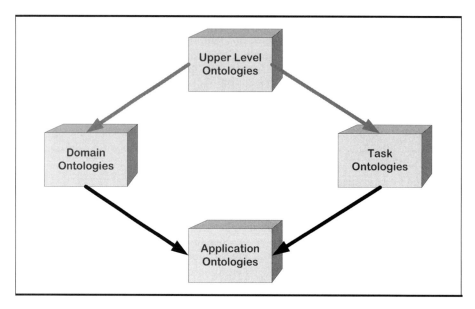

Fig. 2.8 Ontology classification as proposed by Nicola Guarino (1998).

2.3.3 Classifying Ontologies According to the Information Represented

Gómez-Pérez et al. (2004) propose a classification that is partially orthogonal to those discussed in the previous sections, which uses the type of information represented by the ontology as the main classification criteria. They identified the following categories of ontologies.

- *Knowledge representation ontologies* provide primitive modeling elements of knowledge representation models. They offer the modeling constructs used in frame-based representations, such as classes, subclasses, values, attributes (slots), and axioms.

- *Generic and common use ontologies* represent common-sense knowledge that can be used in different domains. They typically include a vocabulary that relates classes, events, space, causality, and behavior, among other concepts. An example is the Time Ontology, available at the DAML public ontology library Web site (URL: http://www.daml.org/ontologies/).

- *Upper ontologies* describe general concepts. Examples of upper ontologies are SUMO and CYC, discussed in Chapter 9. Because there are essential differences in the way each upper ontology treats its concepts, the IEEE proposed the creation of a working group whose focus was the creation of a standard upper ontology, known as SUO. The results of this working group are publicly available (URL: http://suo.ieee.org).

- *Domain ontologies* offer concepts that can be reused within a specific domain (medical, pharmaceutical, law, among others). The frontier between an upper ontology and a domain ontology should be clear.

- *Task ontologies* describe the vocabulary related to a task or activity.

- *Domain-task ontologies* are task ontologies that can be reused in one specific domain, but not generically in similar domains.

- *Method ontologies* provide definitions for concepts and relationships relevant to a process.

- *Application ontologies* contain all the necessary concepts to model the application in question. This kind of ontology is used to specialize and extend domain or task ontologies for a specific application.

2.4 Web Ontology Description Languages

Ontology description languages are specifically designed to define ontologies. They recently received considerable attention, boosted by the emergence of the Semantic Web. This new breed of ontology description languages is sometimes called *lightweight ontology languages*, *Web ontology languages,* or *markup ontology languages*.

The layered model for the Semantic Web (see Fig. 2.9) puts the relationship among ontology description languages, RDF and RDF Schema, and XML in a better perspective. The bottom layer offers character encoding (Unicode) and referencing (URI) mechanisms. The second layer introduces XML as the document exchange standard. The third layer accommodates RDF and RDF Schema as mechanisms to describe the resources available on the Web. As such, they may be classified as lightweight ontology languages. Full ontology description languages appear in the fourth layer as a way to capture more semantics. The topmost layer introduces expressive rule languages.

The brief history of ontology description languages in this section expands the above comments.

William Turncliffe introduced the concept of a *markup language* in 1967. Very briefly, a markup language indicates the structure of a document with help of tags intermixed with the data.

The recent markup languages descend from the *Standard Generalized Markup Language* (SGML), a metalanguage to define markup languages for documents. An ISO standard (ISO 8879), SGML was originally designed to enable the sharing of machine-readable documents, but it has also been used extensively in the printing and publishing industries. The complexity of SGML prevented a more widespread adoption, but it inspired the design of HTML and XML, the best-known markup languages.

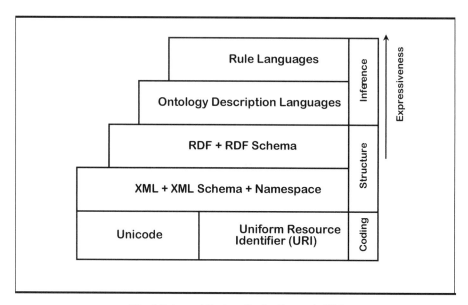

Fig. 2.9 An architecture for the Semantic Web
(adapted from Berners-Lee, T. *Semantic Web - XML2000*. Available at:
http://www.w3.org/2000/Talks/1206-xml2k-tbl/Overview.html).

The *Hypertext Markup Language* (HTML) is a language to format hypertext documents for human reading. HTML was part of an effort to design a hypertext system, carried out by Tim Berners-Lee and Robert Cailau in 1989 at the Conséil Européen pour la Recherche Nucléaire (CERN). In October 1990, this effort came to be known as the World Wide Web (WWW or, simply, the Web). The HTML 4.01 Specification was published as a W3C Recommendation on December, 24th 1999.

The *Extensible Markup Language* (XML) is a general-purpose markup language for creating special-purpose markup languages, which is simpler to parse and process than SGML. The broad goal of XML is to enable generic SGML to be served, received, and processed on the Web in the way that is now possible with HTML. The current W3C Recommendation, XML 1.0 (Third Edition), was published on February 4th, 2004.

The *Resource Description Framework* (RDF) is a general-purpose language for representing information about resources in the Web. It is particularly intended for representing metadata about Web resources, but it can also be used to represent information about objects that can be identified on the Web, even when they cannot be directly retrieved from the Web. To some extent, RDF is a lightweight ontology language designed to support interoperability between applications that exchange machine-understandable information on the Web. RDF is currently defined by a set of W3C recommendations, published on February 10th, 2004.

The lack of expressiveness of RDF was partly eased with the introduction of the *RDF Vocabulary Description Language 1.0: RDF Schema* (RDF Schema or RDF-S), which offers primitives to model hierarchies of classes and properties. RDF-S is currently defined by a W3C recommendation, also published on February 10th, 2004.

Several ontology description languages, such as SHOE, Oil, DAML, DAML+Oil, and OWL, were later defined based on RDF/RDF-S.

Developed at the University of Maryland, the *Simple HTML Ontology Extension* (SHOE) was the first ontology description language created for the Semantic Web. It extends HTML with new tags to semantically annotate Web pages. Software agents can then use such tags to improve the search for Web pages.

The *Ontology Inference Layer* (Oil) is the result of the On-To-Knowledge Project, sponsored by the European Community, which involved several European universities. Oil has a formal semantics based on description logic. In fact, efficient inference mechanisms have been implemented that permit verifying the consistency of an ontology specification written in Oil.

At about the same time Oil was developed, the Defense Advanced Research Projects Agency (DARPA) sponsored the *DARPA Agent Markup Language* (DAML) Program. The goal of the DAML effort was to develop a language by extending RDF/RDF Schema, as well as tools aligned with the concept of the Semantic Web. The first release of DAML dates from August, 2000. It was superseded by the DAML-ONT release of October, 2000.

These two languages were amalgamated into a single language, DAML+Oil, in early 2001. A reformatted version of the March, 2001 release of DAML+Oil was subsequently submitted to W3C as a starting point for the Web Ontology Working Group (WebOnt), whose purpose was to define a new ontology description language for the Semantic Web.

The *Web Ontology Language* (OWL) was the result of the Web Ontology Working Group (now closed). OWL facilitates greater machine interpretability of Web content than that supported by XML and RDF/RDF Schema by providing additional vocabulary, based on description logic. OWL has three increasingly expressive sublanguages: OWL Lite, OWL DL, and OWL Full. OWL is currently defined by a set of W3C recommendations, published on February 10th, 2004.

2.5 Ontologies, Categories, and Intelligence

In Chapter 1, we clarified the distinction between artificial intelligence and the Semantic Web. Briefly, artificial intelligence aims at the construction of software agents capable of showing a level of intelligence that is similar (or superior) to human intelligence. The goal of the Semantic Web, on the other hand, is to develop software that can help human beings in making their decisions. The role of software agents on the Semantic Web will be restricted; the fact that they will be able to process information will not make them able to make decisions, but rather alleviate users from burdensome or cumbersome activities. A simple example is comparing prices. A Semantic Web software agent will be able to: search prices, as well as selling and shipping conditions, from various Web sites; organize the information in a consistent format that facilitates comparison (for example, by currency, shipping costs, and local taxes); and offer a summary, so that the user can make his or her decision.

In the context of the Semantic Web, the role of ontologies is to make the vocabularies used explicit and to provide an information-sharing standard. Indeed, ontologies provide a common model that allows software agents and applications to share data in a significant way. The classification process that underlies ontology construction should take into consideration the automation possibilities, and not the way humans organize their own knowledge.

Furthermore, ontologies do not necessarily reflect the way human beings think or classify their knowledge. If we were to search for a model that reflected the way humans organize their knowledge, Semantic Web ontologies would not be the most adequate model.

Again in the context of the Semantic Web, ontologies categorize concepts into classes, based on common characteristics. The idea that categories are defined by properties (or attributes) forms the basis of what the linguist George Lakoff calls the "classical vision" of categorization. In this vision, a class is defined by a series of properties. The basic condition to belong to a class is to possess all properties associated with the class (Lakoff 1987).

Since Aristotelian times until the beginning of the last century, categories were thought of as abstractions to which one could relate entities. Those entities either belonged or did not belong to a given category, depending on the number of properties that a pair entity-class shared. The set of all properties was sufficient to define any class.

In the beginning of the last century, the Viennese philosopher Wittgenstein contested the classical vision of categorization. In the classical vision, each category is very well bounded, that is, has very clear frontiers, so that it is possible to determine whether an entity belongs to a category. Conversely, any category could be described by its property set. Wittgenstein argued that some concepts do not adapt to such a definition. The example he used, which became a classic in this kind of discussion, is the concept of *game*. There is no set of properties that are shared by all participants of this category. Some games are played just for fun, others are competitive, some use cards, others dice, some involve luck, others strategy, some games involve one player, others more than one, and some games are played indoors and others outdoors. Indeed, there are innumerable variations. To make evident that games lack a common set of properties, we list some of them:

- Chess, video games, and Monopoly™ involve competition, skill, and strategy; they are played for fun and involve more than one player
- Chess and poker involve competition and many players
- Poker, patience, and bridge are card games
- Tennis and golf are played outdoors

Wittgenstein then introduced the concept of family resemblance. According to the philosopher, although there is no single set of properties shared by all games, its members "resemble" each other in many ways. Therefore, games could be thought of as families. Members in a family usually resemble one another is many ways, for example, habits, hair color, tastes, and features, but we can never guarantee the existence of a group of attributes that will be shared by all members of the same family.

Since then, the classical vision has been suffering severe criticism. According to Eleanor Rosch, a researcher in the area of cognitive psychology, the classical vision has two basic implications:

- *First, if categories are defined only by properties all members share, then no members should be better examples of the category than any other members.*

- *Second, if categories are defined only by properties inherent in the members, then categories should be independent of the peculiarities of any beings doing the categorization.*

(Lakoff 1987)

Rosch observed that categories have best examples, called prototypes. In addition, the categorization process by humans is quite dependent on who is doing the classification. If we think of a Dog category, most people would think of a German Shepherd, Labrador, or Dalmatian. Although Chow-Chows and Pekinese also belong to the Dog category, they would hardly be the examples used to illustrate one of its members.

The complete argument in favor of the prototype theory and, above all, its philosophical implications is exposed in Lakoff (1987), the reading of which is highly recommended.

The point of including this discussion about how human beings categorize their knowledge is to show the contrast between the complexities of the issues brought forward by Wittgenstein, Lakoff, and Rosch, and the categorization process underlying Semantic Web ontologies.

In the Semantic Web context, ontologies are fully specified within the boundaries of what Lakoff calls the Classical Vision. Classes are defined by a set of common properties; possessing all of them is the premise for belonging to the class. The set of properties may be defined as necessary and sufficient, that is, a formal definition by which inference mechanisms will automatically identify membership.

Furthermore, Semantic Web ontologies are very useful in sharing and exchanging information between software agents. However, they are not sufficient to model the way human beings categorize information. In this light, Semantic Web ontologies should be understood as an effective means of sharing information, but not representing human intelligence.

References

Barbosa, S.D.J.; Silveira, M.S.; Paula, M.G.; Breitman, K. (2004) Supporting a shared understanding of communication-oriented concerns in human-computer interaction: a lexicon-based approach. In: R. Bastide; N. Graham; J. Röth (Eds.), *Proceedings of the Nineth IFIP Working Conference on Engineering for Human-Computer Interaction*, jointly with the 11th International Workshop on Design, Specification and Verification of

Interactive Systems, EHCI-DSVIS 2004, Schloss Tremsbüttel, Hamburg, Germany, V. 3058, pp. 56–71.

Breitman, K.; Leite, J.C. (2003) Ontology as a requirement engineering product. In: *Proceedings of the Eleventh IEEE International Requirements Engineering Conference.* 8–12 Sept. 2003, Monterey Bay, California, USA, pp. 309–319.

Buranarach, M. (2001) The foundation for semantic interoperability on the world wide web. Doctoral Thesis, Department of Information Science and Telecommunications, School of Information Sciences, University of Pittsburgh. November 8, 2001, 121 pp.

Daconta, M.; Obrst, L.; Smith, K. (2003) The Semantic Web: A Guide to the Future of XML, Web Services, and Knowledge Management. John Wiley & Sons, New York, USA.

Fensel, D. (2001) Ontologies: A Silver Bullet for Knowledge Management and Electronic Commerce. Springer-Verlag, New York, USA.

Gómez-Pérez, A..; Fernadéz-Peréz, M.; Corcho, O. (2004) *Ontological Engineering.* Springer-Verlag, New York, USA.

Gruber, T.R. (1993) A translation approach to portable ontologies. *Knowledge Acquisition,* Vol. 5, No. 2, pp.199–220. Available at: http://ksl-web.stanford.edu/KSL_Abstracts/KSL-92-71.html.

Gruninger, M.; Lee, J. (2002) Introduction to the ontology application and design. *Communications of the ACM,* Vol. 45, No. 2, pp. 39- 41.

Guarino, N. (1998) Formal ontology and information systems. In: *Proceedings of the First International Conference on Formal Ontologies in Information Systems,* FOIS'98, Trento, Italy, pp. 3–15.

Guarino, N.; Carrara, M.; Giaretta, P. (1994) An ontology of meta-level categories In: *Proceedings of the Principles of Knowledge Representation and Reasoning - KR'94.* San Francisco, CA, USA, pp. 270–280.

Lakoff, G. (1987) Women, Fire and Dangerous Things – What Categories Reveal about the Mind. Chicago University Press, Chicago, USA.

Maedche, A. (2002) *Ontology Learning for the Semantic Web.* Kluwer Academic, Boston, MA, USA.

McGuinness, D. L. (2003) Ontologies come of age. In: Fensel, D.; Hendler, J.; Lieberman, H.; Wahlster, W. (Eds). *Spinning the Semantic Web: Bringing the World Wide Web to Its Full Potential.* MIT Press, Cambridge, MA, USA, pp. 171–194.

McGuinness, D.; Harmelen, F.V. (2004) OWL web ontology language overview. W3C Recommendation 10 February 2004. Available at: http://www.w3.org/TR/owl-features/.

Minsky, M. (1975) A framework for representing knowledge. In: P. H. Winston (Ed.) *The Psychology of Computer Vision.* McGraw Hill, New York, USA.

Noy, N.F.; McGuinness, D.L. (2001) Ontology development 101: A guide to creating your first ontology. Technical Report KSL-01-05, Stanford Knowledge Systems Laboratory.

ODP (2006) The Open Directory Project. Available at: http://dmoz.org/.

Sowa, J.F. (1999) Knowledge Representation: Logical, Philosophical and Computational Foundations. Brooks/Cole, Pacific Grove, CA, USA.

Sowa, J.F. (2004) Principles of Ontology. Available at: http://www-ksl.stanford.edu/onto-std/mailarchive/0136.html

UNESCO (1995) UNESCO Thesaurus: A Structured List of Descriptors for Indexing and Retrieving Literature in the Fields of Education, Science, Social and Human Science, Culture, Communication and Information. UNESCO Publishing, Paris, France.

Uschold, M.; Jasper, R. (1999) A framework for understanding and classifying ontology applications. In: *Proceedings of the IJCAI99 Workshop on Ontologies and Problem-Solving Methods (KRR5).* Stockholm, Sweden.

Ushold, M.; Gruninger, M. (1996) Ontologies: Principles, methods and applications. *Knowledge Engineering Review,* Vol. 11, No. 2, pp. 93–136.

3

Knowledge Representation in Description Logic

3.1 Introduction

Description logic denotes a family of knowledge representation formalisms that model the application domain by defining the relevant concepts of the domain and then using these concepts to specify properties of objects and individuals occurring in the domain (Baader and Nutt 2003). As the name implies, research on description logic emphasizes a careful formalization of the notions involved, and a preoccupation with precisely defined reasoning techniques. Note that we prefer the singular form, description logic, rather than the plural form, description logics, in spite of the fact that we are talking about a family of formalisms.

Description logic received renewed attention recently because it provides a formal framework for the Web ontology language OWL, proposed as a standard and discussed in Chapter 5. Indeed, several constructs that OWL introduces cannot be properly appreciated without at least a superficial knowledge of description logic. Furthermore, some of the ontology tools discussed in Chapter 10, notably Protégé, offer a user interface based on notions that description logic supports. This chapter therefore provides the background required for a better understanding of OWL and Protégé, as well as other tools. The emphasis is on the knowledge representation features of description logic, inasmuch as the details of the reasoning techniques are beyond the scope of this book.

The history of description logic goes back to an earlier discussion about knowledge representation formalisms that flourished in the 1980s. At the heart of the discussion was the categorization of such formalisms into two groups: *non-logic-based* and *logic-based formalisms*. The non-logic-based formalisms reflect cognitive notions and claim to be closer to one's intuition and, therefore, easier to comprehend. Such formalisms include semantic networks, frames, and rule-based representations. However, most of them lack a consistent semantics and adopt ad hoc reasoning procedures, which leads to systems that exhibit different behavior, albeit supporting virtually identical languages. The second category includes those formalisms that are variants of first-order logic. They reflect the belief that first-order logic is sufficient to describe facts about the real world. Because they borrow the basic syntax, semantics, and proof theory of first-order logic, formalisms in this second category have a solid foundation.

Semantic networks and frames were later given a formal semantics by mapping them to first-order logic. Moreover, different features of these formalisms correspond to distinct fragments of first-order logic, supported by specialized reasoning techniques with quite different complexity (Brachman and Levesque 1985). In other words, the full power of first-order logic was not necessarily required to achieve an adequate level of expressiveness, as far as knowledge representation is concerned. As a result of this last observation, research on the so-called terminological systems began. Recently, the term Description Logic (DL) was adopted to emphasize the importance of the underlying logical system.

From this perspective, knowledge representation systems can be characterized as *pre-DL systems*, *DL systems,* and *current generation DL systems*. The ancestor of DL systems, KL-ONE, introduced most of the key notions and marked the transition from semantic networks to well-founded terminological systems. In general, pre-DL systems were mainly concerned with concept representation schemes and classification algorithms. DL systems were inspired by theoretical research on the complexity of reasoning in description logic. Systems such as CLASSIC (Brachman et al. 1991) favored efficient reasoning techniques by adopting a description logic with limited expressive power. At the other extreme, systems such as BACK (Nebel and van Luck 1988) emphasized expressiveness and reasoning efficiency, sacrificing completeness (roughly, there were true sentences that the systems could not prove). Current generation DL systems, of which FACT (Horrocks 1998; 2003) and RACER (Haarslev and Moller 2001) are good examples, use optimized reasoning techniques to deal with expressive varieties of description logic and yet retain completeness.

3.2 An Informal Example

The following requirements largely shaped the development of description logic:

- The description language should support the notions of:
  - *Atomic concepts* (denoting sets of individuals)
  - *Atomic roles* (denoting binary relations between individuals)
  - *Constants* (denoting individuals)
- The description language should include constructors to define:
  - *Complex concepts* (denoting sets of individuals)
  - *Complex roles* (denoting binary relations between individuals)

- *Axioms* (defining new concepts or imposing restrictions on the concepts)
- *Assertions* (expressing facts about individuals)
- The reasoning techniques should cover at least:
  - *Concept subsumption* (a concept is a subconcept of another concept)
  - *Concept instantiation* (an individual is an instance of a concept)

In this section, we introduce the basic concepts of description logic with the help of an example, leaving a formal presentation to the next section.

We use the following constructions of description logic to describe our example (see Section 3.3 for the details), where C and D are complex concepts, R is an atomic role, and a and b are constants denoting individuals:

$$\bot \quad \text{(the empty set)}$$
$$\neg C \quad \text{(the set of individuals that are not in set } C\text{)}$$
$$C \sqcap D \quad \text{(the intersection of sets } C \text{ and } D\text{)}$$
$$C \sqcup D \quad \text{(the union of sets } C \text{ and } D\text{)}$$
$$\exists R.C \quad \text{(the set of individuals } a \text{ such that there is}$$
$$\text{an individual b such that } R \text{ relates } a \text{ to } b \text{ and } b \text{ is}$$

in C)

$$\forall R.C \quad \text{(the set of individuals } a \text{ such that,}$$
$$\text{for any individual } b, \text{ if } R \text{ relates } a \text{ to } b, \text{ then } b \text{ is in } C\text{)}$$

$$C \sqsubseteq D \quad \text{(asserts that set } C \text{ is a subset of set } D\text{)}$$
$$C \equiv D \quad \text{(asserts that } C \text{ and } D \text{ are the same set)}$$
$$C(a) \quad \text{(asserts that } a \text{ denotes an individual that is in set } C\text{)}$$
$$R(a,b) \quad \text{(asserts that } R \text{ relates } a \text{ to } b\text{)}$$

The intuitive meaning of all these constructs is immediate, except for $\exists R.C$ and $\forall R.C$, which are given special attention in the examples that follow.

Consider an alphabet consisting of the following atomic concepts, atomic roles, and constants (together with their intended interpretation):

Atomic concepts:	`Book`	(the set B of books)
	`Author`	(the set A of authors)
	`Country`	(the set C of countries)
	`EuroCountry`	(the set E of European countries)
Atomic roles:	`hasAuthor`	(the binary relation H between individuals)
	`publishedIn`	(the binary relation P between individuals)
Constants:	`"The Description Logic Handbook"`	
	`"Principia Mathematica"`	
	`"Franz Baader"`	
	`"Diego Calvanese"`	
	`"Bertrand Russell"`	
	`"Alfred Whitehead"`	
	`"United Kingdom"`	

Note that, strictly speaking, we cannot guarantee that *H* relates books to authors, and that *P* relates books to the countries where they were published. We can only say that *H* and *P* relate individuals to individuals, which is intrinsic to the semantics of description logic.

A *complex concept*, or a *concept description*, is an expression that constructs a new concept out of other concepts. We illustrate how to define complex concepts that are gradually more sophisticated, using the above alphabet and the intended interpretation for the atomic concepts and atomic roles (the sets *B*, *A*, *C*, *E*, *H*, and *P*). That is, in the explanations that follow each example, we use the intended interpretation or intended semantics of the symbols in the alphabet.

The first two examples use just the simple constructs ¬*C* and *C* ⊓ *D*:

(1)   ¬EuroCountry
        (the set of individuals, *not necessarily countries*, that are not European countries)

Observe that negation is always with respect to the set of all individuals, hence the intuitive explanation in (1).

(2)   Country ⊓ ¬EuroCountry
        (the set of countries that are not European countries)

Note that, to define the set of countries that are not European countries, we circumscribed negation to the set of countries in (2). The next examples involve the more sophisticated constructs ∃*R.C* and ∀*R.C*:

(3)   ∀hasAuthor.⊥
        (the set of individuals, *not necessarily books*, that have no known author)

Recall that *H* is a binary relation between individuals that represents the intended interpretation of hasAuthor. The complex concept in (3) denotes the set *S* of individuals such that, for each *s* in *S*, if *H* relates *s* to an individual *b*, then *b* belongs to the empty set (the intended interpretation of ⊥). Because the empty set has no individuals, *S* is the set of individuals that *H* relates to no individual. That is, *S* is the set of individuals for which *H* is undefined, hence the explanation in (3).

(4)   ∃publishedIn.EuroCountry
        (the set of individuals, *not necessarily books*, published in some European country and perhaps elsewhere)

Also recall that *P* is a binary relation between individuals that represents the intended interpretation of publishedIn. The complex concept in (4) denotes the set *T* of individuals that *P* relates to some individual in *E*. However, note that (4) does not guarantee that, given an individual *t* in *T*, *P* relates *t* only to individuals in *E*. That is, *T* is the set of individuals, not necessarily books, that *P* relates to some individual in E and perhaps to other individuals not in E, hence the intuitive explanation in (4).

(5) $\forall$publishedIn.EuroCountry
       (the set of individuals, *not necessarily books*, published only in European countries or not published at all)

The complex concept in (5) denotes the set U of individuals such that, for each u in U, if P relates u to an individual e, then e is in E. However, note that, by definition, U will also include any individual e' such that P does not relate e' to any individual, hence the intuitive explanation in (5).

(6) $\exists$publishedIn.EuroCountry $\sqcap$ $\forall$publishedIn.EuroCountry
       (the set of individuals, *not necessarily books*, published in European countries, and only in European countries)

The complex concept in (6) denotes the set V of individuals that P relates to some individual in E, and only to individuals in E. Therefore, it correctly constructs the set of individuals that are indeed published, and only published in European countries. Finally, note that (6) does not guarantee that the country of publication is unique.

The next two examples use the complex concepts defined in (3) and (6) to specify sets of books with certain properties:

(7)   Book $\sqcap$ $\forall$hasAuthor.$\bot$
       (the set of books that have no known author)

(8)   Book $\sqcap$ $\exists$publishedIn.EuroCountry
            $\sqcap$ $\forall$publishedIn.EuroCountry
       (the set of books published in European countries, and only in European countries)

A *definition* is an axiom that introduces a new *defined concept* with the help of complex concepts. For example, the axioms below define the concepts nonEuroCountry, anonymousBook, nonAnonymousBook, EuroBook, and nonEuroBook:

(9)   nonEuroCountry $\equiv$ Country $\sqcap$ $\neg$EuroCountry
       (the concept of non-European countries is defined as those countries that are not European countries)

(10)   AnonymousBook $\equiv$ Book $\sqcap$ $\forall$hasAuthor.$\bot$
       (the concept of anonymous books is defined as those books that have no known author)

(11)   nonAnonymousBook $\equiv$ Book $\sqcap$ $\neg$AnonymousBook

(the concept of nonanonymous books is defined as those books that are not anonymous)

(12)   EuroBook ≡ Book ⊓ ∃publishedIn.EuroCountry
                          ⊓ ∀publishedIn.EuroCountry
        (the concept of European books is defined as those books that are published in European countries)

(13)   nonEuroBook ≡ Book ⊓ ¬EuroBook
        (the concept of non-European books is defined as those books that are not European books)

Note that the expression in (2) is a complex concept, whereas that in (9) is a definition that introduces a new concept, nonEuroCountry. Definition (11) introduces a new defined concept, nonAnonymousBook, with the help of the defined concept AnonymousBook and the atomic concept Book. Similar observations apply to the other axioms.

An *inclusion* is an axiom that just imposes a restriction on the world being modeled, indicating that a concept is subsumed by another concept. An example of an inclusion is:

(14)   EuroCountry ⊑ Country
        (A European country is also a country)

This restriction obviously corresponds to the observed reality, but it has to be made explicit in the world model, because we started with two unrelated concepts, Country and EuroCountry.

An *assertion* either states that an individual belongs to a concept, or describes that individuals are related to each other by roles. Examples of assertions are:

```
(15)  Book("The Description Logic Handbook")
(16)  Book("Principia Mathematica")
(17)  Author("Franz Baader")
(18)  Author("Diego Calvanese")
(19)  Author("Bertrand Russell")
(20)  Author("Alfred Whitehead")
(21)  Country("United Kingdom")
(22)  EuroCountry("United Kingdom")
(23)  hasAuthor("The Description Logic Handbook",
                "Franz Baader")
(24)  hasAuthor("The Description Logic Handbook",
                "Diego Calvanese")
(25)  hasAuthor("Principia Mathematica", "Bertrand Russell")
(26)  hasAuthor("Principia Mathematica", "Alfred Whitehead")
(27)  publishedIn("The Description Logic Handbook",
                "United Kingdom")
(28)  publishedIn("Principia Mathematica", "United Kingdom")
```

Without assertion (15), we cannot correctly state that the constant "The
Description Logic Handbook" denotes an individual which is indeed an
instance of the concept Book. Likewise, assertion (23) guarantees that "The
Description Logic Handbook" and "Franz Baader" denote individuals that
are related by hasAuthor. Similar observations apply to the other assertions.

A *knowledge base* is a set of axioms and assertions, written using a specific
language. The *terminology*, or *TBox*, of the knowledge base consists of the set of
axioms that define new concepts. The *world description*, *assertional knowledge*, or
ABox of the knowledge base consists of the set of assertions. The TBox expresses
intentional knowledge, which is typically stable, whereas the ABox captures
extensional knowledge, which changes as the world evolves.

For example, the axioms and assertions in (9) to (28) can be organized as a
knowledge base, which we call BOOKS, where the TBox consists of definitions (9) to
(13) and the inclusion (14), and the ABox contains the assertions in (15) to (28).

We now informally exemplify how to deduce concept subsumptions and concept
instantiations from the BOOKS knowledge base. We stress that the examples are just
indicative of what can be proved, but not of how the DL proof procedures operate.

We first prove that every country can be classified as either European or
nonEuropean, but not both. More precisely, we prove that:

(29)   nonEuroCountry ⊑ ¬EuroCountry

(30)   Country ≡ EuroCountry ⊔ nonEuroCountry

The inclusion (29) follows directly from (9) and is equivalent to saying that no
individual is both a European country and a non-European country. To prove (30),
we establish the following sequence of equivalent complex concepts.

(31)   EuroCountry ⊔ nonEuroCountry
       ≡   EuroCountry ⊔ (Country ⊓ ¬EuroCountry)   from (9)
       ≡   (EuroCountry ⊔ Country)
           ⊓ (EuroCountry ⊔ ¬EuroCountry)   (distribution of ⊔ over ⊓)
       ≡   EuroCountry ⊔ Country   (simplification)
       ≡   Country   from (14)

We may likewise prove that every book is either anonymous or nonanonymous,
but not both, using just (10) and (11). In this case, the definitions (10) and (11)
already guarantee that AnonymousBook and nonAnonymousBook are subsumed by
Book. That is, no inclusion similar to (14) is required. More precisely, we can prove
that:

(32)   nonAnonymousBook ⊑ ¬AnonymousBook

(33)   Book ≡ AnonymousBook ⊔ nonAnonymousBook

The inclusion (32) follows directly from (11). To prove (33), we establish the
following sequence of equivalent complex concepts.

(34) AnonymousBook ⊔ nonAnonymousBook
      ≡ AnonymousBook ⊔ (Book ⊓ ¬AnonymousBook)   from (11)
      ≡ (AnonymousBook ⊔ Book)
        ⊓ (AnonymousBook ⊔ ¬AnonymousBook)   (distribution of ⊔ over ⊓)
      ≡ AnonymousBook ⊔ Book   (simplification)
      ≡ Book   from (10)

Finally and omitting the details, we can also prove that:

(35) nonEuroBook ⊑ ¬EuroBook   from (13)
(36) Book ≡ EuroBook ⊔ nonEuroBook   from (12), (13)

We now turn to examples of concept instantiation. Suppose we want to prove that:

(37) nonAnonymousBook("Principia Mathematica")
      ("Principia Mathematica" is an instance of nonAnonymousBook)

We proceed as follows.

(38) nonAnonymousBook ≡ Book ⊓ ¬(Book ⊓ ∀hasAuthor.⊥)
                                                from (10), (11)
(39) nonAnonymousBook ≡ Book ⊓ (¬Book ⊔ ¬∀hasAuthor.⊥)
                                                from (38)
(40) nonAnonymousBook ≡ (Book ⊓ ¬Book)
                        ⊔ (Book ⊓ ¬∀hasAuthor.⊥)   from (39)
(41) nonAnonymousBook ≡ Book ⊓ ¬∀hasAuthor.⊥   from (40)
(42) (¬∀hasAuthor.⊥)("Principia Mathematica")   from (25)
(43) (Book ⊓ ¬∀hasAuthor.⊥)("Principia Mathematica")
                                                from (16), (42)
(44) nonAnonymousBook("Principia Mathematica")   from (41), (43)

Note that, to derive (39) from (38), we used the law ¬($C ⊓ D$) ≡ (¬C ⊔ ¬D), and to derive (39) from (38), the law $C ⊓ (D ⊔ E) ≡ (C ⊓ D) ⊔ (C ⊓ E)$.

In general, the reasoning techniques that DL systems implement should be able to solve several inference problems, which we summarize in Sections 3.4.1 and 3.4.2. However, the details of the reasoning techniques are beyond the scope of this book, and do not necessarily generate the simple deductions we gave as examples in this section.

3.3 The Family of Attributive Languages

3.3.1 Concept Descriptions

Description languages differ by the collection of constructors they offer to define concept descriptions. Following Baader and Nutt (2003), we introduce in this section the syntax and semantics of the *family of attributive languages*, or $\mathcal{AL}$-*family*. The discussion formalizes and expands the notions covered in Section 3.2.

An *attributive language* $\mathcal{L}$ is characterized by an *alphabet* consisting of a set of *atomic concepts*, a set of *atomic roles*, and the special symbols $\top$ and $\bot$, respectively called the *universal concept* and the *bottom concept*.

The set of *concept descriptions* of $\mathcal{L}$ is inductively defined as follows.

(i) Any atomic concept and the universal and bottom concepts are concept descriptions

(ii) If A is an atomic concept, C and D are concept descriptions, and R is an atomic role, then the following expressions are concept descriptions.

$\neg A$	(atomic negation)
$C \sqcap D$	(intersection)
$\forall R.C$	(value restriction)
$\exists R.\top$	(limited existential quantification)

The other classes of languages of the $\mathcal{AL}$-family maintain the same definition of alphabet, but expand the set of concept descriptions to include expressions of the one of the forms.

(iii) If C and D are concept descriptions, R is an atomic role, and n is a positive integer, then the following expressions are concept descriptions.

$\neg C$	(arbitrary negation)
$C \sqcup D$	(union)
$\exists R.C$	(full existential quantification)
$(\geq n\, R)$	(at-least restriction, a type of cardinality restriction)
$(\leq n\, R)$	(at-most restriction, a type of cardinality restriction)

Table 3.1 at the end of this section summarizes the constructions that the various classes of languages of the $\mathcal{AL}$-family allow. The letter in the first column induces a notation for specific classes of languages. For example, a language that allows all constructs of an $\mathcal{AL}$ language, arbitrary negation, and union is called an $\mathcal{ALCU}$ *language*.

An *interpretation* I for an attributive language L consists of a nonempty set Δ^I, the *domain* of I, whose elements are called *individuals*, and an *interpretation function* such that:

(i) $T^I = \Delta^I$ and $\perp^I = \emptyset$

(ii) For every atomic concept A of L, the interpretation function assigns a set $A^I \subseteq \Delta^I$

(iii) For every atomic role R of L, the interpretation function assigns a binary relation $R^I \subseteq \Delta^I \times \Delta^I$

The interpretation function is extended to concept descriptions of L inductively as follows.

$$
\begin{aligned}
(\neg A)^I &= \Delta^I - A^I \\
(C \sqcap D)^I &= C^I \cap D^I \\
(\forall R.C)^I &= \{ a \in \Delta^I \mid (\forall b \in \Delta^I)\,((a,b) \in R^I \Rightarrow b \in C^I\,) \} \\
(\exists R.T)^I &= \{ a \in \Delta^I \mid (\exists b \in \Delta^I)\,((a,b) \in R^I\,) \}
\end{aligned}
$$

In words, $(\neg A)^I$ denotes the complement of A^I with respect to the domain; $(C \sqcap D)^I$ denotes the intersection of C^I and D^I; $(\forall R.C)^I$ denotes the set of individuals that R relates only to individuals in C^I, if any; and $(\exists R.T)^I$ denotes the set of individuals that R relates to some individual of the domain.

For the extended family, we have:

$$
\begin{aligned}
(\neg C)^I &= \Delta^I - C^I \\
(C \sqcup D)^I &= C^I \cup D^I \\
(\exists R.C)^I &= \{ a \in \Delta^I \mid (\exists b \in \Delta^I)\,((a,b) \in R^I \wedge b \in C^I\,) \} \\
(\geq n\,R)^I &= \{ a \in \Delta^I \mid card(\{\, b \in \Delta^I \mid (a,b) \in R^I\,\}) \geq n\,\} \\
(\leq n\,R)^I &= \{ a \in \Delta^I \mid card(\{\, b \in \Delta^I \mid (a,b) \in R^I\,\}) \leq n\,\}
\end{aligned}
$$

where $card(S)$ denotes the cardinality of a set S. In words, we have that:

- $(\neg C)^I$ denotes the complement of C^I with respect to the domain
- $(C \sqcup D)^I$ denotes the union of C^I and D^I
- $(\exists R.C)^I$ denotes the set of individuals that R relates to some individual in C^I
- $(\geq n\,R)^I$ denotes the set of individuals that R relates to at least n individuals
- $(\leq n\,R)^I$ denotes the set of individuals that R relates to at most n individuals

We say that two concept descriptions C and D of L are *equivalent*, denoted $C \equiv D$, iff $C^I = D^I$, for all interpretations I of L.

By inspecting the semantics of the concept descriptions, we observe that union can be expressed with the help of negation and intersection, and full existential quantification with the help of negation and value restriction. Indeed, we have that:

$$(C \sqcup D) \quad \equiv \quad \neg(\neg C \sqcap \neg D)$$
$$\exists R.C \quad \equiv \quad \neg \forall R. \neg C$$

Therefore, the classes of languages are not independent of each other.

As an example, consider the language $\mathcal{P}$ with the following alphabet (see Section 3.2).

Atomic concepts:

Book	(the set of books)
Author	(the set of authors)
Country	(the set of countries)
EuroCountry	(the set of European countries)

Roles:

hasAuthor	(assigns a book to an author)
publishedIn	(assigns a book to the country where it was published)

Strictly speaking, we cannot guarantee that any interpretation I of $\mathcal{P}$ will be such that hasAuthor^I assigns an individual in Book^I to an individual in Author^I. That is, we cannot guarantee that hasAuthor$^I \subseteq$ Book$^I \times$ Author^I. A similar observation holds for publishedIn. This is an intrinsic limitation of the semantics of description logic.

Table 3.2 shows examples of concept descriptions in $\mathcal{P}$, including those already introduced in Section 3.2. Examples (1) to (5) and (10) use only constructions that $\mathcal{AL}$ languages allow. Therefore, if they suffice to capture all domain properties, we may treat $\mathcal{P}$ as an $\mathcal{AL}$ language. Note, however, that we cannot express the concept of single-author books in $\mathcal{AL}$ languages. We have to consider $\mathcal{P}$ as an $\mathcal{ALN}$ language if we want to cover concepts that involve cardinality restrictions. Indeed, examples (6) to (9) illustrate the use of cardinality restrictions. Lastly, the concept descriptions in (10) and (11) exemplify the use of full existential quantification. Again, to include these concept descriptions, we have to consider that $\mathcal{P}$ is at least an $\mathcal{ALE}$ language.

Table 3.1 The family of attributive languages.

Lang.	Constr.	Name	Semantics
$\mathcal{AL}$	$\top$	universal concept	$\top^I = \Delta^I$
			the set of all individuals
	$\bot$	bottom concept	$\bot^I = \varnothing$
			the empty set
	$\neg A$	atomic negation	$\Delta^I - A^I$
			the complement of A^I w.r.t. the domain
	$C \sqcap D$	intersection	$C^I \cap D^I$
			the intersection of C^I and D^I
	$\forall R.C$	value restriction	$\{\, a \in \Delta^I \mid (\forall b \in \Delta^I)\, ((a,b) \in R^I \Rightarrow b \in C^I\,)\,\}$
			the set of individuals that R relates only to individuals of C^I
	$\exists R.\top$	limited existential quantification	$\{\, a \in \Delta^I \mid (\exists b \in \Delta^I)\, ((a,b) \in R^I\,)\}$
			the set of individuals that R relates to some individual
C	$\neg C$	arbitrary negation	$\Delta^I - C^I$
			the complement of C^I with respect to the domain
$\mathcal{U}$	$C \sqcup D$	union	$C^I \cup D^I$
			the union of C^I and D^I
$\mathcal{E}$	$\exists R.C$	full existential quantification	$\{\, a \in \Delta^I \mid (\exists b \in \Delta^I)\, ((a,b) \in R^I \wedge b \in C^I\,)\,\}$
			the set of individuals that R relates to some individual of C^I
$\mathcal{N}$	$(\geq n\, R)$	at-least restriction (cardinality restr.)	$\{\, a \in \Delta^I \mid card(\{\, b \in \Delta^I \mid (a,b) \in R^I\,\}) \geq n\,\}$
			the set of individuals that R relates to at least n individuals
	$(\leq n\, R)$	at-most restriction (cardinality restr.)	$\{\, a \in \Delta^I \mid card(\{\, b \in \Delta^I \mid (a,b) \in R^I\,\}) \leq n\,\}$
			the set of individuals that R relates to at most n individuals

Table 3.2 Examples of Concept Descriptions.

#	Class	Example
(1)	$\mathcal{AL}$	Country ⊓ ¬EuroCountry
		countries that are not European countries
		$\text{Country}^I \cap (\Delta^I - \text{EuroCountry}^I)$
(2)	$\mathcal{AL}$	Book ⊓ ∀hasAuthor.⊥
		books without (known) authors, that is, anonymous books
		$\text{Book}^I \cap \{ a \in \Delta^I \mid (\forall b \in \Delta^I)\,((a,b) \notin \text{hasAuthor}^I) \}$
(3)	$\mathcal{AL}$	Book ⊓ ∃hasAuthor.⊤
		books that hasAuthor assigns to some individual, not necessarily authors
		$\text{Book}^I \cap \{ a \in \Delta^I \mid (\exists b \in \Delta^I)\,((a,b) \in \text{hasAuthor}^I) \}$
(4)	$\mathcal{AL}$	Book ⊓ ∀hasAuthor.Author
		books that hasAuthor assigns only authors, if to any individual at all; that is, books perhaps with authors
		$\text{Book}^I \cap \{ a \in \Delta^I \mid (\forall b \in \Delta^I)\,((a,b) \in \text{hasAuthor}^I \Rightarrow b \in \text{Author}^I) \}$
(5)	$\mathcal{AL}$	Book ⊓ ∃hasAuthor.⊤ ⊓ ∀hasAuthor.Author
		books necessarily with authors
		$\text{Book}^I \cap \{ a \in \Delta^I \mid (\exists b \in \Delta^I)\,((a,b) \in \text{hasAuthor}^I) \}$ $\cap \{ a \in \Delta^I \mid (\forall b \in \Delta^I)\,((a,b) \in \text{hasAuthor}^I \Rightarrow b \in \text{Author}^I) \}$
(6)	$\mathcal{ALN}$	Book ⊓ (≤ 1 hasAuthor)
		books that hasAuthor assigns to at most one individual, not necessarily an author
		$\text{Book}^I \cap \{ a \in \Delta^I \mid card(\{ b \in \Delta^I \mid (a,b) \in \text{hasAuthor}^I \}) \leq 1 \}$
(7)	$\mathcal{ALN}$	Book ⊓ (≥ 1 hasAuthor)
		books that hasAuthor assigns to at least one individual, not necessarily an author
		$\text{Book}^I \cap \{ a \in \Delta^I \mid card(\{ b \in \Delta^I \mid (a,b) \in \text{hasAuthor}^I \}) \geq 1 \}$

Table 3.2 Examples of Concept Descriptions (cont.).

#	Class	Example
(8)	$\mathcal{ALN}$	Book $\sqcap$ (≥ 1 hasAuthor) $\sqcap$ (≤ 1 hasAuthor)$\sqcap$ $\forall$hasAuthor.Author
		books with a single author
		Book$^I \cap \{\, a \in \Delta^I \mid card(\{\, b \in \Delta^I \mid (a,b) \in$ hasAuthor$^I\,\}) = 1\,\}$ $\cap \{\, a \in \Delta^I \mid (\forall b \in \Delta^I)\,((a,b) \in$ hasAuthor$^I \Rightarrow b \in$ Author$^I)\}$
(9)	$\mathcal{ALN}$	Book $\sqcap$ (≥ 2 hasAuthor) $\sqcap$ $\forall$hasAuthor.Author
		books with multiple authors
		Book$^I \cap \{\, a \in \Delta^I \mid card(\{\, b \in \Delta^I \mid (a,b) \in$ hasAuthor$^I\,\}) \geq 2\,\}$ $\cap \{\, a \in \Delta^I \mid (\forall b \in \Delta^I)\,((a,b) \in$ hasAuthor$^I \Rightarrow b \in$ Author$^I)\}$
(10)	$\mathcal{AL}$	Book $\sqcap$ $\forall$publishedIn.EuroCountry
		books that publishedIn assigns only to European countries, if to any individual at all
		Book$^I \cap \{\, a \in \Delta^I \mid$ $(\forall b \in \Delta^I)\,((a,b) \in$ publishedIn$^I \Rightarrow b \in$ EuroCountry$^I)\}$
(11)	$\mathcal{ALE}$	Book $\sqcap$ $\exists$publishedIn.EuroCountry
		books published in some European country (and perhaps elsewhere)
		Book$^I \cap \{\, a \in \Delta^I \mid$ $(\exists b \in \Delta^I)\,((a,b) \in$ publishedIn$^I \wedge b \in$ EuroCountry$^I)\}$
(12)	$\mathcal{ALE}$	Book $\sqcap$ $\forall$publishedIn.EuroCountry $\sqcap$ $\exists$publishedIn.EuroCountry
		books published in European countries
		Book$^I \cap \{\, a \in \Delta^I \mid (\forall b \in \Delta^I)\,((a,b) \in$ publishedIn$^I \Rightarrow$ $b \in$ EuroCountry$^I)\,\}$ $\cap \{\, a \in \Delta^I \mid (\exists b \in \Delta^I)\,((a,b) \in$ publishedIn$^I \wedge$ $b \in$ EuroCountry$^I)\,\}$

3.3.2 Terminologies

Let $\mathcal{L}$ be a language in any of the classes of the $\mathcal{AL}$-family. A *terminological axiom* (written) in $\mathcal{L}$ or, simply, an *axiom*, is an expression of the form $C \sqsubseteq D$, called an *inclusion*, or of the form $C \equiv D$, called an *equality*, where C and D are concept descriptions in $\mathcal{L}$.

Let I be an interpretation for $\mathcal{L}$. Then, I *satisfies* $C \sqsubseteq D$ iff $C^I \subseteq D^I$, and I *satisfies* $C \equiv D$ iff $C^I = D^I$. Let $\mathcal{T}$ be a set of axioms. Then, I *satisfies* $\mathcal{T}$, or I *is a model of* $\mathcal{T}$, iff I satisfies each axiom in $\mathcal{T}$. Two sets of axioms are *equivalent* iff they have the same models.

For example, let $\mathcal{P}$ be the language introduced in Section 3.2. Then, the following expressions are inclusions (in $\mathcal{P}$).

$$\texttt{Book} \sqsubseteq \forall\texttt{hasAuthor.Author}$$
$$\texttt{Book} \sqsubseteq (\geq 1\ \texttt{publishedIn}) \sqcap (\leq 1\ \texttt{publishedIn}) \sqcap$$

$$\forall\texttt{publishedIn.Country}$$

Let I be an interpretation for $\mathcal{P}$ and assume that I satisfies the two axioms. Then, we have that

$$\texttt{Book}^I \subseteq \{\, a \in \Delta^I \mid (\forall b \in \Delta^I)\, ((a,b) \in \texttt{hasAuthor}^I \Rightarrow b \in \texttt{Author}^I)\,\}$$

$$\texttt{Book}^I \subseteq \{\, a \in \Delta^I \mid card(\{\, b \in \Delta^I \mid (a,b) \in \texttt{publishedIn}^I \,\}) = 1 \,\} \cap$$
$$\{\, a \in \Delta^I \mid (\forall b \in \Delta^I)\, ((a,b) \in \texttt{publishedIn}^I \Rightarrow b \in \texttt{Country}^I)\,\}$$

Intuitively, the first axiom guarantees that, for any book a, if a has a known author, then it is an individual of the set $\texttt{Author}^I$. The second axiom guarantees that every book has exactly one country of publication.

A *definition* (written) in $\mathcal{L}$ is an equality $A \equiv D$ such that A is an atomic concept and D is a concept description of $\mathcal{L}$.

A *terminology* or a *TBox* (written) in $\mathcal{L}$ is a set of definitions $\mathcal{D}$ such that, for any atomic concept A of $\mathcal{L}$, there is at most one definition in $\mathcal{D}$ whose left-hand side is A, called *the definition of A* in $\mathcal{D}$. We may therefore partition (with respect to $\mathcal{D}$) the atomic concepts of $\mathcal{L}$ into *defined concepts* (with respect to $\mathcal{D}$) that appear in the left-hand side of the definitions in $\mathcal{D}$ and *primitive concepts* (with respect to $\mathcal{D}$) that do not appear in the left-hand side of the definitions in $\mathcal{D}$. Consistently with the use in Section 3.2, we may extend the notion of TBox to also contain inclusions.

We say that a defined concept A *directly uses* an atomic concept B iff B occurs in the right-hand side of the definition of A. Note that B may itself be a defined concept. We inductively define that A *uses* an atomic concept C iff A *directly uses* a defined concept B and B uses C. A terminology is *acyclic* iff no defined concept uses itself; that is, the uses relationship is acyclic.

In acyclic terminologies, the interpretation of the defined concepts can be constructed from the interpretation of the primitive concepts, as expected. More precisely, let $\mathcal{D}$ be an acyclic terminology in $\mathcal{L}$. A *base interpretation* for $\mathcal{L}$ with respect to $\mathcal{D}$ is an interpretation I of $\mathcal{L}$, except for the defined concepts (with respect to $\mathcal{D}$). An *extension* of I is an interpretation J of $\mathcal{L}$ that has the same domain as I and which is identical to I in all primitive concepts and atomic roles. It is possible to prove that, if $\mathcal{D}$ is an acyclic terminology in $\mathcal{L}$, then every base interpretation for $\mathcal{L}$ with respect to $\mathcal{D}$ has a unique extension that is a model of $\mathcal{D}$.

For example, let $\mathcal{P}$ be the language introduced in Section 3.2, with defined concepts nonEuroCountry, anonymousBook, nonAnonymousBook, EuroBook and nonEuroBook. Assume that $\mathcal{D}$ is a terminology in $\mathcal{P}$ containing the following definitions:

$$
\begin{aligned}
\text{nonEuroCountry} &\equiv \text{Country} \sqcap \neg\text{EuroCountry} \\
\text{AnonymousBook} &\equiv \text{Book} \sqcap \forall\text{hasAuthor}.\bot \\
\text{nonAnonymousBook} &\equiv \text{Book} \sqcap \neg\text{AnonymousBook} \\
\text{EuropeanBook} &\equiv \text{Book} \sqcap \forall\text{publishedIn}.\text{EuroCountry} \\
&\quad\ \sqcap \exists\text{publishedIn}.\text{EuroCountry} \\
\text{nonEuroBook} &\equiv \text{Book} \sqcap \neg\text{EuroBook}
\end{aligned}
$$

Let I be a base interpretation for $\mathcal{P}$ with respect to $\mathcal{D}$. Then, the unique extension of $\mathcal{P}$ that is a model of $\mathcal{D}$ assigns the following interpretations to the defined concepts:

$$
\begin{aligned}
\text{nonEuroCountry}^I &= \text{Country}^I - \text{EuroCountry}^I \\
\text{AnonymousBook}^I &= \text{Book}^I \cap \{a \in \Delta^I \mid (\forall b \in \Delta^I)\, ((a,b) \notin \text{hasAuthor}^I)\} \\
\text{nonAnonymousBook}^I &= \text{Book}^I - \text{AnonymousBook}^I \\
\text{EuropeanBook}^I &= \text{Book}^I \\
&\quad \cap \{a \in \Delta^I \mid (\forall b \in \Delta^I)\, ((a,b) \in \text{publishedIn}^I \Rightarrow \\
&\qquad\quad b \in \text{EuroCountry}^I)\} \\
&\quad \cap \{a \in \Delta^I \mid (\exists b \in \Delta^I)\, ((a,b) \in \text{publishedIn}^I \wedge \\
&\qquad\quad b \in \text{EuroCountry}^I)\} \\
\text{nonEuroBook}^I &= \text{Book}^I - \text{EuroBook}^I
\end{aligned}
$$

Finally, let $\mathcal{D}$ be an acyclic terminology in $\mathcal{L}$. Let A be a defined concept with definition $A \equiv B_0$ in $\mathcal{D}$. Then, we can rewrite $A \equiv B_0$ as a new definition $A \equiv B_1$ where B_1 is obtained from B_0 by replacing a defined concept that occurs in B_0 by its definition in $\mathcal{D}$. Because $\mathcal{D}$ is acyclic, we can continue this process a finite number of steps until we obtain a new definition $A \equiv B_n$ that does not contain any defined

3.3 The Family of Attributive Languages   51

concept. We can repeat this process until we obtain a new terminology $\mathcal{D}'$ where all definitions are of the form $A \equiv B$, where B contains only primitive concepts. We call this new terminology the *expansion* of $\mathcal{D}$. We can also prove the following.

Proposition 3.1: Let $\mathcal{D}$ be an acyclic terminology and $\mathcal{D}'$ be its expansion. Then, we have that:
   (i) $\mathcal{D}$ and $\mathcal{D}'$ have the same primitive and derived concepts.
   (ii) $\mathcal{D}$ and $\mathcal{D}'$ are equivalent.

Therefore, we may assume without loss of generality that acyclic terminologies are such that all definitions are of the form $A \equiv B$, where B contains only primitive concepts.

3.3.3 Assertions

Let $\mathcal{L}$ be a language in any of the classes of the $\mathcal{AL}$-family. We expand the alphabet of $\mathcal{L}$ with *constants*, which will denote individuals. An *assertion* (written) in $\mathcal{L}$ is an expression of the form $C(a)$, called a *concept assertion*, or of the form $R(b,c)$, called a *role assertion*, where a, b, and c are constants of the alphabet of $\mathcal{L}$; C is a concept description in $\mathcal{L}$; and R is an atomic role in $\mathcal{L}$.

A *world description, assertional knowledge,* or *ABox* (written) in $\mathcal{L}$ is a set of assertions $\mathcal{A}$ (written) in $\mathcal{L}$.

An interpretation $\mathcal{I}$, with domain Δ^I, for $\mathcal{L}$ is defined as before, except that $\mathcal{I}$ also assigns an element $a^I \in \Delta^I$, for each constant a of $\mathcal{L}$, in a way that different constants map to distinct individuals in Δ^I. We say that $\mathcal{I}$ *satisfies* $C(a)$ iff $a^I \in C^I$, and that $\mathcal{I}$ *satisfies* $R(b,c)$ iff $(b^I,c^I) \in R^I$. Given an Abox $\mathcal{A}$, we say that $\mathcal{I}$ *satisfies* $\mathcal{A}$, or $\mathcal{I}$ *is a model of* $\mathcal{A}$, iff $\mathcal{I}$ satisfies each assertion in $\mathcal{A}$.

Returning to the language $\mathcal{P}$, consider again assertions (15) and (23) from Section 3.2:

```
Book("Principia Mathematica")
hasAuthor("Principia Mathematica", "Bertrand Russell")
```

Let $\mathcal{I}$ be an interpretation for $\mathcal{P}$ and assume that $\mathcal{I}$ satisfies the two assertions. Then, we have that

```
"Principia Mathematica" I ∈ Book I
("Principia Mathematica" I, "Bertrand Russell" I) ∈ hasAuthor I
```

Finally, a *knowledge base* (written) in $\mathcal{L}$ is a pair $\mathcal{K} = (\mathcal{D},\mathcal{A})$ where $\mathcal{D}$ is a *TBox* and $\mathcal{A}$ is a *ABox* (written) in $\mathcal{L}$. We say that an interpretation $\mathcal{I}$ for $\mathcal{L}$ is a *model of $\mathcal{K}$* iff $\mathcal{I}$ is a model of $\mathcal{D}$ and $\mathcal{A}$.

3.4 Inference Problems

3.4.1 Inference Problems for Concept Descriptions

Let $\mathcal{D}$ be a terminology, and C and D be concept descriptions in a language $\mathcal{L}$ in what follows. We say that:

- C is *satisfiable* with respect to $\mathcal{D}$ iff there is a model $\mathcal{I}$ of $\mathcal{D}$ such that $C^{\mathcal{I}} \neq \varnothing$; otherwise, we say that C is *unsatisfiable* with respect to $\mathcal{D}$

- C is *subsumed* by D with respect to $\mathcal{D}$, denoted $C \sqsubseteq_{\mathcal{D}} D$ or $\mathcal{D} \models C \sqsubseteq D$, iff, for every model $\mathcal{I}$ of $\mathcal{D}$, we have $C^{\mathcal{I}} \subseteq D^{\mathcal{I}}$

- C and D are *equivalent* with respect to $\mathcal{D}$, denoted $C \equiv_{\mathcal{D}} D$ or $\mathcal{D} \models C \equiv D$, iff, for every model $\mathcal{I}$ of $\mathcal{D}$, we have $C^{\mathcal{I}} = D^{\mathcal{I}}$

- C and D are *disjoint* with respect to $\mathcal{D}$ iff, for every model $\mathcal{I}$ of $\mathcal{D}$, we have $C^{\mathcal{I}} \cap D^{\mathcal{I}} = \varnothing$

When $\mathcal{D}$ is empty, we simply say that C is satisfiable, and similarly for the other definitions. The inference problems for concept descriptions are testing for satisfiability, subsumption, equivalence, or disjointness.

The inference problems for concept descriptions can be reduced just to testing for subsumption, because it is possible to prove the following proposition.

Proposition 3.2 (Reduction to Subsumption):
    (i) C is unsatisfiable with respect to $\mathcal{D}$ iff C is subsumed by $\bot$ with respect to $\mathcal{D}$.
    (ii) C and D are equivalent with respect to $\mathcal{D}$ iff C is subsumed by D with respect to $\mathcal{D}$, and D is subsumed by C with respect to $\mathcal{D}$.
    (iii) C and D are *disjoint* with respect to $\mathcal{D}$ iff $C \sqcap D$ is subsumed by $\bot$ with respect to $\mathcal{D}$.

If the language allows negation and intersection, then the inference problems for concept descriptions can also be reduced to testing for unsatisfiability:

Proposition 3.3 (Reduction to Unsatisfiability):
    (i) C is subsumed by D with respect to $\mathcal{D}$ iff $C \sqcap \neg D$ is unsatisfiable with respect to $\mathcal{D}$.
    (ii) C and D are equivalent with respect to $\mathcal{D}$ iff $C \sqcap \neg D$ and $D \sqcap \neg C$ are unsatisfiable.
    (iii) C and D are disjoint with respect to $\mathcal{D}$ iff $C \sqcap D$ is unsatisfiable with respect to $\mathcal{D}$.

If the terminology $\mathcal{D}$ is acyclic we can in fact eliminate $\mathcal{D}$ by replacing each defined concept C by its definition until only primitive concepts occur in the concept expressions. Therefore, in the basic inference problems, we may assume that $\mathcal{D}$ is empty.

More precisely, let $\mathcal{D}$ be a terminology and C be a concept description in a language $\mathcal{L}$. Let $\mathcal{D}'$ be the expansion of $\mathcal{D}$. The *expansion of C with respect to $\mathcal{D}$* is the concept expression C' obtained by replacing each occurrence in C of a defined concept A by the concept description B, where $A \equiv B$ is the definition of A in $\mathcal{D}'$.

Proposition 3.4: Let $\mathcal{D}$ be a terminology and C and D be concept descriptions in a language $\mathcal{L}$. Let C' and D' be the expansions of C and D with respect to $\mathcal{D}$. Assume that $\mathcal{D}$ is acyclic.

(i) C is unsatisfiable with respect to $\mathcal{D}$ iff C' is unsatisfiable.

(ii) C and D are equivalent with respect to $\mathcal{D}$ iff C' and D' are equivalent.

(iii) C and D are disjoint with respect to $\mathcal{D}$ iff C' and D' are disjoint.

Finally, let $\mathcal{D}$ be a terminology, C be a concept description, and S be a set of concept descriptions (all in a language $\mathcal{L}$). Suppose that, for any two concept descriptions $U, V \in S$, it is never the case that U is subsumed by V with respect to $\mathcal{D}$ and V is subsumed by U with respect to $\mathcal{D}$. We say that $U \in S$ is the *most specific concept* that subsumes C with respect to $\mathcal{D}$ iff U subsumes C with respect to $\mathcal{D}$ and there is no $V \in S$ such that U subsumes V with respect to $\mathcal{D}$ and V subsumes C with respect to $\mathcal{D}$. Likewise, we say that $V \in S$ is the *most general concept* that C subsumes with respect to $\mathcal{D}$ iff C subsumes V with respect to $\mathcal{D}$ and there is no atomic concept $U \in S$ such that C subsumes U with respect to $\mathcal{D}$ and U subsumes V with respect to $\mathcal{D}$. We then define the *classification problem* for C in S with respect to $\mathcal{D}$ as follows: "Find $D, E \in S$ such that D is the most specific concept in S that subsumes C with respect to $\mathcal{D}$ and E the most general concepts that C subsumes with respect to $\mathcal{D}$." Intuitively, the classification problem amounts to correctly placing a new concept expression C in a taxonomic hierarchy of concepts. It abstracts the basic task in constructing a terminology.

3.4.2 Inference Problems for Assertions

Let $\mathcal{D}$ be a terminology and $\mathcal{A}$ be a set of assertions in a language $\mathcal{L}$ (with constants). Let α be an assertion, C be a concept description, and a be a constant in $\mathcal{L}$. We say that:

- $\mathcal{A}$ is *consistent* with respect to $\mathcal{D}$ iff there is an interpretation $\mathcal{I}$ of $\mathcal{L}$ that is simultaneously a model of $\mathcal{D}$ and $\mathcal{A}$

- α is *entailed* by $\mathcal{A}$ and $\mathcal{D}$, denoted $\mathcal{A} \cup \mathcal{D} \models \alpha$, iff, for every interpretation $\mathcal{I}$ of $\mathcal{L}$, if $\mathcal{I}$ is simultaneously a model of $\mathcal{D}$ and $\mathcal{A}$ then $\mathcal{I}$ satisfies α
- *a is an instance of C* with respect to $\mathcal{A}$ and $\mathcal{D}$ iff $\mathcal{A} \cup \mathcal{D} \models C(a)$.

The first three inference problems for assertions therefore are testing consistency of a world description with respect to a terminology, testing entailment of an assertion by a world description with respect to a terminology, and testing if a constant is an instance of a concept description with respect to a world description and a terminology.

Finally, let $\mathcal{D}$ be terminology, a be a constant, S be a set of concept descriptions, and $\mathcal{A}$ be a set of assertions (all in a language $\mathcal{L}$). Suppose that, for any two concept descriptions $U, V \in S$, it is never the case that U is subsumed by V with respect to $\mathcal{D}$ and V is subsumed by U with respect to $\mathcal{D}$. We then define the *realization problem* for a in S with respect to $\mathcal{D}$ and $\mathcal{A}$. Find a concept description $C \in S$ such that $\mathcal{A} \cup \mathcal{D} \models C(a)$ and there is no concept description $D \in S$ such that $\mathcal{A} \cup \mathcal{D} \models D(a)$ and $\mathcal{D} \models D \sqsubseteq C$.

Recommended Reading

The basic reference for this chapter is *The Description Logic Handbook* (Baader et al. 2003). We specially recommend reading Chapter 1 (Nardi and Brachman 2003) and Chapter 2 (Baader and Nutt 2003), which lay down the basic concepts in detail, and Chapter 10 (Borgida and Brachman 2003), which covers conceptual modeling with description logic.

The description logic Web site (URL: http://dl.kr.org/) contains a substantial amount of material, including links to courses and tutorials.

For the readers interested in learning more about knowledge representation formalisms, we recommend Brachman and Levesque (2004), and for those wishing to cover the interplay between logic and computer science, we suggest Huth and Ryan (2004).

References

Baader, F.; Calvanese, D.; McGuiness, D.L.; Nardi, D.; Patel-Schneider, P.F. (Eds.) (2003) *The Description Logic Handbook: Theory, Implementation and Applications*. Cambridge University Press, Cambridge, UK.

Baader, F.; Nutt, W. (2003) Basic description logics. In: Baader, F.; Calvanese, D.; McGuiness, D.L.; Nardi, D.; Patel-Schneider, P.F. (Eds) *The Description Logic Handbook: Theory, Implementation and Applications*. Cambridge University Press, Cambridge, UK.

Borgida, A.; Brachman, R.J. (2003) Conceptual Modeling with Description Logics. In: Baader, F.; Calvanese, D.; McGuiness, D.L.; Nardi, D.; Patel-Schneider, P.F. (Eds) *The Description Logic Handbook: Theory, Implementation and Applications*. Cambridge University Press, Cambridge, UK.

Brachman, R.J.; Levesque, H.J. (Eds.) (1985) *Readings in Knowledge Representation*. Morgan Kaufmann, Los Altos, CA, USA.

Brachman, R.J.; McGuinness, D.L.; Patel-Schneider, P.F.; Resnick, L.A.; Borgida, A. (1991) Living with CLASSIC: When and how to use a KL-ONE like language. In: Sowa, J.F. (Eds) *Principles of Semantic Networks*. Morgan Kaufmann, Los Altos, CA, USA, pp. 401–456 .

Brachman, R.J.; Levesque, H.J. (2004) *Knowledge Representation and Reasoning*. Morgan Kaufmann, Los Altos, CA, USA.

Haarslev, V.; Moller, R. (2001) RACER system description. In: *Proceedings of the Sixth International Joint Conference on Automated Reasoning*, Siena, Italy. Lecture Notes in Computer Science, Vol. 2083. Springer-Verlag, Berlin, Germany, pp. 701–705.

Horracks, I. (1998) Using an expressive description logic: FaCT or fiction? In: *Proceedings of the Sixth International Conference on Principles of Knowledge Representation and Reasoning*, pp. 636–647.

Horracks, I. (2003) The FaCT System. Available at: ttp://www.cs.man.ac.uk/~horrocks/FaCT/

Huth, M.; Ryan, M. (2004) *Logic in Computer Science: Modelling and Reasoning about Systems*. Cambridge University Press, Cambridge, UK.

Nardi, D.; Brachman, R.J. (2003) An introduction to description logics. In: Baader, F.; Calvanese, D.; McGuiness, D.L.; Nardi, D.; Patel-Schneider, P.F. (Eds) *The Description Logic Handbook: Theory, Implementation and Applications.* Cambridge University. Press, Cambridge, UK.

Nebel, B.; van Luck, K. (1988) Hybrid reasoning in BACK. In: *Proceedings of the Third International Symposium on Methodologies for Intelligent Systems*, pp. 260–269.

4

RDF and RDF Schema

4.1 Introduction

The *Resource Description Framework* (RDF) is a general-purpose language for representing information about resources in the Web. It is particularly intended for representing metadata about Web resources, but it can also be used to represent information about objects that can be identified on the Web, even when they cannot be directly retrieved from the Web. To some extent, RDF is a lightweight ontology language designed to support interoperability between applications that exchange machine-understandable information on the Web. RDF is currently defined by a set of W3C recommendations, published on February 10th, 2004.

The lack of expressiveness of RDF was partly eased with the introduction of the *RDF Vocabulary Description Language 1.0: RDF Schema* (RDF-S or RDF Schema), which offers primitives to model hierarchies of classes and properties. RDF-S is currently defined by a W3C recommendation, also published on February 10th, 2004.

This chapter describes both RDF and RDF Schema, after a very brief introduction to some essential XML concepts, including the concepts of URI and namespaces. The syntax of the examples in this chapter was validated with the W3C RDF validation service (available at http://www.w3.org/RDF/Validator/).

4.2 XML Essentials

4.2.1 Elements and Attributes

The *Extensible Markup Language* (XML) is a general-purpose markup language, designed to describe structured documents. Unlike HTML, users may create their own tags in XML, creating specific markup languages, such as the ontology description languages described in this and the next chapters. Also, unlike HTML, tags in XML have no semantics indicating how to present documents through a Web browser.

An *XML document* consists of plain text and markup, in the form of tags, which is interpreted by application programs. A simple XML document would be as follows:

```
1.    <?xml version="1.0" encoding="UTF-8" ?>
2.    <cat>
3.       <item docid="www.cat.com/docs#R1">
4.          <description>My homepage</description>
5.          <creator>R051156</creator>
6.       </item>
7.       <item docid="www.cat.com/docs#R2">
8.          <description>My Book</description>
9.          <creator/>
10.      </item>
11.   </cat>
```

An XML document may start with an optional *processing instruction* tag that indicates, for example, the XML version of the document and the character encoding used, as shown in line 1.

An *element* typically consists of a *start-tag*, the element *content*, and a matching *end-tag*, as in line 4. An element may have an *empty content*, in which case it may be denoted by the *empty-element tag*, as in line 9. Elements may be nested, defining a structure for the document, as in the above example. An element is named after the start-tag. For example, lines 3 to 6 define an `<item>` element, whereas lines 7 to 10 define a second `<item>` element. The start-tag, or the empty-element tag, may have zero or more *attributes* consisting of a *name*, followed by the equal sign, followed by a *value*, enclosed in (double) quotes. For example, the start-tag of the `<item>` element in line 3 has the attribute `docid="www.cat.com/docs#R1"`.

An XML document must satisfy certain syntactic constraints, such as every start-tag must have a matching end-tag, and elements must be nested within other elements. In addition, an XML document may optionally include an XML schema declaration that defines additional constraints on the document structure. A discussion about XML Schema is beyond the scope of this very simple introduction. It suffices to say that the XML Schema specification includes a set of datatypes, which the ontology description languages borrow.

Table 4.1 List of terms and abbreviations.

Abbreviation	Term	Explanation
	resource	anything that has identity, be it a retrievable digital entity or a physical entity
URI	Uniform Resource Identifier	identifies a resource in the Web
URIref	URI Reference	URI with an optional fragment identifier
	Namespace	a collection of names, identified by a URIref
QName	Qualified Name	identifies a name in a namespace; has the syntax n:p, where n is a *namespace prefix* and p is the *local part;* expands to the URIref obtained by concatenating the URIref of the namespace with the local part

4.2.2 URIs and Namespaces

The concepts of URI, URI reference, namespace, and qualified name are fundamental for structuring the Semantic Web as a distributed, federated information space, because they provide an addressing scheme that is stable, distributed, and effective. We make extensive use of these concepts throughout the book because they also play a core role in the ontology description languages we adopt. To help the reader, Table 4.1 serves as a guide to the concepts we introduce in this section.

A *resource* is anything that has an identity, be it a retrievable digital entity (such as an electronic document, an image, or a service), a physical entity (such as a book) or a collection of other resources.

A *Uniform Resource Identifier* (URI) is a character string that identifies an abstract or physical resource on the Web. Examples of URIs following different *URI schemes* are:

- A URI following the FTP scheme for File Transfer Protocol services:
  `ftp://ftp.mysite.com/files/foobar.txt`

- A URI following the HTTP scheme for Hypertext Transfer Protocol services:
  `http://www.mysite.com/pub/foobar.html`

- A URI following the MAILTO scheme for e-mail addresses:
  `mailto:em@w3.org`

A *URI reference* (URIref) denotes the common usage of a URI, with an optional *fragment identifier* attached to it and preceded by the character "#". However, the URI that results from such a reference includes only the URI after removing the fragment identifier.

Examples of URIrefs are:

- A URIref identifying an individual:
  `http://www.w3.org/People/EM/contact#me`

- A URIref identifying a class (or type):
  `http://www.w3.org/2000/10/swap/pim/contact#Person`

- A URIref identifying a property:
  `http://www.w3.org/2000/10/swap/pim/contact#mailbox`

- A URIref identifying a property value:
  `http://www.example.org/staffem/85741`

An *absolute* URIref identifies a resource independently of the context in which the URIref appears. A *relative* URIref is a URIref with some prefix omitted; hence, information from the context in which the URIref appears is required to fill in the omitted prefix. In particular, a relative URIref consisting of just a fragment identifier is equivalent to the URIref of the document in which it appears, with the fragment identifier appended to it. For example, the relative URIref `#PrivateDoc`, appearing in a document identified by the URIref `http://www.cat.com/schema` is considered equivalent to the URIref:

`http://www.cat.com/schema#PrivateDoc`

An *XML namespace*, or simply a *namespace*, is a collection of names. A namespace is identified by a URIref. Table 4.2 shows examples of namespaces we use throughout this book.

Names from namespaces may appear as *qualified names* (QNames) of the form `P:L`, containing a single colon "`:`", that separates the name into a *namespace prefix* `P` and a *local part* `L`. The namespace prefix must be associated with a namespace URIref `N` in a namespace declaration (see below). We say that the qualified name *represents* the absolute URIref constructed by concatenating `N` and `L`.

Table 4.2 Examples of commonly used namespaces.

Namespace	URIref	Prefix
RDF	`http://www.w3.org/1999/02/22-rdf-syntax-ns#`	`rdf`
RDF Schema	`http://www.w3.org/2000/01/rdf-schema#`	`rdfs`
DAML	`http://www.daml.org/2001/03/daml+oil#`	`daml`
OWL	`http://www.w3.org/2002/07/owl#`	`owl`
Dublin Core	`http://purl.org/dc/elements/1.1/`	`dc`

Examples are (see Table 4.2 for the namespace prefixes and the associated URIref):

- The QName `rdf:description` has namespace prefix `rdf` and local part `description`. It expands to the URIref:
  `http://www.w3.org/1999/02/22-rdf-syntax-ns#description`

- The QName `dc:creator` has namespace prefix `dc` and local part `creator`. It expands to the URIref:
  `http://purl.org/dc/elements/1.1/creator`

A namespace is declared using a family of reserved attributes, whose name must either be `xmlns` or have `xmlns:` as a prefix, and whose value is a URIref identifying the namespace.

For example, the following code fragment shows the namespace declarations of the catalogue ontology, which is the last example of this chapter.

```
1.  <rdf:RDF
2.      xmlns="http://www.cat.com/docs"
3.      xml:base="http://www.cat.com/docs"
4.      xmlns:cs="http://www.cat.com/schema/"
5.      xmlns:dc="http://purl.org/dc/elements/1.1/"
6.      xmlns:rdf="http://www.w3.org/1999/02/22-rdf-syntax-ns#"
7.      xmlns:rdfs="http://www.w3.org/2000/01/rdf-schema#"
8.      xmlns:owl ="http://www.w3.org/2002/07/owl#"
9.      xmlns:xsd ="http://www.w3.org/2001/XMLSchema#">
```

Line 2 indicates that the *default namespace* of the catalogue ontology is the URI `http://www.cat.com/docs`. All unqualified terms used in the XML document that defines the catalogue ontology will belong to this namespace. Line 3 identifies the base URI for the catalogue ontology.

In general, the *base URI* of an XML document is the value of the attribute `xml:base` or, by default, the URI of the document itself. If R is a relative URIref and B is the base URI of a document, the equivalent absolute URIref is B concatenated with R. In the above example, if `#R20301` is a relative URIref occurring in a document with base URI `http://www.cat.com/docs`, then the equivalent absolute URIref is `http://www.cat.com/docs#R20301`.

Returning to our example, Line 4 assigns the namespace prefix `cs` to the namespace `http://www.cat.com/schema/`. Line 5 defines the namespace prefix `dc` and assigns it to another URI, which identifies the namespace of a second ontology (the Dublin Core metadata scheme) from which the catalogue ontology will import concepts. Lines 6 to 9 define namespace prefixes for the namespaces of RDF, RDF Schema, OWL, and XML Schema, respectively. RDF and RDF Schema are covered in this chapter, whereas OWL is addressed in the next chapter. XML Schema is important in this context because it provides a type system for ontology description languages.

4.3 RDF

The *Resource Description Framework* (RDF) is a general-purpose language for representing information in the Web. It is particularly intended for representing metadata about Web resources, but it can also be used to represent information about objects that can be identified on the Web, even when they cannot be directly retrieved from the Web. To some extent, RDF is a lightweight ontology language to support interoperability between applications that exchange machine-understandable information on the Web.

RDF has a very simple and flexible data model, based on the central concept of the RDF statement. We also consider the concept of vocabulary as part of the RDF data model, due to its relevance to ontology modeling. RDF offers three equivalent notations: RDF triples, RDF graphs, and RDF/XML. We cover all these topics, starting with the RDF data model.

4.3.1 RDF Statements and Vocabularies

An *RDF statement* (or simply a *statement*) is a triple *(S, P, O),* where

- *S* is a URIref, called the *subject* of the statement
- *P* is a URIref, called the *property* (also called the *predicate*) of the statement, that denotes a binary relationship
- *O* is either a URIref or a literal, called the *object* of the statement; if *O* is a literal, then *O* is also called the *value* of the property *P*

Let *s* be the resource identified by the URIref *S.* We also say that *s has a P property of O*, or that *s has a P property with value O.*

Literals are character strings that represent datatype values. Literals may not be used as subjects or properties in RDF statements.

A *vocabulary* is a set of URIrefs and is therefore synonymous with an XML namespace. Note that, because a vocabulary is a set, each URIref must be unique within a vocabulary. A vocabulary *V* is frequently specified in two alternative ways. The first alternative uses qualified names to define *V* as follows.

- Select a fixed URIref U and a prefix p for it
- Define a set of qualified names with prefix p
- Define *V* as the set of URIrefs represented by such qualified names

We say that *V* is a *qualified name vocabulary* (a nonstandard term), U is the *URIref* of the vocabulary, and p is the *name* of the vocabulary. Sometimes the URIref of a vocabulary is actually the URL of a Web resource that provides further information about that vocabulary. For example, the URL of the Dublin Core vocabulary is `http://purl.org/dc/elements/1.1/`.

The second alternative is similar, but uses fragment identifiers to define a vocabulary *V* as follows

- Select a fixed URIref U and a prefix p for it
- Define a set of fragment identifiers
- Define *V* as the set of URIrefs obtained by concatenating U, the character "#" and each fragment identifier

We say that *V* is a *fragment identifier vocabulary* (also a nonstandard term), U is *URIref* of the vocabulary, and p is the *name* of the vocabulary. Because of the syntactical subtleties of RDF/XML, qualified name vocabularies are frequently used to define URIrefs used as properties of RDF statements, whereas fragment identifier vocabularies are preferred to define URIrefs that will denote subjects or objects of RDF statements.

RDF, RDF Schema, and OWL are actually defined as vocabularies. For example, the RDF vocabulary has URIref http://www.w3.org/1999/02/22-rdf-syntax-ns#, typically has the prefix rdf, and contains the qualified names listed in Table 4.5 at the end of this section.

A set *R* of RDF statements should be understood as expressing the conjunction of the statements. The URIrefs used in the RDF statements in *R* may be taken from *native* vocabularies, that is, vocabularies defined exclusively for *R*, or from *imported* vocabularies, that is, vocabularies defined elsewhere.

Throughout this chapter, we use a running example that models a document metadata catalogue, that is, a catalogue that describes documents with the help of metadata, but that does not contain the documents themselves. Formally, the catalogue is defined as a set of RDF statements, based on three native vocabularies (see Table 4.3):

- docid is a fragment identifier vocabulary containing URIrefs that uniquely identify documents; a fragment identifier of the form R20301, for example, stands for the URIref http://www.cat.com/docs#R20301 that identifies a document within the docid vocabulary
- authid is a fragment identifier vocabulary containing URIrefs that uniquely identify authorities (persons or institutions) that are the creators of the documents; a fragment identifier of the form R051156, for example, stands for the URIref http://www.cat.com/auth#R051156 that identifies an authority within the authid vocabulary
- cs is a qualified name vocabulary containing URIrefs that uniquely identify document types; a qualified name of the form cs:PersonalDoc, for example, stands for the URIref http://www.cat.com/schema/PersonalDoc that identifies a document type within the cs vocabulary

The docid and authid vocabularies contain URIrefs that will be used as subjects and objects of the RDF statements that comprise the catalogue. The cs vocabulary contains URIrefs that will be used as properties of RDF statements that describe documents.

Table 4.3 Vocabularies of the document metadata catalogue.

Native Vocabularies	
Name / URIref	**Prefix**
Catalogue Document IDs `http://www.cat.com/docs`	`docid`
Catalogue Document Authorities `http://www.cat.com/auth`	`authid`
Catalogue Document Schema `http://www.cat.com/schema/`	`cs`
Imported Vocabularies	
Name / URIref	**Prefix**
RDF `http://www.w3.org/1999/02/22-rdf-syntax-ns#`	`rdf`
Dublin Core `http://purl.org/dc/elements/1.1/`	`dc`

The catalogue also uses two imported vocabularies:

- `rdf` is the RDF vocabulary, as explained in this chapter
- `dc` is the Dublin Core vocabulary containing the qualified names used as properties to describe document metadata. We use only three such qualified names:

  `dc:title` — a name given to the resource
  `dc:creator` — an entity that creates the content of the resource
  `dc:date` — a date associated with an event in the life cycle of the resource

For example, the qualified name `dc:title` expands to the URIref

  `http://purl.org/dc/elements/1.1/title`

Note that our very simple example already illustrates three interesting features of RDF and the Semantic Web technology in general. First, our catalogue reuses a vocabulary, the Dublin Core, which is standardized by a large community. We are therefore using the terms "title", "creator", and "date" according to a well-established meaning (and not according to our personal taste). Second, our catalogue uses universal IDs, the URIrefs, to identify the documents and authorities. Third, we introduce document IDs and authorities as vocabularies, which other applications can reuse, just as our catalogue reused the Dublin Core vocabulary.

Table 4.4 contains three RDF statements that form a fragment of the catalogue. Note that they all have `http://www.cat.com/docs#R20301` as the subject, which is a URIref that identifies a certain document. Also note that the object of statement S1 is a URIref, whereas the objects of statements S2 and S3 are literals.

Table 4.4 Examples of RDF statements.

Stmt	Element	Value (Absolute URIref or Literal)	Value (QName)
S1	Subject	`http://www.cat.com/docs#R20301`	
	Property	`http://purl.org/dc/elements/1.1/creator`	`dc:creator`
	Value	`http://www.cat.com/auth#R051156`	
S2	Subject	`http://www.cat.com/docs#R20301`	
	Property	`http://purl.org/dc/elements/1.1/title`	`dc:title`
	Value	`Karin Homepage`	
S3	Subject	`http://www.cat.com/docs#R20301`	
	Property	`http://purl.org/dc/elements/1.1/date`	`dc:date`
	Value	`2021-01-20`	

4.3.2 RDF Triples and Graphs

The RDF triples notation translates RDF statements directly into character strings. More precisely, the *RDF triple* for an RDF statement *(S, P, O)* is a string of one of the two forms:

> *<S> <P> <O>* .   if *O* is an absolute or relative URIref
> *<S> <P> "O"* .   if *O* is a literal

The RDF triples notation for a set ***R*** of RDF statements is simply the concatenation of the RDF triples that represent each RDF statement in ***R***, in any order.

For example, the RDF triples corresponding to the RDF statements of Table 4.4 are (as a convenience, the subject, property, and object of an RDF triple appear in separated lines):

```
<http://www.cat.com/docs#R20301>
   <http://purl.org/dc/elements/1.1/creator>
      <http://www.cat.com/auth#R051156> .

<http://www.cat.com/docs#R20301>
   <http://purl.org/dc/elements/1.1/title>
      "Karin Homepage" .

<http://www.cat.com/docs#R20301>
   <http://purl.org/dc/elements/1.1/date>
      "2021-01-20" .
```

or, using qualified names for the URIrefs in the dc vocabulary:

```
<http://www.cat.com/docs#R20301>
   dc:creator <http://www.cat.com/auth#R051156> .

<http://www.cat.com/docs#R20301>
   dc:title   "Karin Homepage" .

<http://www.cat.com/docs#R20301>
   dc:date    "2021-01-20" .
```

The RDF graphs notation translates a set of RDF statements into a graph, with nodes representing subjects or objects, and arcs representing properties. More precisely, the *RDF graph* for a set *R* of RDF statements is a labeled graph where:

- The set of nodes of the graph is constructed as follows:
  - For each URIref *U* that occurs as subject or as object of an RDF statement in *R*, there is a node in the graph labeled with *U* ;
  - For each literal *L* that occurs as object of an RDF statement in *R*, there is a node in the graph labeled with *L* ;
  - These are the only nodes in the graph.
- The set of arcs of the graph is constructed as follows:
  - For each RDF statement *(S, P, O)* in *R*, there is an arc directed from the node labeled with *S* to the node labeled with *O*, and the arc is labeled with *P* ;
  - These are the only arcs in the graph.

Only absolute URIrefs are allowed to label nodes and arcs in RDF graphs. Furthermore, when drawing RDF graphs, nodes labeled with URIrefs are shown as ellipses, whereas nodes labeled with literals are shown as boxes. Figure 4.1 contains the RDF graph for the statements in Table 4.4.

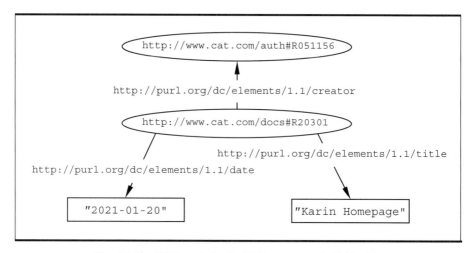

Fig. 4.1 The RDF graph for the RDF statements in Table 4.4.

4.3.3 RDF/XML

RDF/XML provides an XML notation for RDF statements and is the preferred notation in the context of software agents exchanging data, as in the Semantic Web, or in open distributed environments in general. RDF/XML is based on the RDF vocabulary, partly summarized in Table 4.5 at the end of this section. In spite of the fact that we are using XML, we still prefer the term "RDF vocabulary" to the term "XML namespace", although we have already noted that they are synonyms.

We introduce the details of RDF/XML with the help of our running example. The three RDF statements shown in Table 4.4 can be written in RDF/XML as

```
1.  <?xml version="1.0"?>
2.  <rdf:RDF
3.      xmlns:rdf="http://www.w3.org/1999/02/22-rdf-syntax-ns#"
4.      xmlns:dc="http://purl.org/dc/elements/1.1/">
5.    <rdf:Description
6.        rdf:about="http://www.cat.com/docs#R20301">
7.      <dc:creator
8.        rdf:resource="http://www.cat.com/auth#R051156"/>
9.    </rdf:Description>
10.   <rdf:Description
11.       rdf:about="http://www.cat.com/docs#R20301">
12.     <dc:title>Karin Homepage</dc:title>
13.   </rdf:Description>
14.   <rdf:Description
15.       rdf:about="http://www.cat.com/docs#R20301">
16.     <dc:date>2021-01-20</dc:date>
17.   </rdf:Description>
18. </rdf:RDF>
```

Lines 3 and 4 introduce the `rdf` and `dc` vocabularies so that we may use qualified names to abbreviate URIrefs in these vocabularies (we reinforce that vocabulary and namespace are synonyms, but we prefer the former term).

Lines 5 to 9 define the RDF statement S1 of Table 4.4:

- Line 5 uses the qualified name `rdf:Description` of the RDF vocabulary to indicate the beginning of a new RDF statement
- Line 6 uses the qualified name `rdf:about` of the RDF vocabulary to indicate the subject of S1, which is the absolute URIref that is the value of `rdf:about`
- Line 7 indicates that the qualified name `dc:creator` of the Dublin Core vocabulary is the property of S1
- Line 8 uses the qualified name `rdf:resource` of the RDF vocabulary to indicate the object of S1, which is the absolute URIref that is the value of `rdf:resource`
- Line 9 indicates that the definition of the RDF statement is completed

Lines 10 to 13 define the RDF statement S2 of Table 4.4. The explanation is similar to that of statement S1, except that line 12 indicates that the qualified name dc:title of the Dublin Core vocabulary is the property of S2; line 12 also indicates that the value "Karin Homepage" of the XML element dc:title is the object of S2. Lines 14 through 16 likewise define the RDF statement S3 of Table 4.4.

Unlike RDF graphs, RDF/XML allows the use of a relative URIref R as a value of rdf:about or rdf:resource. The equivalent absolute URIref is obtained by concatenating R with the base URI (recall, from the end of Section 4.2.2, that the base URI of an XML document is the value of the attribute xml:base or, by default, the URI of the document itself).

We may then rewrite the previous example in a more concise way, as follows

```
1.  <?xml version="1.0"?>
2.  <rdf:RDF
3.      xml:base="http://www.cat.com/docs"
4.      xmlns:rdf="http://www.w3.org/1999/02/22-rdf-syntax-ns#"
5.      xmlns:dc="http://purl.org/dc/elements/1.1/">
6.    <rdf:Description rdf:about="#R20301">
7.      <dc:creator
8.        rdf:resource="http://www.cat.com/auth#R051156"/>
9.    </rdf:Description>
10.   <rdf:Description rdf:about="#R20301">
11.     <dc:title>Karin Homepage</dc:title>
12.   </rdf:Description>
13.   <rdf:Description rdf:about="#R20301">
14.     <dc:date>2021-01-20</dc:date>
15.   </rdf:Description>
16. </rdf:RDF>
```

Line 3 declares http://www.cat.com/docs as the base URI of the document, which means that lines 6, 10, and 13 may use the relative URIref #R20301 to identify the subject of the RDF statements. The absolute URIref corresponding to the value of rdf:about is http://www.cat.com/docs#R20301.

By contrast, the value of rdf:resource in line 8 still is the absolute URIref http://www.cat.com/auth#R051156, that identifies the object of the RDF statement S1. Indeed, the authid vocabulary is not the base URI of the document, and RDF/XML allows the use of a relative URIref in rdf:resource only with respect to the base URI.

RDF/XML also contains the qualified name rdf:ID, which can be used as an attribute of rdf:Description, instead of rdf:about. The value of rdf:ID is an XML name V which must be unique, relative to the current base URI, and which defines the relative URIref #V. However, note that a valid XML name must start with a letter or the underscore symbol, "_". Hence, rdf:ID="V" and rdf:about="#V" are equivalent notations. If B is the base URI, the value of both attributes are equivalent to the absolute URIref B#V. Note that a QName cannot be used as the value of rdf:about, rdf:resource, or rdf:ID.

An RDF/XML element that represents the property of an RDF statement is called a *property* element. In the above example, the property elements are all from

the Dublin Core vocabulary, dc:creator, dc:title and dc:date. To simplify
the notation further, RDF/XML allows property elements to be nested within an
rdf:Description element, indicating that the properties apply to the same
resource. Our running example would then be rewritten as

```
1.  <?xml version="1.0"?>
2.  <rdf:RDF xml:base="http://www.cat.com/docs"
3.      xmlns:rdf="http://www.w3.org/1999/02/22-rdf-syntax-ns#"
4.      xmlns:dc="http://purl.org/dc/elements/1.1/">
5.    <rdf:Description rdf:ID="R20301">
6.      <dc:creator
7.         rdf:resource="http://www.cat.com/auth#R051156"/>
8.      <dc:title>Karin Homepage</dc:title>
9.    <dc:date>2021-01-20</dc:date>
10.   </rdf:Description>
11. </rdf:RDF>
```

Note the use of rdf:ID in line 6, whose value is R20301, without the symbol "#".
This is entirely equivalent to the use of rdf:about with value #R20301. Both are
equivalent to the URIref http://www.cat.com/docs#R20301.

The RDF vocabulary also contains other names, besides those our running
example illustrates, which capture additional semantics or introduce new syntactical
constructs. We discuss some of these names in the rest of this section. The reader is
referred to Table 4.5 for a partial summary of the RDF vocabulary.

The qualified name rdf:type of the RDF vocabulary is a built-in property with
a predefined semantics. An RDF statement of the form *(S,* rdf:type, *O)* indicates
that resource *O* represents a *category* or a *class* of resources, of which resource *S* is
an *instance*. Such resources are called *typed node elements* in RDF/XML
documents.

We may add an rdf:type property (line 9) to our running example to indicate
that Karin's homepage is a personal document, which is represented as the name
http://www.cat.com/schema/PersonalDoc. Also note that, in this case, the
RDF vocabulary is http://www.cat.com/schema/

```
1.  <?xml version="1.0"?>
2.  <rdf:RDF xml:base="http://www.cat.com/docs"
3.      xmlns:rdf="http://www.w3.org/1999/02/22-rdf-syntax-ns#"
4.      xmlns:dc="http://purl.org/dc/elements/1.1/">
5.    <rdf:Description rdf:about="#R20301">
6.      <rdf:type
7.  rdf:resource="http://www.cat.com/schema/PersonalDoc"/>
8.      <dc:creator
9.      rdf:resource="http://www.cat.com/auth#R051156"/>
10.     <dc:title>Karin Homepage</dc:title>
11.     <dc:date>2021-01-20</dc:date>
12.   </rdf:Description>
13. </rdf:RDF>
```

RDF/XML provides a special abbreviation where the `rdf:type` property and its value are removed, and the `rdf:Description` element is replaced by an element whose name is the qualified name corresponding to the value of the removed `rdf:type` property. In this abbreviated syntax, our running example becomes:

```
1.  <?xml version="1.0"?>
2.  <rdf:RDF
3.      xml:base="http://www.cat.com/docs"
4.      xmlns:cs="http://www.cat.com/schema/"
5.      xmlns:rdf="http://www.w3.org/1999/02/22-rdf-syntax-ns#"
6.      xmlns:dc="http://purl.org/dc/elements/1.1/">
7.    <cs:PersonalDoc rdf:about="#R20301">
8.      <dc:creator
9.         rdf:resource="http://www.cat.com/auth#R051156"/>
10.     <dc:title>Karin Homepage</dc:title>
11.     <dc:date>2021-01-20</dc:date>
12.   </cs:PersonalDoc>
13. </rdf:RDF>
```

Now, the qualified name `rdf:datatype` of the RDF vocabulary is an attribute of a property element and assumes as value an XML Schema datatype. It permits defining the type of a literal assigned as the value of a property element. For example, we may indicate that the value of the property `dc:date` (in line 11) is of the XML Schema type `date` (in line 12):

```
1.  <?xml version="1.0"?>
2.  <rdf:RDF
3.      xml:base="http://www.cat.com/docs"
4.      xmlns:cs="http://www.cat.com/schema/"
5.      xmlns:rdf="http://www.w3.org/1999/02/22-rdf-syntax-ns#"
6.      xmlns:dc="http://purl.org/dc/elements/1.1/">
7.    <cs:PersonalDoc rdf:about="#R20301">
8.      <dc:creator
9.        rdf:resource="http://www.cat.com/auth#R051156"/>
10.     <dc:title>Karin Homepage</dc:title>
11.     <dc:date
12.       rdf:datatype="http://www.w3.org/2001/XMLSchema#date">
13.         2021-01-20
14.     </dc:date>
15.   </cs:PersonalDoc>
16. </rdf:RDF>
```

We now turn to the last topic about RDF we cover. Applications sometimes need to represent information about the RDF statements themselves, such as when the statements were made, who made them, or other provenance information. RDF provides a built-in vocabulary intended for describing RDF statements. A description of a statement using this vocabulary is called a *reification* of the statement.

The *RDF reification vocabulary* consists of the type rdf:Statement, and the properties rdf:subject, rdf:predicate, and rdf:object (see Table 4.5). For example, a reification of the statement S1 in Table 4.4 would be given by assigning the statement a qualified name, such as stmts:S1, and then describing the statement as follows

```
stmts:S1 rdf:type       rdf:Statement .
stmts:S1 rdf:subject    docid:R20301 .
stmts:S1 rdf:predicate  dc:creator .
stmts:S1 rdf:object     authid:R051156 .
```

These four statements say that the resource identified by the qualified name stmts:S1 is an RDF statement (line 1), whose subject is the resource identified by qualified name docid:R20301 (line 2), whose predicate (or property) is the resource identified by the qualified name dc:creator, and whose object is the resource identified by the qualified name authid:R051156. In general, the four statements representing the reification of an RDF statement are referred to as a *reification quad*.

4.4 RDF Schema

RDF offers enormous flexibility but, apart from the rdf:type property, which has a predefined semantics, it provides no means for defining application-specific classes and properties. Instead, such classes and properties, and hierarchies thereof, are described using extensions to RDF provided by the *RDF Vocabulary Description Language 1.0: RDF Schema* (RDF Schema or RDF-S).

RDF Schema is defined as a (qualified name) vocabulary (see Table 4.6), whose URIref is http://www.w3.org/2000/01/rdf-schema#, and whose name typically is rdfs.

4.4.1 Classes

In RDF Schema, a *class* is any resource having an rdf:type property whose value is the qualified name rdfs:Class of the RDF Schema vocabulary.

A class *C* is defined as a *subclass* of a class *D* by using the predefined rdfs:subClassOf property to relate the two classes. The rdfs:subClassOf property is transitive in RDF Schema.

We may use RDF Schema to define a set *CP* of classes and properties for our document metadata catalogue. The result is very similar to a conceptual database schema, with the major difference that the definitions in *CP* are not mandatory, in the sense that we may have catalogue instances that do not exactly follow the classes and properties in *CP*.

In the examples that follow, we continue to use the vocabularies introduced in Table 4.3. Using the RDF triples notation, we may then define several classes of documents for our catalogue as follows

```
cs:Publication       rdf:type           rdfs:Class .
cs:Book              rdf:type           rdfs:Class .
cs:JournalPaper      rdf:type           rdfs:Class .
cs:ConfPaper         rdf:type           rdfs:Class .
cs:ShortPaper        rdf:type           rdfs:Class .
cs:Book              rdfs:subClassOf    cs:Publication .
cs:JournalPaper      rdfs:subClassOf    cs:Publication .
cs:ConfPaper         rdfs:subClassOf    cs:Publication .
cs:ShortPaper        rdfs:subClassOf    cs:JournalPaper .
cs:ShortPaper        rdfs:subClassOf    cs:ConfPaper .
```

Using the RDF/XML unabbreviated notation, this class hierarchy would be defined as follows

```
1.  <?xml version="1.0"?>

2.  <rdf:RDF
3.      xml:base="http://www.cat.com/schema/"
4.      xmlns:rdf="http://www.w3.org/1999/02/22-rdf-syntax-ns#"
5.      xmlns:rdfs="http://www.w3.org/2000/01/rdf-schema#"
6.      xmlns:dc="http://purl.org/dc/elements/1.1/">

7.    <rdf:Description rdf:about="Publication">
8.        <rdf:type
9.  rdf:resource="http://www.w3.org/2000/01/rdf-schema#Class"/>
10.   </rdf:Description>

11.   <rdf:Description rdf:about="Book">
12.       <rdf:type
13. rdf:resource="http://www.w3.org/2000/01/rdf-schema#Class"/>
14.       <rdfs:subClassOf rdf:resource="Publication"/>
15.   </rdf:Description>

16.   <rdf:Description rdf:about="JournalPaper">
17.       <rdf:type
18. rdf:resource="http://www.w3.org/2000/01/rdf-schema#Class"/>
19.       <rdfs:subClassOf rdf:resource="Publication"/>
20.   </rdf:Description>

21.   <rdf:Description rdf:about="ConfPaper">
22.       <rdf:type
23. rdf:resource="http://www.w3.org/2000/01/rdf-schema#Class"/>
24.       <rdfs:subClassOf rdf:resource="Publication"/>
25.   </rdf:Description>

26.   <rdf:Description rdf:about="ShortPaper">
27.       <rdf:type
28. rdf:resource="http://www.w3.org/2000/01/rdf-schema#Class"/>
29.       <rdfs:subClassOf rdf:resource="JournalPaper"/>
30.       <rdfs:subClassOf rdf:resource="ConfPaper"/>
31.   </rdf:Description>
32. </rdf:RDF>
```

Recall that RDF/XML allows the value of `rdf:about` or `rdf:resource` to be a relative URIref R, which is equivalent to the absolute URIref obtained by concatenating R with the base URI.

Line 3 declares the base URI is `http://www.cat.com/schema/`, differently from the running example of Section 4.3. Moreover, lines 7, 11, 16, 21, and 26 use the attribute `rdf:about`, rather than `rdf:ID`, which indicate that the absolute URIref that identifies each class must be obtained by concatenating the base URI with the value of `rdf:about` (without an intermediate "#" character). Taken together, this means that the above document defines a vocabulary with URIref `http://www.cat.com/schema/`, which contains five names, represented by the URIrefs:

```
http://www.cat.com/schema/Publication
http://www.cat.com/schema/Book
http://www.cat.com/schema/JournalPaper
http://www.cat.com/schema/ConfPaper
http://www.cat.com/schema/ShortPaper
```

In the RDF/XML abbreviated notation, we may rewrite the above example as follows

```
1.  <?xml version="1.0"?>

2.  <rdf:RDF
3.      xml:base="http://www.cat.com/schema/"
4.      xmlns:rdf="http://www.w3.org/1999/02/22-rdf-syntax-ns#"
5.      xmlns:rdfs="http://www.w3.org/2000/01/rdf-schema#"
6.      xmlns:dc="http://purl.org/dc/elements/1.1/">

7.  <rdfs:Class rdf:about="Publication"/>

8.  <rdfs:Class rdf:about="Book">
9.      <rdfs:subClassOf rdf:resource="Publication"/>
10. </rdfs:Class>

11. <rdfs:Class rdf:about="JournalPaper">
12.     <rdfs:subClassOf rdf:resource="Publication"/>
13. </rdfs:Class>

14. <rdfs:Class rdf:about="ConfPaper">
15.     <rdfs:subClassOf rdf:resource="Publication"/>
16. </rdfs:Class>

17. <rdfs:Class rdf:about="ShortPaper">
18.     <rdfs:subClassOf rdf:resource="JournalPaper"/>
19.     <rdfs:subClassOf rdf:resource="ConfPaper"/>
20. </rdfs:Class>

21. </rdf:RDF>
```

4.4.2 Properties

A *property* is any instance of the class rdfs:Property. The rdfs:domain property is used to indicate that a particular property applies to a designated class, and the rdfs:range property is used to indicate that the values of a particular property are instances of a designated class or, alternatively, are instances (i.e., literals) of an XML Schema datatype.

To define that an instance *I* of a class has a property *P* with value *V*, we simply define an RDF statement *(I, P, V)*, in any of the notations we introduced.

The specialization relationship between two properties is described using the predefined rdfs:subPropertyOf subproperty. An RDF property may have zero or more subproperties; all RDF Schema rdfs:range and rdfs:domain properties that apply to an RDF property also apply to each of its subproperties.

In our running example, we may add a property whose value is the number of pages of a publication, and a property whose value is the place of publication of a conference paper, as follows

```
1.  <?xml version="1.0"?>
2.  <!DOCTYPE rdf:RDF
3.      [<!ENTITY xsd "http://www.w3.org/2001/XMLSchema#">]>

4.  <rdf:RDF
5.      xml:base="http://www.cat.com/schema/"
6.      xmlns:rdf="http://www.w3.org/1999/02/22-rdf-syntax-ns#"
7.      xmlns:rdfs="http://www.w3.org/2000/01/rdf-schema#"
8.      xmlns:dc="http://purl.org/dc/elements/1.1/">

9.   <rdfs:Class rdf:about="Publication"/>
10.  <rdfs:Class rdf:about="JournalPaper">
11.     <rdfs:subClassOf rdf:resource="Publication"/>
12.  </rdfs:Class>
13.  <rdfs:Class rdf:about="ConfPaper">
14.     <rdfs:subClassOf rdf:resource="Publication"/>
15.  </rdfs:Class>
16.  <rdfs:Class rdf:about="ShortPaper">
17.     <rdfs:subClassOf rdf:resource="JournalPaper"/>
18.     <rdfs:subClassOf rdf:resource="ConfPaper"/>
19.  </rdfs:Class>

20.  <rdf:Property rdf:about="noPages">
21.     <rdfs:domain rdf:resource="Publication"/>
22.     <rdfs:range rdf:resource="&xsd;positiveInteger"/>
23.  </rdf:Property>
24.  <rdf:Property rdf:about="placeOfPublication">
25.     <rdfs:domain rdf:resource="ConfPaper"/>
26.     <rdfs:range rdf:resource="&xsd;string"/>
27.  </rdf:Property>

28. </rdf:RDF>
```

Lines 2 and 3 define xsd as an abbreviation for the XML Schema vocabulary. Lines 20 to 23 define the number of pages property, identified by the URIref

```
http://www.cat.com/schema/noPages
```

Likewise, lines 24 to 27 define the place of publication property, identified by the URIref

```
http://www.cat.com/schema/placeOfPublication.
```

4.4.3 Individuals

An *instance* of a class *C* is a resource having an rdf:type property whose value is *C*. A resource may be an instance of more than one class.

For example, the following RDF Schema fragment defines an individual of the class city, declared in the vocabulary http://www.cat.com/schema/,

```
<rdf:Description rdf:ID="c32">
   <rdf:type
          rdf:resource="http://www.cat.com/schema/City"/>
</rdf:Description>
```

If we associate the abbreviation cs with the above vocabulary, we may rewrite the definition as

```
<cs:City rdf:ID="c32"/>
```

As a more comprehensive example, recall from Table 4.3 that the metadata document catalogue is based on three vocabularies:

- http://www.cat.com/schema/ defines the *catalogue schema*, that is, the set of classes and properties of the catalogue
- http://www.cat.com/docs defines a *catalogue extension*, that is, a set of instances of the classes and properties defined in the catalogue schema
- http://www.cat.com/auth defines a *list of authorities*, that is, a list of authors' names, publishers' names, and so on

The example in Section 4.4.2 defined a sample of the catalogue schema, whereas our last example defines a sample of the catalogue extension.

```
1.  <?xml version="1.0"?>

2.  <!DOCTYPE rdf:RDF
3.       [<!ENTITY xsd "http://www.w3.org/2001/XMLSchema#">]>

4.  <rdf:RDF
5.       xml:base="http://www.cat.com/docs"
```

```
6.        xmlns:cs="http://www.cat.com/schema/"
7.        xmlns:rdf="http://www.w3.org/1999/02/22-rdf-syntax-ns#"
8.        xmlns:rdfs="http://www.w3.org/2000/01/rdf-schema#"
9.        xmlns:dc="http://purl.org/dc/elements/1.1/">

10.   <cs:Book
11.       rdf:about="#R20301">
12.       <dc:creator
13.         rdf:resource="http://www.cat.com/auth#R051156"/>
14.       <dc:title>
15.         SEMANTIC WEB: CONCEPTS AND TECHNOLOGIES
16.         FOR THE GEOGRAPHIC INFORMATION SCIENCES
17.       </dc:title>
18.       <dc:date rdf:datatype="&xsd;date">
19.         2021-01-20
20.       </dc:date>
21.       <cs:noPages>
22.         324
23.       </cs:noPages>
24.   </cs:Book>

25.   <cs:ConfPaper
26.       rdf:about="#R20302">
27.       <dc:creator
28.         rdf:resource="http://www.cat.com/auth#R051156"/>
29.       <dc:title>
30.         USING GAZETTEERS TO ANNOTATE GEOGRAPHIC
31.         CATALOGUE ENTRIES
32.       </dc:title>
33.       <dc:date rdf:datatype="&xsd;date">
34.         2021-01-21
35.       </dc:date>
36.       <cs:noPages>
37.         6
38.       </cs:noPages>
39.       <cs:placeOfPublication>
40.         Chipre
41.       </cs:placeOfPublication>
42.   </cs:ConfPaper>

43. </rdf:RDF>
```

Line 5 declares that the base URI is http://www.cat.com/docs/, the catalogue extension. Line 6 declares that http://www.cat.com/schema/, the catalogue schema, is a namespace, with abbreviation cs. Any other application wishing to reuse the catalogue classes and properties should likewise declare the catalogue schema as a namespace.

4.5 A Summary of the RDF/RDF Schema Vocabulary

Table 4.5 summarizes the RDF/RDF Schema vocabulary covered in this chapter. A comprehensive account can be found in Manola and Miller (2004).

Table 4.5 A partial account of the RDF/RDF Schema vocabulary.

Basic RDF Vocabulary	
Term	**Description**
rdf:RDF	indicates an RDF/XML document
rdf:Description	indicates the beginning of the description of an RDF statement
rdf:about	an attribute of rdf:Description; indicates the subject of the RDF statement, which is the URIref obtained as follows - the value of rdf:about, if it is a URIref - the concatenation of the base URI and the value of rdf:about, if it is not a URIref
rdf:ID	an attribute of rdf:Description; indicates the subject of the RDF statement, which is URIref obtained by concatenating the base URI, the symbol "#" and the value of rdf:ID
property elements	elements nested within the element rdf:Description; indicate properties that apply to the subject being described
rdf:resource	an attribute of a property element; indicates the object of the RDF statement, which is the URIref obtained as follows - the value of rdf:resource, if it is a URIref - the concatenation of the base URI and the value of rdf:resource, if it is not a URIref
rdf:type	a built-in property element with a predefined semantics; has as attribute rdf:resource, whose value represents a class of resources
rdf:datatype	an attribute of a property element, whose value is a XML Schema datatype; permits defining the type of a literal assigned as value of a property element

Table 4.5 A partial account of the RDF/RDF Schema vocabulary (cont.).

RDF Reification Vocabulary	
Term	**Description**
`rdf:Statement`	type indicating that the RDF statement is about another RDF statement
`rdf:subject`	property indicating the subject of an RDF statement
`rdf:predicate`	property indicating the predicate of an RDF statement
`rdf:object`	property indicating the object of an RDF statement
RDF Container Vocabulary	
Term	**Description**
`rdf:Seq`	indicates a sequence of resources or literals
`rdf:Bag`	indicates a "bag" (set with repetitions) of resources or literals
`rdf:alt`	indicates a list of resources or literals that represent alternatives
`rdf:li`	indicates an element of a sequence, bag, or alternative list
Basic RDF Schema Vocabulary	
Term	**Description**
`rdfs:Class`	a resource denoting the class of all classes
`rdfs:subClassOf`	a property that defines a class as a subclass of another class
`rdf:Property`	a resource denoting the class of all properties (actually, of the RDF vocabulary)
`rdfs:domain`	a property used to indicate that a particular property applies to a designated class (the domain of the property)
`rdfs:range`	a property used to indicate that the values of a particular property are instances of a designated class (the range of the property) or, alternatively, are instances (that is, literals) of an XML Schema datatype (also called the range of the property in the second case)
`rdfs:subPropertyOf`	a property that indicates that a property is a subproperty of another property
`rdfs:Datatype`	a resource used to indicate that a given URIref identifies a datatype
`rdfs:seeAlso`	a property used to relate a resource to another that contains a definition for the first
`rdfs:isDefinedBy`	a subproperty of rdfs:seeAlso used to relate a resource to a place where its definition is located, usually an RDF Schema
`rdfs:comment`	a property used to associate a comment with a resource
`rdfs:label`	a property used to assign a different name to a resource

Recommended Reading

The literature about XML, and related technologies, is enormous. To be economical, we suggest reading a small sample of W3C documents directly related to the topics discussed here (Fallside and Walmsley 2004; Manola and Miller 2004), or visiting the W3 Schools Website for online tutorials on XML (W3 Schools - XML) and XML Schema (W3 Schools - XML Schema). The official Dublin Core documents are also very readable references (Dublin Core 2004; ISO 2003).

References

DCMI (2004) Dublin Core Metadata Element Set, Version 1.1: Reference Description. Dublin Core Metadata Initiative. Available at: http://dublincore.org/documents/2004/12/20/dces/.

Fallside, D.C.; Walmsley, P. (Eds) (2004) XML Schema Part 0: Primer Second Edition. W3C Recommendation, 28 October 2004. Available at: http://www.w3.org/TR/xmlschema-0/.

ISO (2003) Information and documentation - The Dublin Core metadata element set. ISO Draft International Standard. ISO 15836:2003(E) / ISO TC 46/SC 4 N515. Available at: http://www.niso.org/international/SC4/n515.pdf.

Manola, F.; Miller, E. (Eds) (2004) RDF Primer. W3C Recommendation, 10 February 2004. Available at: http://www.w3.org/TR/rdf-primer/.

W3 Schools (2006a) XML Schema Tutorial. Available at: http://www.w3schools.com/schema/default.asp.

W3 Schools (2006b) XML Tutorial. Available at: http://www.w3schools.com/xml/default.asp.

5

OWL

5.1 Introduction

The *Web Ontology Language* (OWL) describes classes, properties, and relations among these conceptual objects in a way that facilitates machine interpretability of Web content. OWL is the result of the Web Ontology Working Group (now closed) and descends from DAML+Oil, which is in turn an amalgamation of DAML and OIL.

OWL is defined as a vocabulary, just as are RDF and RDF Schema, but it has a richer semantics. Hence, an ontology in OWL is a collection of RDF triples, which uses such vocabulary. The definition of OWL is organized as three increasingly expressive sublanguages:

- *OWL Lite* offers hierarchies of classes and properties, and simple constraints with enough expressive power to model thesauri and simple ontologies. However, it imposes limitations on how classes are related to each other, for example

- *OWL DL* increases expressiveness and yet retains decidability of the classification problem (see Section 3.4.1). OWL DL offers all OWL constructs, under certain limitations

- *OWL Full* is the complete language, without limitations, but it ignores decidability issues

OWL Full can be viewed as an extension of RDF, whereas OWL Lite and OWL DL are extensions of restricted forms of RDF. In more detail, we have that: every OWL (Full, DL, or Lite) document is an RDF/XML document; every RDF/XML document is an OWL Full document; not all RDF/XML documents are OWL DL (or OWL Lite) documents.

RDF is more expressive than OWL Lite and OWL DL exactly because the RDF data model imposes no limitations on how resources (URIrefs) can be related to each other. For example, in RDF, a class can be an instance of another class, whereas OWL DL and OWL Lite require that the sets of URIrefs that denote classes, properties, and individuals be mutually disjoint. Therefore, care must be taken when translating from RDF to OWL Lite or OWL DL.

This chapter introduces the OWL constructs, indicating the limitations that characterize OWL Lite and OWL DL. Table 5.4, at the end of this chapter, is a quick guide to OWL. The syntax of the OWL examples listed in this chapter was checked with the help of the WonderWeb OWL Ontology Validator (available at http://phoebus.cs.man.ac.uk:9999/OWL/Validator).

5.2 Requirements for Web Ontology Description Languages

The specification of OWL reflects a set of requirements that the W3C Consortium defined for ontology description languages for the Semantic Web (Heflin 2004), which we reproduce in Table 5.1.

The major points behind the requirements are:

1. The design of the language should be compatible with XML, in the sense that:
   1.1 An ontology should have an XML serialization syntax.
   1.2 An ontology should use the XML Schema datatypes, where applicable.

2. The design of the language should follow description logic, in the sense that:
   2.1 The language should be based on the notions of concept (or class), role (or property), and individual.
   2.2 The language should support expressions thereof.

3. The design of the language should support the definition of ontology vocabularies, in the sense that:
   3.1 An ontology should be identified by a URI reference.
   3.2 The classes, properties, and individuals of an ontology should be identified by URI references.

4. The design of the language should facilitate:
   4.1 The development of ontologies in a distributed fashion.
   4.2 The definition of different versions of the same ontology.
   4.3 The reuse of previously defined ontologies.

Table 5.1 Requirements for ontology description languages for the Semantic Web (Heflin 2004).

R1. Ontologies as distinct resource
Ontologies must be resources that have their own unique identifiers, such as a URI reference.

R2. Unambiguous concept referencing with URIs
Two concepts in different ontologies must have distinct absolute identifiers (although they may have identical relative identifiers). It must be possible to uniquely identify a concept in an ontology using a URI reference.

R3. Explicit ontology extension
Ontologies must be able to explicitly extend other ontologies in order to reuse concepts while adding new classes and properties. Ontology extension must be a transitive relation; if ontology A extends ontology B, and ontology B extends ontology C, then ontology A implicitly extends ontology C as well.

R4. Commitment to ontologies
Resources must be able to commit explicitly to specific ontologies, indicating precisely which set of definitions and assumptions is made.

R5. Ontology metadata
It must be possible to provide metadata for each ontology, such as author, publishing date, etc. These properties may or may not be borrowed from the Dublin Core element set.

R6. Versioning information
The language must provide features for comparing and relating different versions of the same ontology. This should include features for relating revisions to prior versions, explicit statements of backwards-compatibility, and the ability to deprecate identifiers (i.e., to state they are available for backwards-compatibility only, and should not be used in new applications/documents.)

R7. Class definition primitives
The language must be able to express complex definitions of classes. This includes, but is not limited to, subclassing and Boolean combinations of class expressions (i.e., intersection, union, and complement).

R8. Property definition primitives
The language must be able to express the definitions of properties. This includes, but is not limited to, subproperties, domain and range constraints, transitivity, and inverse properties.

R9. Datatypes
The language must provide a set of standard datatypes. These datatypes may be based on the XML Schema datatypes.

R10. Class and property equivalence
The language must include features for stating that two classes or properties are equivalent.

Table 5.1 Requirements for ontology description languages for the Semantic Web (cont.).

R11. Individual equivalence
The language must include features for stating that pairs of identifiers represent the same individual. Due to the distributed nature of the Web, it is likely that different identifiers will be assigned to the same individual.

R12. Attaching information to statements
The language must provide a way to allow statements to be "tagged" with additional information such as source, timestamp, confidence level, etc. The language need not provide a standard set of properties that can be used in this way, but it should instead provide a general mechanism for users to attach such information.

R13. Classes as instances
The language must support the ability to treat classes as instances. This is because the same concept can often be seen as a class or an individual, depending on the perspective of the user. For example, in a biological ontology, the class Orangutan may have individual animals as its instances. However, the class Orangutan may itself be an instance of the class Species.

R14. Cardinality constraints
The language must support the specification of cardinality restrictions on properties. These restrictions set minimum and maximum numbers of individuals that any single individual can be related to via the specified property.

R15. XML syntax
The language should have an XML serialization syntax. XML has become widely accepted by industry and numerous tools for processing XML have been developed. If the Web ontology language has an XML syntax, then these tools can be extended and reused.

R16. User-displayable labels
The language should support the specification of multiple alternative user-displayable labels for the resources specified by an ontology. This can be used, for example, to view the ontology in different natural languages.

R17. Supporting a character model
The language should support the use of multilingual character sets.

R18. Supporting a uniqueness of Unicode strings
In some character encodings (e.g., Unicode-based encodings), there are some cases where two different character sequences look the same and are expected, by most users, to compare equally. Given that the W3C I18N WG has decided on early uniform normalization (to Unicode Normal Form C) as the usual approach to solving this problem; any other solution needs to be justified.

5.3 Header Information, Versioning, and Annotation Properties

An OWL ontology usually starts with a set of namespace declarations and includes a collection of sentences about the ontology itself, grouped under the tag `owl:Ontology`. Such sentences register comments and version information, and may indicate that the current ontology imports other ontologies. OWL Lite includes all such constructs.

If an ontology O_1 imports another ontology O_2, then the entire set of declarations in O_2 is appended to O_1 and so on, recursively. Usually, O_1 also includes a namespace declaration pointing to the URIref of O_2 so that O_1 may use the vocabulary of O_2 in its own declarations. Importing another ontology, O_2, will also import all of the ontologies that O_2 imports.

For example, consider the following fragment.

```
1.    <?xml version="1.0"?>
2.    <!DOCTYPE rdf:RDF [
3.        <!ENTITY xsd "http://www.w3.org/2001/XMLSchema#">] >
4.    <rdf:RDF
5.        xml:base="http://www.cat.com/owl-schema/"
6.        xmlns:dc="http://purl.org/dc/elements/1.1/"
7.        xmlns:owl="http://www.w3.org/2002/07/owl#"
8.        xmlns:rdf="http://www.w3.org/1999/02/22-rdf-syntax-ns#"
9.        xmlns:rdfs="http://www.w3.org/2000/01/rdf-schema#">
10.   <owl:Ontology rdf:about="">
11.       <rdfs:comment>The Metadata Catalogue in OWL
12.       </rdfs:comment>
13.       <rdfs:label>Metadata Catalogue</rdfs:label>
14.       <owl:priorVersion
15.           rdf:resource="http://www.cat.com/schema/"/>
16.       <owl:imports
17.           rdf:resource="http://www.cat.com/auth/"/>
18.   </owl:Ontology>
19.   ...
```

Line 3 defines `xsd` as an abbreviation for the XML Schema vocabulary, and lines 5 to 9 declare the namespaces, as in the examples in Chapter 4.

The value of the `rdf:about` attribute of `owl:Ontology` indicates the URIref of the ontology. If the value is empty, as in line 10, the URIref of the ontology is the base URI of the document (recall from Section 4.2.2 that the base URI of an XML document is the value of the attribute `xml:base` or, by default, the URI of the document itself).

Lines 11 and 13 use qualified names of the `rdfs` vocabulary. Line 11 is self-explanatory. Line 13 provides a perhaps more readable name for the ontology. Lines 14 and 15 indicate the URIref of a previous version of the ontology, if any. Finally, lines 16 and 17 say that the current ontology imports the ontology identified by the URIref `http://www.cat.com/auth/`.

5.4 Properties

5.4.1 Datatype and Object Properties

OWL Lite offers the same class constructors as RDF Schema. However, unlike RDF Schema, OWL Lite distinguishes between a property whose range is a set of datatype values (or RDF literals) and a property whose range is a set of resources (identified by URIrefs). We stress that, as in RDF Schema, properties do not denote functions, but generic binary relations.

More precisely, a *datatype property* is a binary relation between the set of instances of a class and a set of instances of a datatype (see Section 5.7), declared with the help of the owl:DatatypeProperty constructor. An *object property* is a binary relation between the set of instances of two classes, declared with the help of the owl:ObjectProperty constructor.

OWL Lite uses the RDF Schema terms rdfs:domain and rdfs:range to declare the domain and range of a property, and the term rdfs:subPropertyOf to declare property hierarchies. These terms have the same semantics in OWL Lite and RDF Schema. In particular, if a property has multiple domain declarations (or range declarations), the property domain is the intersection of the domains (or ranges) that were declared. Property equivalence is declared with the help of the constructor owl:equivalentProperty.

With the adaptations to accommodate datatype and object properties, under certain circumstances, a set of class and property definitions in RDF Schema can be translated to OWL Lite almost directly, by changing from the vocabulary of one language to the vocabulary of the other. For example, the class declarations of the catalogue schema, introduced in Chapter 4, would be rewritten as follows

```
1.  <?xml version="1.0"?>
2.  <!DOCTYPE rdf:RDF [
3.     <!ENTITY xsd "http://www.w3.org/2001/XMLSchema#">] >
4.  <rdf:RDF
5.      xml:base="http://www.cat.com/owl-schema/"
6.      xmlns:dc="http://purl.org/dc/elements/1.1/"
7.      xmlns:owl="http://www.w3.org/2002/07/owl#"
8.      xmlns:rdf="http://www.w3.org/1999/02/22-rdf-syntax-ns#"
9.      xmlns:rdfs="http://www.w3.org/2000/01/rdf-schema#">
10. <owl:Ontology rdf:about="">
11.     <rdfs:comment>The Metadata Catalogue in OWL
12.     </rdfs:comment>
13.     <rdfs:label>Metadata Catalogue</rdfs:label>
14. </owl:Ontology>
15. <owl:Class rdf:about="Publication"/>
16. <owl:Class rdf:about="Book">
17.     <rdfs:subClassOf rdf:resource="Publication"/>
18. </owl:Class>
19. <owl:Class rdf:about="JournalPaper">
20.     <rdfs:subClassOf rdf:resource="Publication"/>
21. </owl:Class>
22. <owl:Class rdf:about="ConfPaper">
```

```
23.        <rdfs:subClassOf rdf:resource="Publication"/>
24.    </owl:Class>
25.    <owl:Class rdf:about="ShortPaper">
26.        <rdfs:subClassOt rdt:resource="JournalPaper"/>
27.        <rdfs:subClassOf rdf:resource="ConfPaper"/>
28.    </owl:Class>
29.    <owl:Class rdf:about="City"/>
30.    <owl:DatatypeProperty rdf:about="noPages">
31.        <rdfs:domain rdf:resource="Publication"/>
32.        <rdfs:range rdf:resource="&xsd;positiveInteger"/>
33.    </owl:DatatypeProperty>
34.    <owl:ObjectProperty rdf:about="placeOfPublication">
35.        <rdfs:domain rdf:resource="ConfPaper"/>
36.        <rdfs:range rdf:resource="City"/>
37.    </owl:ObjectProperty>
38. </rdf:RDF>
```

Lines 30 to 33 define the `noPages` property as a datatype property from the `Publication` class to `positiveInteger`, one of the recommended XML Schema datatypes (see Section 5.7). Lines 34 to 37 define `placeOfPublication` as an object property from the `ConfPaper` class to the `city` class.

5.4.2 Property Characteristics

In OWL Lite, properties may themselves have properties (also called characteristics, or metaproperties) that correspond to set-theoretic concepts, as shown in Table 5.1. However, only OWL Full allows `owl:InverseFunctionalProperty` to be specified for datatype properties, which means that datatype values can be defined as unique keys for a class only in OWL Full.

Table 5.1 OWL vocabulary for property characteristics.

Term	Definition
`owl:TransitiveProperty`	R is *transitive* iff, for any x, y and z, if $R(x,y)$ and $R(y,z)$ then $R(x,z)$
`owl:SymmetricProperty`	R is *symmetric* iff, for any x, y, $R(x,y)$ iff $R(y,x)$
`owl:FunctionalProperty`	R is *functional* iff, for any x, y and z, if $R(x,y)$ and $R(x,z)$ then $y=z$
`owl:InverseFunctional Property`[1]	R is *inverse functional* iff, for any x, y and z, if $R(y,x)$ and $R(z,x)$ then $y=z$
`owl:InverseOf`	S is the *inverse* of R iff, for any x, y, $R(x,y)$ iff $S(y,x)$

[1]Restricted to object properties in OWL Lite and OWL DL.

Returning to our running example, the property declarations of the catalogue schema introduced in Chapter 4 would be rewritten as (we omit the class declarations of the running example from the fragment below)

```
1. <?xml version="1.0"?>

2. <!DOCTYPE rdf:RDF [
3. <!ENTITY xsd "http://www.w3.org/2001/XMLSchema#">
4. <!ENTITY owl "http://www.w3.org/2002/07/owl#">] >

5. <rdf:RDF xml:base="http://www.cat.com/owl-schema/"
6.  xmlns:owl="http://www.w3.org/2002/07/owl#"
7.  xmlns:rdf="http://www.w3.org/1999/02/22-rdf-syntax-ns#"
8.  xmlns:rdfs="http://www.w3.org/2000/01/rdf-schema#">
9.  ...
10.   <owl:DatatypeProperty rdf:about="noPages">
11.       <rdf:type rdf:resource="&owl;FunctionalProperty"/>
12.       <rdfs:domain rdf:resource="Publication"/>
13.       <rdfs:range rdf:resource="&xsd;positiveInteger"/>
14.   </owl:DatatypeProperty>

15.   <owl:ObjectProperty rdf:about="placeOfPublication">
16.       <rdf:type rdf:resource="&owl;FunctionalProperty"/>
17.       <rdfs:domain rdf:resource="ConfPaper"/>
18.       <rdfs:range rdf:resource="City"/>
19.   </owl:ObjectProperty>

20. </rdf:RDF>
```

Line 4 defines `owl` as an abbreviation for the OWL vocabulary. Line 11 indicates that the `noPages` property is functional, which means that `noPages` associates each individual of the `Publication` class with at most one positive integer, its number of pages. Likewise, line 15 defines that the `placeOfPublication` property is functional, which implies that `placeOfPublication` associates each individual of the `ConfPaper` class with at most one individual of the `city` class.

Note that we do not require that datatype or object properties be total. For example, there may be an individual p of the `Publication` class for which the property `noPages` is not defined (that is, the number of pages of p may not be indicated). Likewise, there may be an individual c of the `ConfPaper` class for which the property `placeOfPublication` is not defined.

5.5 Classes

OWL DL and, to some extent, OWL Lite offer constructs to specify complex class descriptions and to define class restrictions and axioms, as summarized in Table 5.2. This section introduces these constructs, with the help of examples, also translated to description logic and naïve set theory, where applicable.

Table 5.2 Class constructors.

Term	Set Theory	DL	Description
`owl:Thing`	U	$\top$	the set of all individuals
`owl:Nothing`	$\varnothing$	$\bot$	the empty set
`owl:oneOf`	$\{x_1,\ldots,x_n\}$		the set of $x_1,\ldots,x_n$
`rdfs:subClassOf`	$A \subseteq B$	$A \sqsubseteq B$	A is a subset of B

`<owl:Restriction>`
`... R ...`
`</owl:Restriction>`
	$\{x/R\}$		the set of all things satisfying R

`owl:equivalentClass`	$A = B$	$A \equiv B$	A is equal to B
`owl:intersectionOf`	$A \cap B$	$A \sqcap B$	A intersection B
`owl:unionOf`	$A \cup B$	$A \sqcup B$	A union B
`owl:complementOf`	$\sim B$ $A \sim B$	$\neg B$ $A \sqcap \neg B$	complement of B w.r.t. U complement of B w.r.t A
`owl:disjointWith`	$A \cap B = \varnothing$	$A \sqcap B \equiv \bot$	A and B are disjoint

5.5.1 Class Descriptions

Top and Bottom Classes

OWL Lite introduces `owl:Thing` to denote the OWL universe, or the top class, and `owl:Nothing` to denote the empty set, or the bottom class. Therefore, all OWL individuals belong to `owl:Thing`, and no individual belongs to `owl:Nothing`.

Enumeration

OWL DL, but not OWL Lite, permits defining a class by enumeration, using the construct `owl:oneOf`. For example, we may categorize conferences as levels `"A"`, `"B"`, or `"C"`, by first defining the `Grade` class by enumeration as follows.

```
1. <owl:Class rdf:about="Grade">
2.   <owl:oneOf rdf:parseType="Collection">
3.       <owl:Thing rdf:about="A"/>
4.       <owl:Thing rdf:about="B"/>
5.       <owl:Thing rdf:about="C"/>
6.   </owl:oneOf>
7. </owl:Class>
```

Set Theory: Grade = {A,B,C}

We may then define the object type property `ConfGrade` that assigns grades to conferences as follows

```
1.  <owl:ObjectProperty rdf:about="hasGrade">
2.     <rdf:type rdf:resource="&owl;FunctionalProperty"/>
3.     <rdfs:domain rdf:resource="Conf"/>
4.     <rdfs:range rdf:resource="Grade"/>
5.  </owl:ObjectProperty>
```

Set Theory: hasGrade: Conf→Grade
              (a function with domain Conf and range Grade)

Property Restrictions

OWL Lite allows the description of a class C to include a restriction R on the individuals that may belong to C. The specification of R is always based on some property P of C and, as such, R is called a *property restriction* (in the sense of a restriction defined with the help of a property). In set-theoretic notation, this is equivalent to saying that C is subjected to a restriction of the form $C \subseteq \{x \,/\, R\}$.

Note that the above set inclusion allows the existence of individuals that satisfy R and yet are not in C. In other words, R defines a necessary, but not sufficient, condition for an individual to be in C.

In OWL notation, a class definition with a restriction has the following pattern.

```
1.  <owl:Class rdf:about=C >
2.     ...
3.     <rdfs:subClassOf>
4.        <owl:Restriction>
5.           <owl:onProperty rdf:resource=P>
6.           ... declaration of restriction R...
7.        </owl:Restriction>
8.     </rdfs:subClassOf>
9.     ...
10. </owl:Class>
```

Set Theory: $C \subseteq \{x \,/\, R\}$

Lines 4 to 7 define the (unnamed) class of all things that satisfy R, and line 3 indicates that C is a subclass of such a (unnamed) class. The pattern in lines 3 to 8 may be repeated to define multiple restrictions for the same class.

Restriction declarations may be of three types: quantified restrictions; cardinality restrictions; and value restrictions (also called filler information).

A *quantified restriction* may be an existential or a universal restriction, declared with the help of `owl:someValuesFrom` and `owl:allValuesFrom`, respectively. An *existential restriction* for C, P, and D requires that every instance c of C must have at least one occurrence of property P whose value is an instance of D. An existential restriction therefore corresponds to a description logic inclusion of the form $C \sqsubseteq \exists P.D$.

A *universal restriction* for C, P, and D requires that, for every instance c of C, if c has an occurrence of a property P whose value is d, then d must be an instance of D. Note that a universal restriction does not require c to have at least one occurrence of property P. A universal restriction therefore corresponds to a description logic inclusion of the form $C \sqsubseteq \forall P.D$.

For example, assume that we have two classes, Conf and EuropeanCity, whose instances represent conferences and cities in Europe, respectively, and a property, heldIn, which maps conferences into cities. We may then define a new class, heldInEuropeConf, and restrict it to contain only individuals that are conferences held at least once in a European city as follows

```
1.  <owl:Class rdf:about="heldInEuropeConf">
2.    <rdfs:subClassOf rdf:resource="Conf"/>
3.    <rdfs:subClassOf>
4.      <owl:Restriction>
5.        <owl:onProperty rdf:resource="heldIn"/>
6.        <owl:someValuesFrom rdf:resource="EuropeanCity"/>
7.      </owl:Restriction>
8.    </rdfs:subClassOf>
9.  </owl:Class>
```

Set Theory: heldInEuropeConf $\subseteq$
                   Conf $\cap \{x\, /\, \exists y\, (\text{heldIn}\,(x, y) \wedge y \in \text{EuropeanCity})\}$

Description Logic: heldInEuropeConf $\sqsubseteq$ Conf $\sqcap \exists$heldIn.EuropeanCity

Lines 4 to 7 define the (unnamed) class of all things with at least one occurrence (there may be more than one) of the heldIn property whose value is an instance of the EuropeanCity class. Lines 2 and 3 indicate that the heldInEuropeConf class is a subclass of the intersection of this (unnamed) class and the Conf class. Note that the OWL fragment in lines 1 to 9 does not guarantee that heldInEuropeConf contains all individuals that are conferences held at least once in a European city (that is, it is a necessary, but not sufficient condition).

We may define a second class, EuropeanConf, and restrict it to contain individuals that are conferences held only in European cities as follows

```
1.  <owl:Class rdf:about="EuropeanConf">
2.    <rdfs:subClassOf rdf:resource="Conf"/>
3.    <rdfs:subClassOf>
4.      <owl:Restriction>
5.        <owl:onProperty rdf:resource="heldIn"/>
6.        <owl:allValuesFrom rdf:resource="EuropeanCity"/>
7.      </owl:Restriction>
8.    </rdfs:subClassOf>
9.  </owl:Class>
```

Set Theory: EuropeanConf $\subseteq$
                   Conf $\cap \{x\, /\, \forall y\, (\text{heldIn}\,(x, y) \Rightarrow y \in \text{EuropeanCity})\}$

Description Logic: EuropeanConf $\sqsubseteq$ Conf $\sqcap \forall$heldIn.EuropeanCity

Lines 4 to 7 define the (unnamed) class of all things *t* such that, if the `heldIn` property is defined for *t*, then the value of such a property is an instance of the `EuropeanCity` class. Lines 2 and 3 indicate that the `EuropeanConf` class is a subclass of both this (unnamed) class and the `Conf` class.

Note that, syntactically, the two definitions are almost identical, but semantically they are quite different. Indeed, for every instance *r* of the `heldInEuropeConf` class, `heldIn` must associate *r* with at least one instance *s* of the `EuropeanCity` class (and perhaps with instances of other classes as well). By contrast, for every instance *p* of the `EuropeanConf` class, if `heldIn` associates *p* with *q*, then *q* must be an instance of the `EuropeanCity` class (but `heldIn` may not be defined for *p*).

A *cardinality restriction* (or *cardinality constraint*) for *C* imposes limitations on the number of occurrences of property *P* each instance of *C* must have. An *exact cardinality restriction*, declared with the help of `owl:cardinality`, specifies the exact number of occurrences of property *P* each instance of *C* must have. A *maximum* (or *minimum*) *cardinality restriction*, declared with the help of `owl:maxCardinality` (or `owl:minCardinality`) specifies the maximum (or minimum) number of occurrences of property *P* each instance of *C* must have.

For example, we may redefine `Publication` to be a class whose instances have exactly one occurrence of `noPages` as follows

```
1.  <owl:Class rdf:about="Publication">
2.     <rdfs:subClassOf>
3.        <owl:Restriction>
4.           <owl:onProperty rdf:resource="noPages"/>
5.           <owl:cardinality
6.              rdf:datatype="&xsd;nonNegativeInteger">
7.              1
8.           </owl:cardinality>
9.        </owl:Restriction>
10.    </rdfs:subClassOf>
11. </owl:Class>
```

Set Theory: $\mathtt{Publication} \subseteq \{\ x\ /\ card(\{\ y\ /\ \mathtt{noPages}\ (x, y)\ \}) = 1\ \}$

Description Logic: $\mathtt{Publication} \sqsubseteq (\leq 1\ \mathtt{noPages}) \sqcap (\geq 1\ \mathtt{noPages})$

Lines 3 to 8 define the (unnamed) class of all things with exactly one occurrence of the `noPages` property, and line 2 indicates that the `Publication` class is a subclass of such a (unnamed) class.

OWL Lite allows only 0 or 1 as values of cardinality restrictions. For example, a minimum cardinality restriction with value 1 captures the semantics of "at least one," whereas a maximum cardinality restriction with value 1 captures the semantics of "at most one." OWL DL goes further and permits any positive integer as the value of cardinality restrictions.

Finally, a *value restriction* or *filler information* for *C* imposes limitations on the values the occurrences of property *P* may have. Value restrictions are not part of OWL Lite, however.

For example, we may define `ConfInBerlin` to be a class whose instances must be conferences held in Berlin as follows

```
1.  <owl:Class rdf:about="ConfInBerlin">
2.    <rdfs:subClassOf rdf:resource="Conf"/>
3.    <rdfs:subClassOf>
4.      <owl:Restriction>
5.        <owl:onProperty rdf:resource="heldIn"/>
6.        <owl:hasValue rdf:resource="Berlin"/>
7.      </owl:Restriction>
8.    </rdfs:subClassOf>
9.  </owl:Class>
```

Set Theory: $\texttt{ConfInBerlin} \subseteq \texttt{Conf} \cap \{x\,/\,\texttt{heldIn}(x,\text{`Berlin'})\}$

The above fragment defines necessary conditions for a thing to be an instance of the `ConfInBerlin` class. That is, if some object I is an instance of the `heldInBerlin` class, then I is an instance of the `Conf` class (by line 2) and I has `Berlin` as the value of the `heldIn` property (by lines 3 to 8). But, there might be an object I of the `Conf` class that has `Berlin` as the value of the `heldIn` property, and yet I is not an instance of the `heldInBerlin` class. This follows directly from the semantics of `rdfs:subClassOf`.

Class Intersection, Union, and Complement

OWL Lite only allows using `owl:intersectionOf` with named (simple) classes and unnamed classes defined by property restrictions. OWL Lite does not support `owl:unionOf` and `owl:complementOf`.

Consider again the `Conf` and `EuropeanCity` classes, and the `heldIn` property, which maps conferences into cities. We may redefine the class of conferences that were held only in a European city as follows

```
1.  <owl:Class rdf:about="trulyEuropeanConf">
2.    <owl:intersectionOf rdf:parseType="Collection">
3.      <owl:Class rdf:about="Conf"/>
4.      <owl:Restriction>
5.        <owl:onProperty rdf:resource="heldIn"/>
6.        <owl:allValuesFrom rdf:resource="EuropeanCity"/>
7.      </owl:Restriction>
8.    </owl:intersectionOf>
9.  </owl:Class>
```

Set Theory: $\texttt{trulyEuropeanConf} =$
$\quad\quad\quad\quad\quad\quad \texttt{Conf} \cap \{x\,/\,\forall y\,(\texttt{heldIn}(x,y) \Rightarrow y \in \texttt{EuropeanCity})\}$

Description Logic: $\texttt{trulyEuropeanConf} \equiv \texttt{Conf} \sqcap \forall\texttt{heldIn.EuropeanCity}$

This definition of the `trulyEuropeanConf` class differs from the definition of the `EuropeanConf` class in a fundamental way. Intuitively, it asserts that the `trulyEuropeanConf` class consists of exactly those individuals that are conferences and that are held in a European city. By contrast, according to the definition of the `EuropeanConf` class, there might be a conference held in a European city that is not a member of the `EuropeanConf` class, because the definition uses the subset construct of RDF Schema.

The use of the `owl:unionOf` construct is entirely similar to that of the `owl:intersectionOf` construct.

The `owl:complementOf` construct corresponds to set difference. For example, we may define the set of all things that are not conferences as follows

```
1.  <owl:Class rdf:about="notConf">
2.    <owl:complementOf rdf:resource="Conf" />
3.  </owl:Class>
```

This example may sound a bit strange, because the `notConf` class contains every individual (of the `owl:Thing` class) that does not belong to the `Conf` class. Indeed, one typically defines a new set as the complement of another set (rather than the universe, or the set of all things). A better example would be the set of all conferences that are not held in European cities, defined as follows

```
1.  <owl:Class rdf:about="nonEuropeanConf">
2.    <owl:intersectionOf rdf:parseType="Collection">
3.        <owl:Class rdf:about="Conf"/>
4.        <owl:Class>
5.          <owl:complementOf>
6.            <owl:Restriction>
7.              <owl:onProperty rdf:resource="heldIn"/>
8.              <owl:allValuesFrom
                        rdf:resource="EuropeanCity"/>
9.            </owl:Restriction>
10.         </owl:complementOf>
11.       </owl:Class>
12.   </owl:intersectionOf>
13. </owl:Class>
```

Set Theory: nonEuropeanConf =
$$\text{Conf} \cap \{ x \,/\, \neg\forall y\,(\text{heldIn}\,(x, y) \Rightarrow y \in \text{EuropeanCity}) \}$$

or, equivalently: nonEuropeanConf =
$$\text{Conf} \cap \{ x \,/\, \exists y\,(\text{heldIn}\,(x, y) \wedge y \notin \text{EuropeanCity}) \}$$

Description Logic: $\text{nonEuropeanConf} \equiv \text{Conf} \sqcap \neg\forall\text{heldIn}.\text{EuropeanCity}$

5.5.2 Class Axioms

In addition to the RDF Schema class subset, `rdfs:subClassOf`, OWL includes a construct, `owl:equivalentClass`, to define class equivalence, and a construct, `owl:disjointWith`, to express set disjointness. OWL DL puts no restrictions on the types of class descriptions that can be used with `rdfs:subClassOf` or `owl:equivalentClass`. However, in OWL Lite, the subject must be a class name and the object must be either a class name or a property restriction. OWL Lite does not support `owl:disjointWith`.

Note that, because classes and properties may themselves be treated as individuals in OWL Full, one may use `owl:sameAs` (see Section 5.6) to indicate that two classes (or two properties) are indeed the same. However, declarations of this sort must be used with care because they suffice to characterize the ontology as OWL Full.

Class equivalence is useful, for example, when an ontology O imports another ontology O'. In this case, the user may want to define that a class C from O and a class C' from O' denote the same set of objects. For example, the following fragment indicates that `Publication` and `pubs` are equivalent classes.

```
1.  <owl:Class rdf:about="Publication">
2.    <owl:equivalentClass rdf:resource="&dept;pubs"/>
3.  </owl:Class>
```

where `&dept` is an abbreviation for the URIref of a second, independently developed ontology that uses `&dept;pubs` to denote the class of all publications.

The `owl:disjointWith` construct may be applied to multiple classes. For example, we may define that `ConfPaper` is disjoint with `JournalPaper` and `Book` as follows

```
1.  <owl:Class rdf:about="ConfPaper">
2.    <rdfs:subClassOf rdf:resource="Publication"/>
3.    <owl:disjointWith rdf:resource="JournalPaper"/>
4.    <owl:disjointWith rdf:resource="Book"/>
5.  </owl:Class>
```

Set Theory:

$$\text{ConfPaper} \subseteq \text{Publication}$$
$$\text{ConfPaper} \cap \text{JournalPaper} = \varnothing$$
$$\text{ConfPaper} \cap \text{Book} = \varnothing$$

Description Logic:

$$\text{ConfPaper} \sqsubseteq \text{Publication}$$
$$\text{ConfPaper} \sqcap \text{JournalPaper} \equiv \bot$$
$$\text{ConfPaper} \sqcap \text{Book} \equiv \bot$$

Note that the above assertions do not guarantee that `JournalPaper` and `Book` are disjoint, or that `Publication` is the union of `ConfPaper`, `JournalPaper`, and `Book`.

The following example shows how to define `Publication` as the union of `ConfPaper`, `JournalPaper`, and `Book`, and how to indicate that these three classes are mutually disjoint.

```
1.  <owl:Class rdf:about="ConfPaper">
2.    <owl:disjointWith rdf:resource="JournalPaper"/>
3.    <owl:disjointWith rdf:resource="Book"/>
4.  </owl:Class>

5.  <owl:Class rdf:about="JournalPaper">
6.    <owl:disjointWith rdf:resource="ConfPaper"/>
7.    <owl:disjointWith rdf:resource="Book"/>
8.  </owl:Class>

9.  <owl:Class rdf:about="Book">
10.   <owl:disjointWith rdf:resource="ConfPaper"/>
11.   <owl:disjointWith rdf:resource="JournalPaper"/>
12. </owl:Class>

13. <owl:Class rdf:about="Publication">
14.   <owl:unionOf rdf:parseType="Collection">
15.       <owl:Class rdf:about="ConfPaper"/>
16.       <owl:Class rdf:about="JournalPaper"/>
17.       <owl:Class rdf:about="Book"/>
18.   </owl:unionOf>
19. </owl:Class>
```

Set Theory:

$$\text{ConfPaper} \cap \text{JournalPaper} = \emptyset$$
$$\text{ConfPaper} \cap \text{Book} = \emptyset$$
$$\text{JournalPaper} \cap \text{Book} = \emptyset$$
$$\text{Publication} = \text{ConfPaper} \cup \text{JournalPaper} \cup \text{Book}$$

Description Logic:

$$\text{ConfPaper} \sqcap \text{JournalPaper} \equiv \bot$$
$$\text{ConfPaper} \sqcap \text{Book} \equiv \bot$$
$$\text{JournalPaper} \sqcap \text{Book} \equiv \bot$$
$$\text{Publication} \equiv \text{ConfPaper} \sqcup \text{JournalPaper} \sqcup \text{Book}$$

Since $A \sqcap B \equiv \bot$ is equivalent to $A \sqsubseteq \neg B$, we may rewrite the above inclusions as

Description Logic:

$$\text{ConfPaper} \sqsubseteq \neg\text{JournalPaper}$$
$$\text{ConfPaper} \sqsubseteq \neg\text{Book}$$
$$\text{JournalPaper} \sqsubseteq \neg\text{Book}$$
$$\text{Publication} \equiv \text{ConfPaper} \sqcup \text{JournalPaper} \sqcup \text{Book}$$

5.6 Individuals

OWL Lite individuals and property instances are declared as in RDF Schema. For example, the following OWL Lite fragment defines an individual of the `City` class, declared in the vocabulary `http://www.cat.com/owl-schema/`

```
1. <owl:Thing rdf:about="#Rio-de-Janeiro-Brazil">
2.     <rdf:type
               rdf:resource="http://www.cat.com/owl-schema/City"/>
3. </owl:Thing>
```

If `http://www.cat.com/owl-schema/` is abbreviated as `cs`, we may rewrite the above definition as

```
<cs:City rdf:about="#Rio-de-Janeiro-Brazil"/>
```

Recall that, in OWL (as in RDF), the fact that two URIrefs are different does not imply that they denote different individuals. OWL Lite offers three constructs to capture such restrictions.

To declare that two URIrefs denote the same individual, OWL Lite offers the `owl:sameAs` property. For example, if a city has a nickname we may equate the two names as follows

```
1. <owl:Thing rdf:about="#Rio-de-Janeiro-Brazil">
2.     <owl:sameAs rdf:resource="#Cidade-Maravilhosa" />
3. </owl:Thing>
```

By contrast, to declare that two URIrefs denote different individuals, OWL Lite includes the `owl:differentFrom` property, as in the following fragment

```
1. <owl:Thing rdf:about="#Rio-de-Janeiro-Brazil">
2.     <owl:differentFrom rdf:resource="#Rio-de-Janeiro-Peru"/>
3. </owl:Thing>
```

The `owl:AllDifferent` property, also in OWL Lite, defines a set of mutually distinct URIrefs, as in the example

```
1. <owl:AllDifferent>
2.     <owl:distinctMembers rdf:parseType="Collection">
3.         <cs:City rdf:about="#Rio-de-Janeiro-Brazil"/>
4.         <cs:City rdf:about="#Rio-de-Janeiro-Peru"/>
5.         <cs:City rdf:about="#Rio-de-Janeiro-Colombia"/>
6.     </owl:distinctMembers>
7. </owl:AllDifferent>
```

5.7 Datatypes

Table 5.3 shows the datatypes of the XML Schema vocabulary recommended for use with OWL (recall that the URIref of the XML Schema vocabulary is http://www.w3.org/2001/XMLSchema, and that xsd is the namespace prefix typically used).

Table 5.3 XML Schema recommended datatypes.

xsd:integer	
xsd:int	xsd:decimal
xsd:unsignedInt	xsd:float
xsd:negativeInteger	xsd:double
xsd:nonNegativeInteger	xsd:string
xsd:positiveInteger	xsd:normalizedString
xsd:nonPositiveInteger	xsd:boolean
xsd:long	xsd:time
xsd:unsignedLong	xsd:date
xsd:short	xsd:dateTime
xsd:unsignedShort	xsd:gYear
xsd:byte	xsd:gMonth
xsd:unsignedByte	xsd:gDay
xsd:hexBinary	xsd:gMonthDay
xsd:base64Binary	xsd:gYearMonth
xsd:anyURI	xsd:language
xsd:token	xsd:Name
xsd:NMTOKEN	xsd:NCName

OWL DL (but not OWL Lite) provides a construct to define an enumerated datatype (not a class), with the help of the owl:oneOf construct. The subject of owl:oneOf is a blank node of owl:DataRange class and the object is a list of literals.

The example below redefines `hasGrade` as a datatype property with range {"A", "B", "C"}:

```
1. <?xml version="1.0"?>
2. <!DOCTYPE rdf:RDF [
3. <!ENTITY xsd "http://www.w3.org/2001/XMLSchema#">] >

4. <rdf:RDF xml:base="http://www.cat.com/owl-schema/"
5.     xmlns:owl="http://www.w3.org/2002/07/owl#"
6.     xmlns:rdf="http://www.w3.org/1999/02/22-rdf-syntax-ns#"
7.     xmlns:rdfs="http://www.w3.org/2000/01/rdf-schema#">

8.     <owl:Class rdf:about="Conf"/>

9.     <owl:DatatypeProperty rdf:ID="hasGrade">
10.      <rdfs:range>
11.        <owl:DataRange>
12.          <owl:oneOf>
13.            <rdf:List>
14.              <rdf:first
15.                rdf:datatype="&xsd;string">
16.                A
17.              </rdf:first>
18.              <rdf:rest>
19.               <rdf:List>
20.                 <rdf:first
21.                   rdf:datatype="&xsd;string">
22.                   B
23.                 </rdf:first>
24.                 <rdf:rest>
25.                   <rdf:List>
26.                     <rdf:first
27.                       rdf:datatype="&xsd;string">
28.                       C
29.                     </rdf:first>
30.                     <rdf:rest rdf:resource="&rdf;nil" />
31.                   </rdf:List>
32.                 </rdf:rest>
33.               </rdf:List>
34.              </rdf:rest>
35.            </rdf:List>
36.          </owl:oneOf>
37.        </owl:DataRange>
38.      </rdfs:range>
39.    </owl:DatatypeProperty>
40. </rdf:RDF>
```

Set Theory: hasGrade: Conf→{"A","B","C"}
              (a function with domain Conf and range {"A","B","C"}

5.8 A Summary of the OWL Vocabulary

Table 5.4 summarizes the OWL vocabulary covered in this chapter. A full account can be found in Dean and Schreiber (2004) and in McGuinness and Harmelen (2004).

Table 5.4 A partial account of the OWL vocabulary.

OWL Lite [1]	
Term	**Description**
Ontology	indicates the URIref of the ontology
imports	indicates an imported ontology
versionInfo priorVersion backwardCompatibleWith incompatibleWith DeprecatedClass DeprecatedProperty	indicates versioning information
rdfs:label rdfs:comment rdfs:seeAlso rdfs:isDefinedBy AnnotationProperty OntologyProperty	indicates annotation properties
ObjectProperty	defines a binary relation between the set of instances of two classes
DatatypeProperty	defines a binary relation between the set of instances of a class and a set of instances of a datatype
rdfs:domain	declares the domain of a property
rdfs:range	declares the range of a property
rdfs:subPropertyOf	defines that a property is a subset of another
equivalentProperty	defines that two properties are equivalence
inverseOf	declares that a property is the inverse of another
TransitiveProperty	declares that a property is transitive
SymmetricProperty	declares that a property is symmetric
FunctionalProperty	declares that a property is functional
Class	defines a named class
Thing	the class of all things
Nothing	the empty set

Table 5.4 A partial account of the OWL vocabulary (cont.).

Term	Description
Restriction onProperty	defines a property restriction
someValuesFrom	an *existential restriction* for C, P, and D requires that every instance c of C must have at least one occurrence of property P whose value is an instance of D; corresponds to $C \sqsubseteq \exists P.D$ in description logic
allValuesFrom	a *universal restriction* for C, P, and D requires that, for every instance c of C, if c has an occurrence of a property P whose value is d, then d must be an instance of D; corresponds to $C \sqsubseteq \forall P.D$ in description logic
cardinality	an *exact cardinality restriction* specifies the exact number of occurrences of property P each instance of C must have; OWL Lite allows 0 or 1 only
minCardinality	a *maximum cardinality restriction* specifies the maximum number of occurrences of property P each instance of C must have; OWL Lite allows 0 or 1 only
maxCardinality	a *minimum cardinality restriction* specifies the minimum number of occurrences of property P each instance of C must have; OWL Lite allows 0 or 1 only
rdfs:subClassOf	defines that a named class is a subset of a named class or that a named class is a subset of an unnamed class defined by a property restriction
equivalentClass	defines that two named classes are equivalent or that a named class and an unnamed class defined by a property restriction are equivalent
intersectionOf	Class intersection of named classes or a named class and an unnamed class defined by a property restriction
sameAs	declares that two URIrefs denote the same individual
differentFrom	declares that two URIrefs denote different individuals
AllDifferent	declares that several URIrefs denote different individuals
xsd datatypes	the range of a datatype property is taken from a set of recommended XML Schema datatypes

Table 5.4 A partial account of the OWL vocabulary (cont.).

OWL DL and OWL Full [2,3]	
Term	**Description**
`oneOf`	defines a class by enumeration
`cardinality` `minCardinality maxCardinality`	(same as for OWL Lite, except that OWL DL allows cardinality restrictions with any nonnegative integer)
`hasValue`	a value restriction or filler information imposes limitations on the values that the occurrences of a class property may have

`unionOf`
`complementOf`
`intersectionOf`
`disjointWith`
	define set theoretic combinations of arbitrary class expressions

`equivalentClass` `rdfs:subClassOf`	(same as for OWL Lite, except that OWL DL allows any class expression to be used)
`dataRange`	defines a set of datatype values

(Adapted from McGuinness and Harmelen (2004)).

Notes:

1. The prefixes `rdf:` or `rdfs:` indicate terms already present in the RDF or RDF Schema vocabularies. Terms of the OWL vocabulary are not prefixed.
2. The list of OWL DL and OWL Full language constructs are in addition to those of OWL Lite.
3. OWL DL and OWL Full use the same vocabulary, but OWL DL requires that:
   a. Classes cannot be individuals or properties, and properties cannot be individuals or classes.
   b. Properties must be either ObjectProperties or DatatypeProperties, but not both.

Recommended Reading

The literature about OWL, and related technologies, is enormous. To be economical and unbiased, we suggest reading Heflin (2004) and McGuinness and Harmelen (2004), or visiting the W3 Schools Web site for an online tutorial on OWL (W3 Schools 2006). Another excellent tutorial is Horridge et al. (2004).

References

Carroll, J.J.; De Roo, J. (Eds) (2004) OWL Web Ontology Language Test Cases. W3C Recommendation, 10 February 2004. Latest version available at: http://www.w3.org/TR/owl-test/.

Dean, M.; Schreiber, G. (Eds) (2004) OWL Web Ontology Language Reference. W3C Recommendation, 10 February 2004. Latest version available at: http://www.w3.org/TR/owl-ref/.

Heflin, J. (Ed) (2004) OWL Web Ontology Language Use Cases and Requirements. W3C Recommendation, 10 February 2004. Latest version available at: http://www.w3.org/TR/webont-req/.

Horridge, M.; Knublauch, H. ; Rector, A.; Stevens, R.; Wroe, C. (2004) A Practical Guide To Building OWL Ontologies Using The Protégé-OWL Plugin and CO-ODE Tools Edition 1.0, The University Of Manchester, Stanford University.

McGuinness, D.L.; Harmelen, F.V. (Eds) (2004) OWL Web Ontology Language Overview. W3C Recommendation, 10 February 2004. Latest version available at: http://www.w3.org/TR/owl-features/.

Patel-Schneider, P.F.; Hayes, P.; Horrocks, I. (Eds.) (2004) OWL Web Ontology Language Semantics and Abstract Syntax. W3C Recommendation, 10 February 2004. Latest version available at: http://www.w3.org/TR/owl-semantics/.

W3 Schools (2006) Introduction to OWL. Available at: http://www.w3schools.com/rdf/rdf_owl.asp

6

Rule Languages

6.1 Introduction

Knowledge representation languages, such as RDF Schema and OWL, are designed to specify descriptions of application domains. They typically offer constructs to describe classes, properties, and relationships, as well as constructs to capture class and property restrictions and to define complex classes. By contrast, rule languages are designed to specify data transformation rules that define how to synthesize new facts from those stored in the knowledge base. In this chapter, we introduce four rule languages, *Datalog*, the *Rule Markup Language (RuleML)*, the *Semantic Web Rule Language (SWRL)*, and *TRIPLE*, the last three developed in the context of the Semantic Web.

These rule languages are based on concepts that stem from logic programming (Lloyd 1987), of which Prolog is the archetypal implementation (SWI-Prolog 2006; GNU Prolog 2006).

Datalog is a syntactically restricted subset of logic programming where function symbols are not allowed (Ullman 1988). Datalog was originally defined as a query and rule language for knowledge bases. Query evaluation in Datalog usually follows bottom-up strategies, which operate efficiently even for large databases.

RuleML is a markup language for publishing and sharing knowledge bases on the Web, built on top of Datalog. The language is developed under the auspices of The Rule Markup Initiative (Boley et al. 2001; 2005).

SWRL combines RuleML with OWL and includes a high-level abstract syntax, a model-theoretic semantics, and an XML syntax. SWRL enables Datalog-like rules to be combined with an OWL knowledge base.

TRIPLE also adopts Datalog-like rules, cast in an RDF-based data model, but it offers more sophisticated constructs than SWRL (Sintek and Decker 2002). TRIPLE is in fact a hybrid rule language that permits interaction with external reasoning components, such as those developed for description logic. Also, TRIPLE has no fixed semantics for classes and class hierarchies, but it allows such features to be defined within the language.

6.2 Usage Scenarios for Rule Languages

This section briefly describes four scenarios where rule languages can be profitably used, following mostly Decker et al. (2005). Although knowledge representation languages suffice to address some of the problems these scenarios pose, rule languages provide simpler, more intuitive solutions.

Defining User Views over Ontologies

A complete ontology is often large and complex, accommodating aspects relevant to various groups of users. This situation is entirely similar to a large database conceptual schema and, as such, can be addressed by defining user views that focus on some aspects of the application domain, hiding details in which the user is not interested.

A user view is just another, perhaps simpler, ontology together with a set of sentences that define the view concepts in terms of the base ontology concepts. Rules provide a convenient way to specify view concept definitions. Hence, users will have direct contact with the view concepts, whereas the rule processor will be responsible for implementing the mappings.

Interoperability Among Different Data Sources

In the context of the Semantic Web or of a federation of databases, the user is confronted with a collection of data sources, which were defined independently of each other most of the time. The task of interpreting the description of each data source and formulating sequences of queries to locate the desired data is often burdensome, if not too difficult.

The traditional approach is to define a mediator that has sufficient knowledge about the data sources to automatically translate user queries into local queries, and to combine the partial results into a single answer, which is then passed to the user. The problem becomes that of constructing a mediator with such functionality.

In the context of the Semantic Web, where data sources are described by ontologies, mediation becomes a problem of defining mappings between concepts from different ontologies. This new problem is in fact a generalization of the problem of defining user views over ontologies. Rule languages provide an interesting alternative to define such mappings.

Personalization Services for the Semantic Web

Personalization services for the Semantic Web are cast in a service-based architecture that provides recommendations for the users about how to access or use some resource. The architecture incorporates user models, context models, and resource models.

Personalization services can be realized using rules for personalization, user modeling, and interpreting user requests at runtime.

Ontology-Based Resource Matching

Grids provide protocols to combine geographically distributed computational and data resources, and to deliver such resources to heterogeneous user communities. The resources may belong to different institutions, have different usage policies and pose different requirements on acceptable requests. On the other hand, grid applications may have different constraints on the resources they require. Therefore, an agent is required to match the resources an application needs with the resources available on the grid.

Resource descriptions, request descriptions, and usage policies can be independently modeled and described in an ontology description language. Rules for reasoning about the characteristics of a request, available resources, and usage policies can then be defined appropriately to find a resource that satisfies the request requirements.

6.3 Datalog

Datalog is a syntactically restricted subset of logic programming, originally defined as a query and rule language for deductive databases. In this section, we introduce just the basic Datalog concepts, as a preparation for the next sections. Ullman (1988) is the standard reference for Datalog.

A *Datalog alphabet* $\mathcal{A}$ is a set of predicate symbols, constants, and variables. The *arity* of a predicate symbol is a nonnegative integer that indicates the number of arguments of the predicate. Note that, unlike Prolog, function symbols are not allowed in (basic) Datalog.

To simplify the notation, we do not explicitly list variables and constants of an alphabet, adopting the convention that variables are denoted as strings of lowercase letters and constants are enclosed in double quotation marks. With this convention, an alphabet reduces to a set of predicate symbols. Table 6.1 shows the alphabet of the BOOKS knowledge base, which we use in our examples. All definitions that follow are relative to a given alphabet.

A *term* is a variable or constant. Note that, because Datalog does not admit function symbols, it disallows more complex terms.

Table 6.1 The alphabet of the BOOKS knowledge base.

Predicate	Arity	Intended Interpretation
Book	3	Book(t,c,y) indicates a book with title t, country of publication c, and year of publication y
hasAuthor	2	hasAuthor(t,n) indicates that a book with title t has author n
references	2	references(t,r) indicates that a book with title t references another book with title r
trReferences	2	trReferences(t,r) indicates that a book with title t transitively references another book with title r
UKBook	1	UKBook(t) indicates a book with title t that has as country of publication "United Kingdom"

An *atom* is an expression of the form $P(t_1,\ldots,t_n)$, where P is an n-ary predicate symbol and $t_1,\ldots,t_n$ are terms. Examples of atoms in the BOOKS alphabet are (where, according to our convention, "Semantic Web", "Brazil", and "2005" are constants, and title and country are variables):

1.   Book("Semantic Web","Brazil","2005")
2.   Book(title,country,"2005")

A *clause* is either a fact or a rule. A *fact* is an expression of the form

B.

where B is a variable-free atom. A *rule* is an expression of the form

$$C \leftarrow A_1,\ldots,A_m.$$

where $A_1,\ldots,A_m$ and C are atoms; $A_1,\ldots,A_m$ is called the list of *antecedents* and C is called the *consequent* or *head* of the rule. Variables are treated as universally quantified, with their scope limited to the rule. Variables are *range restricted*, in the sense that only variables that occur in the antecedent of a rule may occur in the consequent of the rule.

A fact must always hold, whereas a rule indicates that, if the antecedent holds, then the consequent must also hold.

A *Datalog knowledge base* is a set of clauses. Unlike Prolog, the ordering of the clauses is irrelevant in Datalog. A rule is *recursive* iff the predicate symbol that occurs in the consequent also occurs in the list of antecedents. A set $S_0,\ldots,S_{n-1}$ of rules is *mutually recursive* iff there are predicate symbols $P_0,\ldots,P_{n-1}$ such that P_i occurs in the consequent of S_i and in the list of antecedents of S_{i+1}, for $i\in[0,n-1]$ (where the sum is module *n*).

Mutually recursive rules considerably increase the expressive power of Datalog, but they create difficulties in defining the semantics of Datalog knowledge bases, not to mention the construction of Datalog processors. We refer the reader to Ullman (1988) for a comprehensive discussion about Datalog processors.

At a given point in time, the BOOKS knowledge base might consist of the following set of clauses.

```
1.    Book("The Description Logic Handbook",
          "United Kingdom", "2003").
2.    Book("Principia Mathematica", "United Kingdom", "1910").
3.    Book("Semantic Web","Brazil","2005").
4.    hasAuthor("The Description Logic Handbook",
              "Franz Baader").
5.    hasAuthor("The Description Logic Handbook",
              "Diego Calvanese").
6.    hasAuthor("Principia Mathematica", "Bertrand Russell").
7.    hasAuthor("Principia Mathematica", "Alfred Whitehead").
8.    hasAuthor("Semantic Web", "Karin Breitman").
9.    references("Semantic Web",
              "The Description Logic Handbook").
10.   references("The Description Logic Handbook",
              "Principia Mathematica").
11.   trReferences(x,y) ← references(x,y).
12.   trReferences(x,y) ← references(x,z), trReferences(z,y).
13.   UKBook(x) ← Book(x, "United Kingdom", y).
```

Note that Clauses 1 to 10 are facts. Clauses 11 and 12 capture what it means to be a transitive reference. Clause 12 is a recursive rule. Finally, Clause 13 is a non-recursive rule that captures what it means to be a book published in the UK.

A Datalog processor would be able to deduce the following facts from the above knowledge base.

```
14.   trReferences("Semantic Web",
              "The Description Logic Handbook").
15.   trReferences("The Description Logic Handbook",
              "Principia Mathematica").
16.   trReferences("Semantic Web", "Principia Mathematica").
17.   UKBook("The Description Logic Handbook").
18.   UKBook("Principia Mathematica").
```

Note that, to deduce Clause 16, the Datalog processor would have to use Clause 12 (a recursive rule), as well as Clauses 9, 10, and 11.

6.4 RuleML

The *Rule Markup Language (RuleML)* basically provides an XML syntax for Datalog clauses. In this section, we introduce the XML syntax of RuleML with the help of examples, based on the BOOKS alphabet of Table 6.1. Each example is expressed in the RuleML XML syntax and in Datalog. The full details can be found in (Hirtle and Boley 2005).

An *atom* in RuleML is expressed with the help of the tags `<atom>`, `<rel>`, `<var>`, and `<ind>`, as in the following examples.

```
1.    <Atom>
2.        <Rel>Book</Rel>
3.        <Ind>Semantic Web</Ind>
4.        <Ind>Brazil</Ind>
5.        <Ind>2005</Ind>
6.    </Atom>
```

Datalog notation: `Book("Semantic Web","Brazil","2005")`

```
7.    <Atom>
8.        <Rel>Book</Rel>
9.        <Var>title</Var>
10.       <Var>publ</Var>
11.       <Ind>2005</Ind>
12.   </Atom>
```

Datalog notation: `Book(title,publ,"2005")`

The values of the `<Rel>` tag in lines 2 and 8 indicate a predicate symbol; the values of the `<Ind>` tag in lines 3, 4, 5, and 11 indicate constants; and the values of the tag `<Var>` in lines 9 and 10 indicate that title and publ should be understood as variables. Hence, variables and constants need not follow any syntactical convention, as in Section 6.3, because they are explicitly indicated with the help of the tags `<Ind>` and `<Var>`.

A *rule* in RuleML is expressed with the help of tags `<Implies>`, `<head>`, and `<body>`, as in:

```
1.    <Implies>
2.        <head>
3.            <Atom>
4.                <Rel>UKBook</Rel>
5.                <Var>x</Var>
6.            </Atom>
7.        </head>
8.        <body>
9.            <Atom>
10.               <Rel>Book</Rel>
11.               <Var>x</Var>
12.               <Ind>United Kingdom</Ind>
13.               <Var>y</Var>
14.           </Atom>
15.       </body>
16.   </Implies>
```

Datalog notation: `UKBook(x) ← Book(x, "United Kingdom", y).`

Rules can be more complex and involve conjunctions, indicated by the tag
<And> nested inside <body>, as in the following example.

```
1.    <Implies>
2.       <head>
3.          <Atom>
4.             <Rel>trReferences</Rel>
5.             <Var>x</Var>
6.             <Var>y</Var>
7.          </Atom>
8.       </head>
9.       <body>
10.         <And>
11.            <Atom>
12.               <Rel>references</Rel>
13.               <Var>x</Var>
14.               <Var>z</Var>
15.            </Atom>
16.            <Atom>
17.               <Rel>trReferences</Rel>
18.               <Var>z</Var>
19.               <Var>y</Var>
20.            </Atom>
21.         </And>
22.      </body>
23.   </Implies>
```

Datalog notation: trReferences(x,y) ← references(x,z),
                                         trReferences(z,y).

The following RuleML document contains the complete BOOKS knowledge base
introduced in Section 6.3. It was checked with the W3C validator for XML schema
(available at http://www.w3.org/2001/03/webdata/xsv), as suggested in Hirtle et al.
(2006).

```
1. <?xml version="1.0" encoding="UTF-8"?>
2. <RuleML
3.    xmlns="http://www.ruleml.org/0.91/xsd"
4.    xmlns:xsi="http://www.w3.org/2001/XMLSchema-instance"
5.    xsi:schemaLocation="http://www.ruleml.org/0.91/xsd
6.    http://www.ruleml.org/0.91/xsd/datalog.xsd">
7. <Assert mapClosure="universal">
8.    <Atom>
9.       <Rel>Book</Rel>
10.      <Ind>The Description Logic Handbook</Ind>
11.      <Ind>United Kingdom</Ind>
12.      <Ind>2003</Ind>
13.   </Atom>
14.   <Atom>
15.      <Rel>Book</Rel>
16.      <Ind>Principia Mathematica</Ind>
```

```
17.        <Ind>United Kingdom</Ind>
18.        <Ind>1910</Ind>
19.     </Atom>
20.     <Atom>
21.        <Rel>Book</Rel>
22.        <Ind>Semantic Web</Ind>
23.        <Ind>Brazil</Ind>
24.        <Ind>2005</Ind>
25.     </Atom>
26.     <Atom>
27.        <Rel>hasAuthor</Rel>
28.        <Ind>The Description Logic Handbook</Ind>
29.        <Ind>Franz Baader</Ind>
30.     </Atom>
31.     <Atom>
32.        <Rel>hasAuthor</Rel>
33.        <Ind>The Description Logic Handbook</Ind>
34.        <Ind>Diego Calvanese</Ind>
35.     </Atom>
36.     <Atom>
37.        <Rel>hasAuthor</Rel>
38.        <Ind>Principia Mathematica</Ind>
39.        <Ind>Bertrand Russell</Ind>
40.     </Atom>
41.     <Atom>
42.        <Rel>hasAuthor</Rel>
43.        <Ind>Principia Mathematica</Ind>
44.        <Ind>Alfred Whitehead</Ind>
45.     </Atom>
46.     <Atom>
47.        <Rel>hasAuthor</Rel>
48.        <Ind>Semantic Web</Ind>
49.        <Ind>Karin Breitman</Ind>
50.     </Atom>
51.     <Atom>
52.        <Rel>references</Rel>
53.        <Ind>Semantic Web</Ind>
54.        <Ind>The Description Logic Handbook</Ind>
55.     </Atom>
56.     <Atom>
57.        <Rel>references</Rel>
58.        <Ind>The Description Logic Handbook</Ind>
59.        <Ind>Principia Mathematica</Ind>
60.     </Atom>

61.     <Implies>
62.        <head>
63.           <Atom>
64.              <Rel>trReferences</Rel>
65.              <Var>x</Var>
66.              <Var>y</Var>
67.           </Atom>
68.        </head>
```

```
69.     <body>
70.        <Atom>
71.           <Rel>References</Rel>
72.           <Var>x</Var>
73.           <Var>y</Var>
74.        </Atom>
75.     </body>
76.  </Implies>

77.  <Implies>
78.     <head>
79.        <Atom>
80.           <Rel>trReferences</Rel>
81.           <Var>x</Var>
82.           <Var>y</Var>
83.        </Atom>
84.     </head>
85.     <body>
86.        <And>
87.           <Atom>
88.              <Rel>references</Rel>
89.              <Var>x</Var>
90.              <Var>z</Var>
91.           </Atom>
92.           <Atom>
93.              <Rel>trReferences</Rel>
94.              <Var>z</Var>
95.              <Var>y</Var>
96.           </Atom>
97.        </And>
98.     </body>
99.  </Implies>

100. <Implies>
101.    <head>
102.       <Atom>
103.          <Rel>UKBook</Rel>
104.          <Var>x</Var>
105.       </Atom>
106.    </head>
107.    <body>
108.       <Atom>
109.          <Rel>Book</Rel>
110.          <Var>x</Var>
111.          <Ind>United Kingdom</Ind>
112.          <Var>y</Var>
113.       </Atom>
114.    </body>
115. </Implies>

116. </Assert>
117. </RuleML>
```

6.5 SWRL

The *Semantic Web Rule Language (SWRL)* extends the set of OWL axioms to include Datalog-like clauses. In this section, we briefly present an RDF concrete syntax for SWRL, using the same examples as in Section 6.3, but now cast as an OWL ontology. The discussion follows Horrocks et al. (2004).

Since SWRL is a direct extension of OWL, we have to model the knowledge base as an OWL ontology, with the classes and properties summarized in Table 6.2, and the namespaces shown in Table 6.3.

Table 6.2 Concepts of the BOOKS ontology.

Resource	OWL Object	Intended Interpretation
Book	Simple Class	the class of all books
Title	datatype property with domain Book and range string	maps books into their titles
CountryOfPub	datatype property with domain Book and range string	maps books into their country of publication
YearOfPub	datatype property with domain Book and range gYear	maps books into their year of publication
has Author	datatype property with domain Book and range string	maps books into their author's names
references	object property with domain Book and range Book	maps books into the books they reference
trReferences	object property with domain Book and range Book	transitive closure of references
UKBook	Complex Class	the class of all books published in the UK

Table 6.3 SWRL XML Concrete Syntax namespaces.

Namespace	Abbreviation
the SWRL vocabulary `http://www.w3.org/2003/11/swrl#`	`swrl`
the XML Schema vocabulary `http://www.w3.org/2001/XMLSchema`	`xsd`
the BOOKS vocabulary `http://books.org/terms`	`bk`

Using Datalog-like notation, an *atom* in SWRL is an expression of one of the forms:

`C(x)`	`C` is an OWL class description or data range
`P(x,y)`	`P` is an OWL property
`sameAs(x,y)`	`sameAs` belongs to the OWL vocabulary
`differentFrom(x,y)`	`differentFrom` belongs to the OWL vocabulary
`builtIn(r,x,...)`	`r` is a built-in relation

where x and y are either variables, OWL individuals, or OWL data values.

Therefore, the definition of atoms in SWRL differs from that in RuleML in two ways. First, atoms involve only unary predicates (for OWL class descriptions or data ranges) or binary predicates (for OWL properties, `sameAs` and `differentFrom`), whereas in RuleML predicates may have any arity. Second, OWL class descriptions can be viewed as unary predicates introduced by definition, as discussed in Section 5.4, a concept not supported in RuleML.

Informally, an atom `C(x)` holds iff x is an instance of the class description or data range `C`; an atom `P(x,y)` holds iff x is related to y by property `P`; an atom `sameAs(x,y)` holds iff x is interpreted as the same object as y; an atom `differentFrom(x,y)` holds iff x and y are interpreted as different objects; and `builtIn(r,x,...)` holds iff the built-in relation `r` holds for the interpretations of the arguments.

As an example, consider the Datalog atom.

```
Book("Semantic Web","Brazil","2005").
```

To represent this atom in SWRL RDF Concrete Syntax, we first rewrite it as four distinct atoms that match the OWL definition of the BOOKS knowledge base.

```
1.    Book(B3).
2.    Title(B3,"Semantic Web").
3.    CountryOfPub(B3,"Brazil").
4.    YearOfPub(B3,"2005").
```

Then, we translate these four atoms to OWL, obtaining

```
1. <Book rdf:about="B3">
2.    <Title>Semantic Web</Title>
3.    <CountryOfPub>Brazil</CountryOfPub>
4.    <YearOfPub>2005</YearOfPub>
1. </Book>
```

SWRL allows a complex concept to be defined as a complex class of the underlying OWL ontology, in which case SWRL offers a richer solution than RuleML. For example, instead of using a rule as in Section 6.3, we may include the definition of the complex concept UKBooks in the BOOKS ontology as follows.

```
1. <owl:Class rdf:about="UKBook">
2.    <owl:intersectionOf rdf:parseType="Collection">
3.       <owl:Class rdf:about="Book"/>
4.       <owl:Restriction>
5.          <owl:onProperty rdf:resource="CountryOfPub"/>
6.          <owl:hasValue rdf:datatype="&xsd;string">
7.             United Kingdom
8.          </owl:hasValue>
9.       </owl:Restriction>
10.   </owl:intersectionOf>
1. </owl:Class>
```

A rule in SWRL may have a list of atoms as consequent. But this does not increase the expressive power of the language because any such rule may be equivalently replaced by a set of rules with just one atom as consequent. For example, the following Datalog rule

$$\text{trReferences}(x,z) \leftarrow \text{references}(x,y), \text{trReferences}(y,z).$$

is written in SWRL RDF Concrete Syntax as

```
1.       <swrl:Imp rdf:about="Rule-1">
2.         <swrl:head>
3.           <swrl:AtomList>
4.             <rdf:first>
5.               <swrl:IndividualPropertyAtom>
6.                 <swrl:propertyPredicate
                        rdf:resource="trReferences"/>
7.                 <swrl:argument1>
8.                   <swrl:Variable rdf:about="x"/>
9.                 </swrl:argument1>
10.                <swrl:argument2>
11.                  <swrl:Variable rdf:about="z"/>
12.                </swrl:argument2>
13.              </swrl:IndividualPropertyAtom>
14.            </rdf:first>
15.            <rdf:rest rdf:resource="&rdf;nil"/>
16.          </swrl:AtomList>
```

```
17.      </swrl:head>
18.      <swrl:body>
19.        <swrl:AtomList>
20.          <rdf:first>
21.            <swrl:IndividualPropertyAtom>
22.              <swrl:propertyPredicate
                     rdf:resource="references"/>
23.              <swrl:argument1 rdf:resource="x"/>
24.              <swrl:argument2>
25.                <swrl:Variable rdf:about="y"/>
26.              </swrl:argument2>
27.            </swrl:IndividualPropertyAtom>
28.          </rdf:first>
29.          <rdf:rest>
30.            <swrl:AtomList>
31.              <rdf:first>
32.                <swrl:IndividualPropertyAtom>
33.                  <swrl:propertyPredicate
                         rdf:resource="trReferences"/>
34.                  <swrl:argument1 rdf:resource="y"/>
35.                  <swrl:argument2 rdf:resource="z"/>
36.                </swrl:IndividualPropertyAtom>
37.              </rdf:first>
38.              <rdf:rest rdf:resource="&rdf;nil"/>
39.            </swrl:AtomList>
40.          </rdf:rest>
41.        </swrl:AtomList>
42.      </swrl:body>
43.    </swrl:Imp>
```

The complete BOOKS knowledge base introduced in Section 6.3 is represented in SWRL RDF Concrete Syntax as follows (validated using Protégé 3.1.1 with the SWRL Plugin).

```
1. <?xml version="1.0"?>
2. <!DOCTYPE rdf:RDF [
3.  <!ENTITY xsd "http://www.w3.org/2001/XMLSchema#">
4.  <!ENTITY owl "http://www.w3.org/2002/07/owl#">
5.  <!ENTITY rdf "http://www.w3.org/1999/02/22-rdf-syntax-ns#">
6. ]>
7. <rdf:RDF xmlns:swrlb="http://www.w3.org/2003/11/swrlb#"
8.   xmlns:swrl="http://www.w3.org/2003/11/swrl#"
9.   xmlns:rdf="http://www.w3.org/1999/02/22-rdf-syntax-ns#"
10.   xmlns:rdfs="http://www.w3.org/2000/01/rdf-schema#"
11.   xmlns:owl="http://www.w3.org/2002/07/owl#"
12.   xmlns="http://books.org/"
13.   xml:base="http://books.org/">
14.   <owl:Ontology rdf:about="">
15.     <owl:imports rdf:resource=
            "http://www.daml.org/rules/proposal/swrlb.owl"/>
16.     <owl:imports rdf:resource=
            "http://www.daml.org/rules/proposal/swrl.owl"/>
```

```
17.     <rdfs:comment rdf:datatype="&xsd;string">
18.         The BOOKS knowledge base in OWL
19.     </rdfs:comment>
20.     <rdfs:label rdf:datatype="&xsd;string">
21.         BOOKS ontology
22.     </rdfs:label>
23.  </owl:Ontology>
24.  <owl:Class rdf:about="Book"/>
25.  <owl:Class rdf:about="UKBook">
26.   <owl:equivalentClass>
27.    <owl:Class>
28.      <owl:intersectionOf rdf:parseType="Collection">
29.         <owl:Class rdf:about="Book"/>
30.         <owl:Restriction>
31.           <owl:hasValue rdf:datatype="&xsd;string">
32.             United Kingdom
33.           </owl:hasValue>
34.           <owl:onProperty>
35.           <owl:FunctionalProperty
                     rdf:about="CountryOfPub"/>
36.           </owl:onProperty>
37.         </owl:Restriction>
38.       </owl:intersectionOf>
39.     </owl:Class>
40.    </owl:equivalentClass>
41.  </owl:Class>
42.  <owl:ObjectProperty rdf:about="references">
43.     <rdfs:range rdf:resource="Book"/>
44.     <rdfs:domain rdf:resource="Book"/>
45.  </owl:ObjectProperty>
46.  <owl:ObjectProperty rdf:about="trReferences">
47.     <rdfs:range rdf:resource="Book"/>
48.     <rdfs:domain rdf:resource="Book"/>
49.  </owl:ObjectProperty>
50.  <owl:DatatypeProperty rdf:about="Title">
51.     <rdf:type rdf:resource="&owl;FunctionalProperty"/>
52.     <rdfs:range rdf:resource="&xsd;string"/>
53.     <rdfs:domain rdf:resource="Book"/>
54.  </owl:DatatypeProperty>
55.  <owl:DatatypeProperty rdf:about="hasAuthor">
56.     <rdfs:range rdf:resource="&xsd;string"/>
57.     <rdfs:domain rdf:resource="Book"/>
58.   </owl:DatatypeProperty>
59.   <owl:FunctionalProperty rdf:about="CountryOfPub">
60.     <rdf:type rdf:resource="&owl;DatatypeProperty"/>
61.     <rdfs:domain rdf:resource="Book"/>
62.     <rdfs:range rdf:resource="&xsd;string"/>
63.   </owl:FunctionalProperty>
64.   <owl:FunctionalProperty rdf:about="YearOfPub">
65.     <rdf:type rdf:resource="&owl;DatatypeProperty"/>
66.     <rdfs:domain rdf:resource="Book"/>
67.     <rdfs:range rdf:resource="&xsd;gYear"/>
68.   </owl:FunctionalProperty>
```

```
69.    <swrl:Imp rdf:about="Rule-1">
70.       <swrl:head>
71.          <swrl:AtomList>
72.             <rdf:first>
73.                <swrl:IndividualPropertyAtom>
74.                   <swrl:argument1>
75.                      <swrl:Variable rdf:about="x"/>
76.                   </swrl:argument1>
77.                   <swrl:argument2>
78.                      <swrl:Variable rdf:about="z"/>
79.                   </swrl:argument2>
80.                   <swrl:propertyPredicate
   rdf:resource="trReferences"/>
81.                </swrl:IndividualPropertyAtom>
82.             </rdf:first>
83.             <rdf:rest rdf:resource="&rdf;nil"/>
84.          </swrl:AtomList>
85.       </swrl:head>
86.       <swrl:body>
87.          <swrl:AtomList>
88.             <rdf:first>
89.                <swrl:IndividualPropertyAtom>
90.                   <swrl:argument1 rdf:resource="x"/>
91.                   <swrl:argument2>
92.                      <swrl:Variable rdf:about="y"/>
93.                   </swrl:argument2>
94.                   <swrl:propertyPredicate
   rdf:resource="trReferences"/>
95.                </swrl:IndividualPropertyAtom>
96.             </rdf:first>
97.             <rdf:rest>
98.                <swrl:AtomList>
99.                   <rdf:first>
100.                      <swrl:IndividualPropertyAtom>
101.                         <swrl:argument2 rdf:resource="z"/>
102.                         <swrl:argument1 rdf:resource="y"/>
103.                         <swrl:propertyPredicate
   rdf:resource="references"/>
104.                      </swrl:IndividualPropertyAtom>
105.                   </rdf:first>
106.                   <rdf:rest rdf:resource="&rdf;nil"/>
107.                </swrl:AtomList>
108.             </rdf:rest>
109.          </swrl:AtomList>
110.       </swrl:body>
111.    </swrl:Imp>
112.
113.    <swrl:Imp rdf:about="Rule-2">
114.       <swrl:head>
115.          <swrl:AtomList>
116.             <rdf:rest rdf:resource="&rdf;nil"/>
117.             <rdf:first>
118.                <swrl:IndividualPropertyAtom>
```

```
119.                    <swrl:propertyPredicate
   rdf:resource="trReferences"/>
120.                        <swrl:argument2 rdf:resource="y"/>
121.                        <swrl:argument1 rdf:resource="x"/>
122.                    </swrl:IndividualPropertyAtom>
123.                </rdf:first>
124.              </swrl:AtomList>
125.            </swrl:head>
126.            <swrl:body>
127.              <swrl:AtomList>
128.                <rdf:first>
129.                  <swrl:IndividualPropertyAtom>
130.                    <swrl:argument2 rdf:resource="y"/>
131.                    <swrl:argument1 rdf:resource="x"/>
132.                    <swrl:propertyPredicate
   rdf:resource="references"/>
133.                  </swrl:IndividualPropertyAtom>
134.                </rdf:first>
135.                <rdf:rest rdf:resource="&rdf;nil"/>
136.              </swrl:AtomList>
137.            </swrl:body>
138.        </swrl:Imp>
139.        <Book rdf:about="B1">
140.          <Title rdf:datatype="&xsd;string">
141.              The Description Logic Handbook
142.          </Title>
143.          <hasAuthor rdf:datatype="&xsd;string">
144.              Franz Baader
145.          </hasAuthor>
146.          <hasAuthor rdf:datatype="&xsd;string">
147.              Diego Calvanese
148.          </hasAuthor>
149.          <YearOfPub rdf:datatype="&xsd;gYear">
150.              2003
151.          </YearOfPub>
152.          <CountryOfPub rdf:datatype="&xsd;string">
153.              United Kingdom
154.          </CountryOfPub>
155.          <references rdf:resource="B2"/>
156.        </Book>
157.        <Book rdf:about="B2">
158.          <Title rdf:datatype="&xsd;string">
159.              Principia Mathematica
160.          </Title>
161.          <hasAuthor rdf:datatype="&xsd;string">
162.              Alfred Whitehead
163.          </hasAuthor>
164.          <hasAuthor rdf:datatype="&xsd;string">
165.              Bertrand Russell
166.          </hasAuthor>
167.          <YearOfPub rdf:datatype="&xsd;gYear">
168.              1910
169.          </YearOfPub>
```

```
170.            <CountryOfPub rdf:datatype="&xsd;string">
171.                United Kingdom
172.            </CountryOfPub>
173.        </Book>
174.        <Book rdf:about="B3">
175.            <Title rdf:datatype="&xsd;string">
176.                Semantic Web
177.            </Title>
178.            <hasAuthor rdf:datatype="&xsd;string">
179.                Karin Breitman
180.            </hasAuthor>
181.            <YearOfPub rdf:datatype="&xsd;gYear">
182.                2005
183.            </YearOfPub>
184.            <CountryOfPub rdf:datatype="&xsd;string">
185.                Brazil
186.            </CountryOfPub>
187.            <references rdf:resource="B1"/>
188.        </Book>
189.    </rdf:RDF>
```

6.6 TRIPLE

TRIPLE supports namespaces, sets of RDF statements, reification, and rules with a syntax close to that of first-order logic. In this section, we briefly introduce the basic concepts of TRIPLE, again using the same examples as in Section 6.3. The discussion follows Sintek and Decker (2002) and Decker et al. (2005).

Recall from Chapter 4 that a *resource* can be anything that has identity, a *Uniform Resource Identifier* (URI) is a character string that identifies a resource, and a *URI reference* (URIref) denotes the common usage of a URI. A *namespace* is a collection of names, identified by a URIref.

Names from namespaces may appear as *qualified names* (QNames) of the form P:L, which contain a single colon ":", separating the name into a *namespace prefix* P and a *local part* L. The namespace prefix must be associated with a namespace URIref in a namespace declaration. The qualified name *represents* the absolute URIref constructed by concatenating P and L.

In TRIPLE, these concepts are captured as follows. A *namespace declaration* is an expression of the form "A:=N." that defines A as a namespace prefix for the namespace N. A *resource declaration* is an expression of the form "R:=A:L." that defines R as an abbreviation for the resource identified by the QName "A:L".

Examples of declarations are:

```
1.    bt := "http://books.org/terms#".
2.    b1 := bt:ISBN_0-521-78176-0.
3.    b2 := bt:ISBN_0-521-62606-4.
4.    b3 := bt:ISBN_85-216-1466-7.
5.    BM := bt:BookModel.
```

Line 1 contains a namespace declaration and lines 2 to 5 show four resource declarations. For example, BM abbreviates the URIref

$$\texttt{http://books.org/terms\#BookModel}$$

An *atom* is defined as for Datalog. An *RDF statement* is an expression of the form "S[P→O].", where S is the subject, P is the predicate, and O is the object, and denotes an ordinary RDF triple (S,P,O). Examples of RDF statements in TRIPLE notation are

```
1.    b3[bt:Title→"Semantic Web"].
2.    b3[bt:CountryOfPub→"Brazil"].
3.    b3[bt:YearOfPub→"2005"].
```

A *molecule* abbreviates a list of RDF statements with the same subject, as in

```
b3[   bt:Title→"Semantic Web";
      bt:CountryOfPub→"Brazil";
      bt:YearOfPub→"2005"].
```

RDF statements and molecules can be nested, as in

```
b3[bt:references→b2[bt:Title→
                    "The Description Logic Handbook"]].
```

An *RDF model* is a set of RDF statements. A model can be made explicit in TRIPLE, receive a name (i.e., a resource denoting a model), and be attached to an atom, RDF statement, or molecule to indicate that the statement holds in that model. An example of an RDF model is

```
1.    b3[bt:Title→"Semantic Web"]@BM.
2.    b3[bt:CountryOfPub→"Brazil"]@BM.
3.    b3[bt:YearOfPub→"2005"]@BM.
```

A *model specification* is either a resource (denoting a model) or a Boolean combination of other models (using set union, set intersection, and set different), as in

```
b3[bt:YearOfPub→"2005"]@(BM ∪ NewBM).
```

An *atomic formula* is an atom, an RDF statement, or a molecule. A *formula* is either an atomic formula or an expression recursively defined by composing atomic formulas and formulas with the usual logical connectives (¬, ∧, ∨) and quantifiers (∀, ∃). All variables must be introduced via the universal or existential quantifier.

A *clause* is either a fact or a rule. A *fact* is an atomic formula. A *rule* is an expression of the form $\forall X\ C \leftarrow A$, where X is a list of variables, C is a conjunction of atomic formulas, and A is a formula. Hence, rules in TRIPLE are much more expressive than in the other languages presented earlier because A can be a (complex) formula, and not just a conjunction of atomic formulas.

A *model block* is an expression of the form $@M\{S\}$, where M is a model specification and S is a set of clauses. If the model specification is parameterized, a model block can also be written as $\forall p@M(p)\{S\}$.

A *query* is an expression of the form $\forall X \leftarrow A@M$, where A is a formula with a list X of variables that are not introduced via quantifiers, and M is a model specification.

TRIPLE also supports other features, such as reification and path expressions.

The BOOKS knowledge base, introduced at the end of Section 6.3, would be written in TRIPLE as follows. Just to illustrate some of features, we break the knowledge base into three models, identified by the following URIrefs:

1. `http://books.org/terms#BookData`
   contains all data about books, except references
2. `http://books.org/terms#BookRefs`
   contains all book references
3. `http://books.org/terms#Books`
   the complete model, that imports all statements defined in the other two models, and contains two new rules

The namespace and resource declarations and the model blocks that define these three models are:

```
1.    bt    := "http://books.org/terms#".
2.    Bks   := bt:Books.
3.    BDt   := bt:BookData.
4.    BRf   := bt:BookRefs.

5. @BDt { b1 := bt:ISBN_0-521-78176-0.
6.         b2 := bt:ISBN_0-521-62606-4.
7.         b3 := bt:ISBN_85-216-1466-7.
8.         b1[  Title→"The Description Logic Handbook";
                CountryOfPub→"United Kingdom";
                YearOfPub→"2003").
9.         b2[  Title→"Principia Mathematica";
                CountryOfPub→"United Kingdom";
                YearOfPub→"1910").
10.        b3[  Title→"Semantic Web";
                CountryOfPub→"Brazil";
                YearOfPub→"2005"].
11.        b1[hasAuthor→"Franz Baader"].
12.        b1[hasAuthor→"Diego Calvanese"].
13.        b2[hasAuthor→"Bertrand Russell"].
14.        b2[hasAuthor→"Alfred Whitehead"].
15.        b3[hasAuthor→"Karin Breitman"].
16.    }
```

```
17.    @BRf {
18.           b3[references→b1].
19.           b1[references→b2].
20.           }

21.    @Bks {
22.           FORALL O,P,V   O[P->V]  <-  O[P->V]@BDt.
23.           FORALL O,P,V   O[P->V]  <-  O[P->V]@BRf.
24.           FORALL X,Y     X[trReferences→Y]  ← X[references→Y].
25.           FORALL X,Y,Z  X[trReferences→Y]  ←
26.                          X[references→Z] AND Z[trReferences→Y].
27.           }
```

A query to retrieve all direct or recursive references, defined by `trReferences`, would be formulated in TRIPLE as follows

```
          FORALL X,Y  <-  X[trReferences→Z]@Bks.
```

The output from this query would be the following pairs

```
1.    X = b3, Y = b1
2.    X = b1, Y = b2
3.    X = b3, Y = b2
```

This concludes our brief summary of TRIPLE. A complete account of the language and associated tools can be found at the TRIPLE Web site.

Recommended Reading

Ullman (1988) is the standard reference for Datalog. The RuleML Web site (RuleML 2006) and the TRIPLE Web site (TRIPLE 2006) contain useful tutorials and references, and point to the download sites of the related tools. The reference for SWRL is Horrocks et al. (2004).

References

Boley, H.; Grosof, B.; Tabet, S. (2005) RuleML Tutorial. The RuleML Initiative. Draft Version. Available at: http://www.ruleml.org/papers/tutorial-ruleml.html.

Boley, H.; Tabet, S., Wagner, G. (2001) Design rationale of RuleML: A markup language for Semantic Web rules. In: *Proceedings of the SWWS'01*, Stanford, CA, USA.

Decker, S. et al. (2005) TRIPLE - An RDF rule language with context and use cases. In: *Proceedings of the W3C Workshop on Rule Languages for Interoperability*, Washington, DC, USA, pp. 27–28.

GNU Prolog (2006) The GNU Prolog Web site. Available at: http://gnu-prolog.inria.fr/.

Hirtle, D.; Boley, H. (2005) The modularization of RuleML - Version 0.9. RuleML markup initiative. Available at: http://www.ruleml.org/modularization/#Model.

Hirtle, D.; Boley, H.; Grosof, B.; Kifer, M.; Sintek, M.; Tabet, S.; Wagner, G. (2006) Schema Specification of RuleML 0.91. Available at: www.ruleml.org/spec

Horrocks, I.; Patel-Schneider, P.F.; Boley, H.; Tabet, S.; Grosof, B.; Dean, M. (2004) SWRL: A Semantic Web Rule Language Combining OWL and RuleML. W3C Member Submission 21 May 2004. Available at: http://www.w3.org/Submission/2004/SUBM-SWRL-20040521/.

Lloyd, J.W. (1987) *Foundations of Logic Programming.* Springer-Verlag New York, USA (2nd, Extended Edition).

RuleML (2006) The rule markup initiative. Available at: http://www.ruleml.org/.

Sintek, M.; Decker, S. (2002) TRIPLE - A Query, Inference, and Transformation Language for the Semantic Web. In: *Proceedings of the International Semantic Web Conference (ISWC),* Sardinia, Italy.

SWI-Prolog (2006) What is SWI-Prolog? Available at: http://www.swi-prolog.org/.

TRIPLE (2006) The TRIPLE language. Available at: http://triple.semanticweb.org/.

Ullman, J. (1988) Principles of Database and Knowledge-Base Systems. W.H. Freeman Company.

7

Semantic Web Services

7.1 Introduction

In its early days, the role of the Internet was that of a data provider: weather, finances, education, institutional, government, in addition to text and images about a myriad of other subjects, could be found on Web pages. As it evolved, the Web is no longer just a data provider, but a provider of services as well: buying and selling, auctions, bank transactions, and travel arrangements are among the services that can be performed online today. During the last decade, industry, government, and education sectors have been trying to establish standards for developing and using Web resources through what came to be known as *Web services*. There is no single definition for the expression. We list below those we find more adequate.

A Web service is a software system designed to support interoperable machine-to-machine interaction over a network. It has an interface described in a machine-processable format (specifically WSDL). Other systems interact with the Web service in a manner prescribed by its description using SOAP-messages, typically conveyed using HTTP with an XML serialization in conjunction with other Web-related standards.

(Haas and Brown 2004)

Web services are software components that are developed using specific technologies from three primary technology categories:
— An XML-based description format (for example, WSDL)
— An application messaging protocol (for example, SOAP)
— A collection or transport protocol (for example, HTTP).

(Adams et al. 2002)

A Web Service is a software component that is described via WSDL and is capable of being accessed via standard network protocols such as but not limited to SOAP over HTTP.

(Broberg 2002)

The interest in Web services is justified by the promises of interoperability across computational environments. As computers are becoming ubiquitous at the workplace and at home, the diversity of computer environments (operating systems and software applications) is growing at exponential rate. Because Web service architecture is based on a very specific XML message format, it is:

- Platform independent
- Physical location independent, that is, the place where the message is being sent from is irrelevant
- Application language independent
- Does not require that clients be aware of what kind of processor the server uses

Web service technology enables the use of the Web at a global level. Through Web services, any software application on the Web has the potential to reach any other application. If applications exchange messages in ways compliant with the Web service standards, they will be able to communicate independently of the operating systems, programming languages, processor, and internal protocols.

The goal of semantic Web services is to bring the Web to its full potential. Web service technology brings a dynamic aspect to the use of the Web; on the other hand, Semantic Web technology facilitates information search, retrieval, representation, extraction, interpretation, and maintenance. Today's Web service technology, based on SOAP, WSDL, and the UDDI registry, does not capture enough data semantics or business logic. However, a combination of the two technologies will leverage the potential of the Web service technology. Semantic annotation facilitates service discovery and provides a more sophisticated solution to the selection, composition, and interoperability across heterogeneous services.

To use a Web service, a software agent needs a computer-interpretable description of the service, and the means to access it. An important goal for Semantic Web markup languages is then to establish a framework within which services descriptions are developed and shared. Web sites should be able to employ a standard ontology, consisting of a set of basic classes and properties, for declaring and describing services. In this chapter, we discuss OWL-S, a service upper ontology that resulted from the collaborative effort by researchers at several organizations to define just such an ontology within the context of OWL (Martin et al. 2006).

7.2 Web Service Essentials

7.2.1 Basic Components of a Web Service

The Web service architecture involves many layered and interrelated technologies. In this section, we restrict our discussion to the WSLD specification, the UDDI registry and the SOAP protocol. We refer the reader to Booth et al. (2004) for a more detailed introduction to the Web service technologies.

WSDL — Web Services Description Language

WSDL is a specification that provides the constructs to describe a Web service in terms of method invocations. Those methods are described in an abstract format, so as to make them independent of (1) the language in which they will be implemented and (2) the operating system over which they will operate. WSDL works as the interface to the Web service.

As the communication patterns are becoming standards in the Web, the structured description of communications is becoming a reality. The WSDL contributes greatly to this goal as it provides an XML grammar that describes Web services as a set of information exchange points. In practice, the definitions provided by the WSDL serve as the means to automate communication among software applications.

Besides the abstract definition, a WSDL specification also contains a section that details the concrete elements of communication, that is, how to actually connect to the services. If a service can be accessed using the HTTP and SMTP protocols, an entry for each protocol will be included in the concrete part of the WSDL specification.

Recently, a set of extensions to WSDL, known as WSDL 2.0, was proposed to describe the semantics of service components. Using semantic annotations (i.e., references from an element within a WSDL or XML Schema document to a concept in an ontology), this new specification defines annotation mechanisms for one-to-one and n-to-m mappings between the WSDL inputs and outputs and the concepts defined in an outside ontology. The annotation mechanism is independent of the ontology expression language, and the WSDL 2.0 specification requires no particular ontology language (Farrell and Lausen 2002).

UDDI — Universal Description Discovery and Integration

UDDI is a Web service registry. It works as a catalogue for it allows a potential client to know about functionalities being offered and get to details about the services provided.

UDDI describes business on the Web using physical properties, such as name, address, and services offered. Additionally, those descriptions can be augmented through a new set of properties, called tModels, that describe extra properties, such as those described in the NAICS service taxonomy (see Chapter 9).

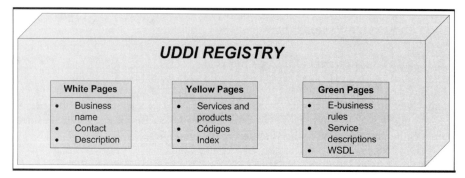

Fig. 7.1 UDDI Registry.

The information provided by a UDDI registry consists of three distinct parts, as illustrated in Fig. 7.1. The first part is the White Pages that contain information about the service provider itself, such as name, phone numbers, address, and contact. The second part is the Yellow Pages, that contain the description of the services offered. Finally, the Green Pages describe the technical details about the services (including the WSDL specification). This standard allows a Web business to:

- Describe its own business
- Describe services offered
- Discover other business that offer desired services
- Integrate with other business, through a business registry and Web services

Despite the fact that the UDDI standard is being used by both IBM and Microsoft, the community is questioning security issues when one displays information on a public registry. Many enterprises fear that they are making publicly available too much information about their assets. This discussion is hindering the acceptance of the UDDI as an open standard. Many believe that the standard should be adopted within the confines of Intranets, rather than making registries publicly available.

SOAP — Simple Object Access Protocol

SOAP is an XML protocol, developed by the W3C Consortium, for decentralized information exchange. It was developed to be independent of any specific programming language. The format of a SOAP message is similar to that of an envelope and is composed of the following elements (Gudgin et al. 2003).

- Envelope: the outermost element information item of a SOAP message
- Header: a collection of zero or more SOAP header blocks each of which might be aimed at any SOAP receiver within the SOAP message path
- Body: a collection of zero or more element information items aimed at an ultimate SOAP receiver in the SOAP message path

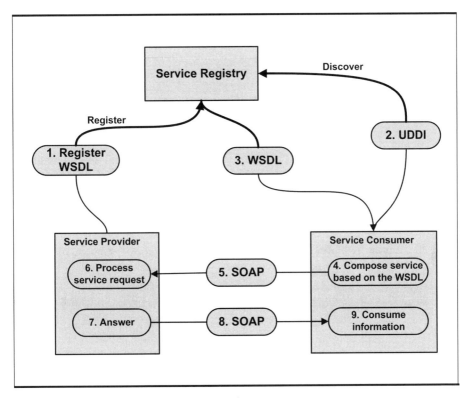

Fig. 7.2 Web service step sequence.

In Fig. 7.2, we illustrate the Web service sequence of steps. Note that each interaction involves at least two of the previously described elements. The first step is to register the service in the UDDI registry. Every service provider should follow this procedure so that other parties may locate the service being offered. Once found, the client receives the service specification (WSDL). Based on the specification, the client will compose a service solicitation that will be sent directly to the service provider, and not to the registry.

Therefore, the role of the UDDI registry is that of a catalogue, because it helps potential clients to find service providers. The actual service negotiation is done directly with the provider. This negotiation process is all based on SOAP message exchanging.

7.2.2 Web Service Security Standards

One of the greatest concerns related to the adoption of Web service technologies is security. In open and distributed environments such as the Web, how can we guarantee the identity of who is manipulating each transaction's data? Among current concerns are authentication, authorization, single sign-on (centralizing the identity registry thereby avoiding the need for multiple-user authentication transactions), confidentiality, and data integrity. As an answer to some of these concerns, Web service security standards were developed. In what follows we list the most significant.

XML Signature

A W3C standard, XML signatures are digital signatures designed for use in XML transactions. The standard defines a schema for capturing the result of a digital signature operation applied to arbitrary (but often XML) data. A fundamental feature of XML signature is the ability to sign only specific portions of the XML tree rather than the complete document. This feature is particularly useful for multiauthor documents. Signatures can be applied to objects other than plaintext, such as images and SOAP messages (Simon et al. 2001).

XML Encryption

XML Encryption is a protocol for encrypting/decrypting digital content (including XML documents and portions thereof) and XML syntax used to represent the (1) encrypted content and (2) information that enables an intended recipient to decrypt it. It also supports secure sessions between more than two parties; each party can maintain secure or insecure states with any of the communicating parties. Both secure and nonsecure data can be exchanged in the same document (Siddiqui 2002). XML Encryption is a W3C standard.

SAML — Security Assertion Markup Language

SAML is an XML-based framework for communicating user authentication, entitlement, and attribute information. As the name suggests, SAML allows business entities to make assertions regarding the identity, attributes, and entitlements of a subject (an entity that is often a human user) to other entities, such as a partner company or another enterprise application (Mishra et al. 2006). This standard is largely accepted and used by the community and is in direct competition with the Liberty Alliance and WS-Security standards.

WS-Security

The WS-Security specification was released in 2002 by the consortium formed by Microsoft, IBM, and VeriSign. This specification combines SOAP messages with cryptography and XML digital signatures in order to protect the integrity, trust, and authentication of messages exchanged on the Web. This standard proposes a series of extensions to the original SOAP header that can be used to place existing and future XML security standards. The goal of the WS-Security standards is to serve as a basis for a complete and customizable security solution. The greatest advantage of this standard is that it imposes some organization on the SOAP message headers. WS-Security includes other standards for policy (WS-Policy), trust (WS-Trust), and information exchange (WS-SecureConversation) (Thompson 2003).

Liberty Alliance Project

The Liberty Alliance, a consortium representing organizations from around the world, was created in 2001 to address the technical, business, and policy challenges around identity and identity-based Web services. The Liberty Alliance specification defines a set of protocols that collectively provide a solution for cross-domain authentication, and session management. This specification also defines provider metadata schemas that may be used for making a priori arrangements between providers (Rouault 2002). We note that this specification relies on the SAML specification.

7.2.3 Web Service Standardization Organizations

In Section 7.1, we provided some definitions for Web service expression. However, the industry has not reached a consensus for a precise definition of a Web service, which has been affecting the development of Web service standards. Characterized by the attempt of many sellers to establish their own Web service standards, this situation has been aggravated over the last years. In order to establish consistent standards, nonprofit consortiums were created, such as those described in what follows.

W3C — World Wide Web Consortium (www.w3.org)

W3C develops interoperable technologies (specifications, guidelines, software, and tools) for the Internet. W3C is a forum for information, commerce, communication, and collective understanding. W3C is responsible for the SOAP, WSDL, XML, XML-Schema, and HTTP standards.

OASIS — Organization for the Advancement of Structured Information Standards (www.oasis-open.org)

OASIS is a nonprofit consortium whose goal is to develop and promote the adoption of e-business standards. OASIS is responsible for the UDDI registry standard, the WS-Security and SAML security specifications.

WS-I — Web Services Interoperability Organization (www.ws-i.org)

WS-I is an open industry organization chartered to promote Web services interoperability across platforms, operating systems, and programming languages. The organization's diverse community of Web services leaders helps customers to develop interoperable Web services by providing guidance, recommended practices, and supporting resources. It has a very large membership including Accenture, DaimlerChrysler, EDS, Fujitsu, Hitachi, HP, France Telecom, Intel, IBM, Oracle, NEC, OMG, SUN, Toshiba, and VeriSign, among many others.

7.2.4 Potential Benefits and Criticism

Some believe that Web service technology will revolutionize the way software is developed. One of the advantages of the approach is its compositional architecture, that is, complex applications can be built by combining simpler services, similarly to pipe architecture, very popular among UNIX users. This construction approach may significantly affect development costs because it promotes software reuse, and it uses a communication protocol (Internet) much less expensive than cable networks. Some of the potential benefits of the Web services technology are:

- Decentralization: Web service technology will allow services to be completely decentralized and distributed.

- Speed: Web service availability is transforming response times into competitive advantage among stakeholders. A positive effect of the increase of business transactions over the Web is forcing the market to adopt a more dynamic and user-centered service model.

- Software packaging: software is usually thought of as closed functionality packages. The Web service compositional model has the potential to review this format and allow software to be developed and marketed as service components.

At the other extreme, Web service technology has received a great deal of criticism for providing an oversimplified model, which leaves out several fundamental concepts, such as:

- Data definition: There are no domain-specific data definitions. XML Schema is used to model the input and output of every application, regardless of the application domain. More severe critics argue that the quality of the services provided would greatly improve if domain ontologies were added. Those ontologies would provide more precise definitions for concepts in use.

- Service invocation behavior: There is no clear definition for the Web service invocation process. The sequence of operations is not defined, so it is not possible to explicit restrictions.

- Mediation: Neither behavior nor information exchanges are mediated.

- Composition: There is a clear need for the construction of complex services. However, today's Web service standards do not provide any support to service composition.

- Service guarantees: There are no guarantees on the services performed, or on the quality of the services. The Web service security initiative, led by WS-Security and Liberty Alliance, provides authentication guarantees. There is no similar effort that guarantees the quality of the services provided.

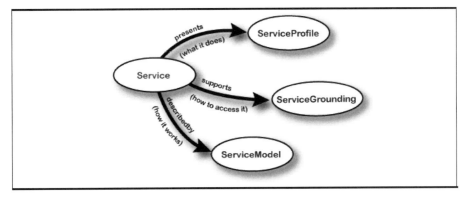

Fig. 7.3 OWL-S service ontology (Martin et al. 2006).

7.3 OWL-S Service Ontology

7.3.1 Overview

OWL-S is an OWL service upper ontology that offers a vocabulary that can be used in conjunction with OWL to describe services in an unambiguous, computer-interpretable format. OWL-S was developed with the goal of allowing discovery, invocation, composition, and automatic monitoring of Web services (Martin et al. 2006). OWL-S treats service composition as processes. There is a very clear distinction among process properties, structure, and implementation in OWL-S, which provides a way to model a process independently of its implementation.

The main class of the service ontology is the `Service` class, as depicted in Fig. 7.3. The current URI for this ontology is:

```
http:// www.daml.org/services/owl-s/1.2/Service.owl
```

which we abbreviate as `&owls` in the examples that follow.

The `ServiceProfile` class describes what the service requires and what it provides to the client. The `Service` and the `ServiceProfile` classes are related by the `present` property and its inverse property, `presentedBy`. The following fragment of OWL code from the service ontology exemplifies this fact.

```
<owl:ObjectProperty rdf:ID="presents">
    <rdfs:comment>
            There are no cardinality restrictions on
            this property.
    </rdfs:comment>
    <rdfs:domain   rdf:resource="&owls;Service" />
    <rdfs:range    rdf:resource="&owls;ServiceProfile" />
    <owl:inverseOf rdf:resource="&owls;presentedBy" />
</owl:ObjectProperty>
```

```
<owl:ObjectProperty rdf:ID="presentedBy">
    <rdfs:comment>
            There are no cardinality restrictions on
            this property.
    </rdfs:comment>
    <rdfs:domain   rdf:resource="&owls;ServiceProfile" />
    <rdfs:range    rdf:resource="&owls;Service" />
    <owl:inverseOf rdf:resource="&owls;presents" />
</owl:ObjectProperty>
```

The ServiceModel class describes how the service works and the consequences of its execution. The Service and the ServiceModel classes are related by the describedBy property and its inverse property, describes. A service can be described by at most one instance of the ServiceModel class. The following extract of OWL code from the service ontology exemplifies this fact.

```
<!-- Being described by a model -->

<owl:ObjectProperty rdf:ID="describedBy">
    <rdfs:domain   rdf:resource="&owls;Service" />
    <rdfs:range    rdf:resource="&owls;ServiceModel" />
    <owl:inverseOf rdf:resource="&owls;describes" />
</owl:ObjectProperty>

<owl:Class rdf:about="#Service">
    <rdfs:comment>
            A service has 0 or 1 models.
            (But note that a service with 0 models does not
            provide automated online access; it exists only
            for discovery purposes; that is, it exists so as
            to provide a Profile.)
    </rdfs:comment>

    <rdfs:subClassOf>
      <owl:Restriction owl:maxCardinality="1">
        <owl:onProperty rdf:resource="#describedBy" />
      </owl:Restriction>
    </rdfs:subClassOf>
</owl:Class>

<owl:ObjectProperty rdf:ID="describes">
    <rdfs:comment>
            There are no cardinality restrictions on
            this property. That is, the same service model
            can be used by many different services.
    </rdfs:comment>
    <rdfs:domain   rdf:resource="&owls;ServiceModel" />
    <rdfs:range    rdf:resource="&owls;Service" />
    <owl:inverseOf rdf:resource="&owls;describedBy"/>
</owl:ObjectProperty>
```

The ServiceGrounding class describes how the service may be accessed. The Service and the ServiceGrounding classes are related by the supports property and its inverse property, supportedBy. An instance of the ServiceGrounding class should be related to exactly one service. The following fragment of OWL code from the service ontology exemplifies this fact.

```
<!--

Supporting a grounding:

Every service model must be grounded in order to be usable,
and there may be multiple groundings for a given model.  But
the relationship between a service model and a grounding is
not expressed directly.  It is expressed indirectly via the
"supports" property of the Service. This allows the service
model  to  be  expressed  independently  of  any  particular
grounding.

-->

<owl:ObjectProperty rdf:ID="supports">
    <rdfs:domain    rdf:resource="&owls;Service" />
    <rdfs:range     rdf:resource="&owls;ServiceGrounding" />
    <owl:inverseOf  rdf:resource="&owls;supportedBy" />
</owl:ObjectProperty>

<owl:ObjectProperty rdf:ID="supportedBy">
    <rdfs:domain    rdf:resource="&owls;ServiceGrounding"/>
    <rdfs:range     rdf:resource="&owls;Service" />
    <owl:inverseOf  rdf:resource="&owls;supports" />
</owl:ObjectProperty>

<owl:Class rdf:about="#ServiceGrounding">
    <rdfs:comment>
                   A Grounding must be associated with exactly
                   one service.
    </rdfs:comment>
    <rdfs:subClassOf>
        <owl:Restriction owl:cardinality="1">
            <owl:onProperty rdf:resource="#supportedBy" />
        </owl:Restriction>
    </rdfs:subClassOf>
</owl:Class>
```

In a nutshell, the profile of a Web service provides all the necessary information for an agent to discover a service. To access the service, the client uses the associated grounding information. We detail each of the elements of the OWL-S service ontology in the next subsections.

7.3.2 Service Profile (What It Does)

The main class of the profile ontology is the ServiceProfile class, responsible for describing the services themselves. The current profile ontology URI is:

http:// www.daml.org/services/owl-s/1.2/Profile.owl

OWL-S defines a subclass of the ServiceProfile class, called Profile, as a possible representation for a service profile. This representation possesses three properties that are used to describe the service in question to human beings, rather than machines. Those properties are: the contactInformation property, that describes who is providing the service in question; the serviceName property, used to identify the process; and the textDescription property, that provides a free text description of the service.

Besides the above-mentioned properties, the Profile class also provides a description of the service functions under two perspectives: information transformation (represented by the inputs and outputs of the service) and changes of state (represented by the preconditions and effects of the service).

OWL-S also introduces the parameter concept. A parameter is a variable type, also used in the rule language context (see Chapter 6). The Parameter class is the superclass of the Input class, that represents the input parameters of a process, as well as the Output class, that represents the output parameters of the same process. The Parameter, Input, and Output classes are part of the OWL-S process ontology. The preconditions and effects of a process, on the other hand, are expressed using logical expressions.

To describe the input and output parameters and the preconditions and effects of a service, the Profile class has the following properties, depicted in Fig. 7.4.

- hasParameter: a property whose domain is the Parameter class from the OWL-S process ontology. This property is not used directly; it serves as the superclass of the rest of the properties.

- hasPrecondition: a property whose range is the Precondition class from the OWL-S process ontology.

- hasResult: a property whose range is the Result class from the OWL-S process ontology. The result of a process specifies the conditions under which its outputs are generated.

- hasInput: a property whose domain is the Input class, subclass of the Parameter class from the OWL-S process ontology. The Input class represents the information required by the process for its execution.

- hasOutput: property whose domain is the Output class, from the OWL-S process ontology.

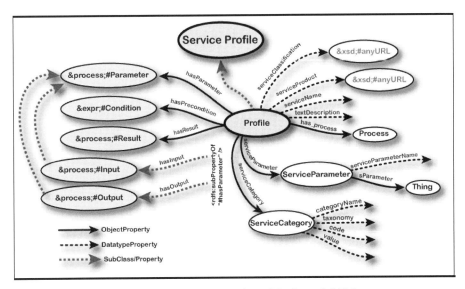

Fig. 7.4 OWL-S profile ontology (Martin et al. 2006).

Ideally, all instances of the `Input`, `Output`, `Precondition`, and `Result` classes are created from the process ontology and referenced by the `Profile` class. Hence, the value for each new property is a reference to an instance of a class from the process ontology. The `Profile` class has a specific set of properties:

- `serviceParameter`: an extensible list of properties whose elements are instances of the `ServiceParameter` class. This class possesses the `serviceParameterName` and the `sParameter` properties (the latter is a pointer to the value of the parameter in some other OWL ontology).

- `serviceCategory`: the value of this property is a reference to an existing service taxonomy. This property is used to describe service categories. It has a name (`categoryName`), a pointer to some taxonomy (`taxonomy`), one or more values in that taxonomy (`value`) and, for each type of associated service, a specific code (`code`).

It is important to note that a service profile may publish only part of the services it provides. However, if not declared, the functionalities will not be discoverable.

7.3.3 Service Model (How It Does)

In OWL-S, a process is a detailed service, described by an instance of the `Process` class, which is a subclass of `ServiceModel`. A process has a number of conditions that determine the situations under which it can be executed. Processes may result in the transformation of input data. A process execution, by the same measure, may transform the world. In other words, the process shifts the world to a different state. To describe a process in OWL-S, it is necessary to specify:

- Input parameters
- Output parameters
- Preconditions
- Effects

which are commonly referred to as IOPEs (Input, Output, Preconditions, and Effects). It is very important to guarantee that, for any given service, the IOPEs represented in the service model are reflected in the service profile.

To describe the relationship between a process and each of its parameters, thus making it possible to specify data transformations, OWL-S provides the `hasInput`, `hasOutput` and, `hasLocal` properties. These are all subproperties of the `hasParameter` property.

In addition to input and output parameters, a process also has preconditions, specified using the `hasPrecondition` property.

When a process is executed, in addition to its outputs, the process can also result in changing the state of the world. These changes are called effects in the OWL-S vocabulary. The effects are different from outputs because, rather than producing data, they change the state of the world (e.g., after receiving a payment, your balance is altered).

To express process preconditions and effects, OWL-S provides a specific expression language, represented by the `Expression` class and all its subclasses, whose URI is `http://www.daml.org/services/owl-s/1.2/generic/Expression.owl`.

The `Expression` class possesses two properties, `expressionLanguage` and `expressionBody`, both with cardinality equal to one, that is, they only accept a single value for language and body. The most common language used as the value for the `expressionLanguage` property is SWRL (see Chapter 6).

In OWL-S, output and effects are not directly related to the processes in question, for they may vary depending on the context of the service being applied. To maintain consistency, a class named `Result` was created. This class maintains a direct relationship with outputs and effects through a property named `hasResult`.

The `Result` class has five properties. The `hasResultVar` allows for the declaration of a variable of the type `ResultVar`, which is a subclass of `Parameter`. This property may be used in conjunction with the `inCondition` property, which defines the conditions under which the desired result may be reached. The `withOutput` property specifies the outputs of the process when the desired result was achieved. Similarly, the `hasEffect` property specifies the execution values of the process over the desired result. Finally, the `resultForm` property provides an abstract XML template for the outputs that have to be sent to the service client.

More than one result may be specified for an OWL-S process. One must be careful, though, to make the conditions under which each result may be achieved mutually exclusive, to avoid ambiguity and dubious execution.

An OWL-S process always involves two agents, namely, an instance of the class TheClient and an instance of the class TheServer.

The Process class corresponds to the union of three OWL-S classes, as is defined by the following OWL fragment,

```
<owl:Class rdf:ID="Process">
    <rdfs:comment> The most general class of processes
    </rdfs:comment>
    <owl:unionOf rdf:parseType="Collection">
        <owl:Class rdf:about="#AtomicProcess"/>
        <owl:Class rdf:about="#SimpleProcess"/>
        <owl:Class rdf:about="#CompositeProcess"/>
    </owl:unionOf>
</owl:Class>
```

Brief explanations for these three OWL-S classes follow.

- AtomicProcess: processes that can be directly invoked, possess no subprocesses, and execute the service in one step. For each atomic process, there should be an associated grounding (how to access it).

- SimpleProcess: processes that can not be directly invoked but, similarly to atomic processes, are considered single-step processes. Simple processes are used as abstraction elements. They may be used to provide a vision over an atomic process or to provide a simplified representation of a composite process. If a simple process is linked to a composite process, this relationship is represented using the realizedBy property. Simple processes may have input or output values associated with them, similarly to the rest of the processes.

- CompositeProcess: processes that can be decomposed into other processes. Control constructors (ControlConstruct) are used to describe composite processes through the composedOf property. Each ControlConstruct, in turn, has a components property, that indicates the process composition.

A composite process may be viewed as a tree whose nonterminal nodes are labeled with control constructs, each node having its offspring labeled using the component property. The leaves of this tree represent other process invocations, indicated as instances of the Perform class. The process property of the Perform class indicates the name of the process to be invoked. The process ontology is depicted in Fig. 7.5.

OWL-S provides the following control constructs: Sequence, Split, Split-Join, Any-Order, Choice, If-Then-Else, Iterate, Repeat-While, Repeat-Until, and AsProcess. An AsProcess object is both a control construct and a process. Considered as a type of control construct, the AsProcess construct has no components. However, if it is a CompositeProcess, it may have a body (the value of its composedOf property). It permits associating outputs, local variables, effects, and even preconditions with an arbitrary subtree of a composite process definition

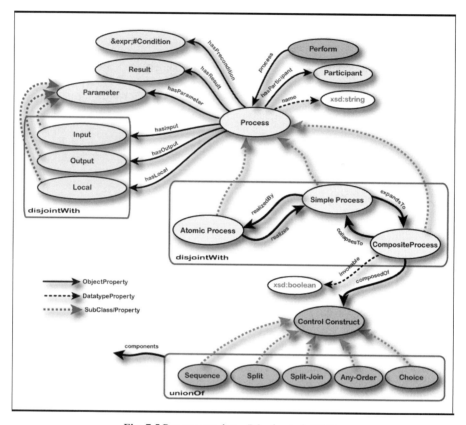

Fig. 7.5 Process ontology (Martin et al. 2006).

(Martin et al. 2006). The control construct semantics is similar to the corresponding constructs in the Business Process Execution Language (BPEL) or Business Process Modeling Languages (BPML) (Andrews et al. 2003).

7.3.4 Service Grounding (How to Access)

How to access an OWL-S service is described by the `ServiceGrounding` class. This class describes the format of the messages that should be exchanged, serialization protocols, transportation, and addressing. An OWL-S grounding may be seen as a mapping from an abstract specification to a concrete service element specification. Among the documents that form an OWL-S specification, the service grounding specification is the only one that deals with concrete implementation details. Both the service profile and service model representations are captured in a more abstract level.

OWL-S does not include an abstract representation for messages. In practice, the message contents are implicitly specified by the `Input` and `Output` properties of the atomic processes. Concrete messages, on the other hand, are specified by a grounding. Messages are specified using WSDL, explained earlier in this chapter. The goal of the grounding is to determine how the inputs and outputs of an atomic process may be described in terms of concrete messages exchanged between processes.

7.4 An OWL-S Example

In this section, we briefly outline the specification of a process application to exemplify the use of OWL-S. The example is partially reproduced from (Vieira 2005a; 2005b).

7.4.1 Scenario Description

Consider the problem of cleaning coastal areas affected by an oil spill. To address this type of accident, we may specify an emergency plan that defines a set of cleaning procedures that take into account the oil type and the characteristics of the coastal area. Table 7.1 provides a schematic example of cleaning procedures, when the type of coastal area is Sand Beach and the oil types are named Type I through Type V. Table cells are filled with a weight indicating the environmental impact of each of the procedures: 0.00 indicates the smallest environmental impact, 0.25 some impact, 0.50 a significant impact, 0.75 the greatest impact, and 1.00 inapplicable.

Now, suppose that an emergency team is assigned to the accident. This team is referred to as the *user* of the emergency plan in what follows.

Suppose that the user comes to a point in the overall emergency plan execution where he needs to select a cleaning procedure for a sand beach affected by an oil spill. The user can then search in Table 7.1 to select the best procedure to clean the beach.

For example, if the oil is of Type II, the best procedures are "VC: Vacuum Cleaning" and "CL: Cold, Low Pressure Cleaning." However, if there is no information about the oil type, Table 7.1 becomes useless. In this case, the user may take an educated guess and assume, say, that the oil is of Type II. He will then proceed with the emergency plan based on this assumption.

Table 7.1 Environmental impact of cleaning procedures for sand beaches.

Oil Type	Type I	Type II	Type III	Type IV	Type V
ND: Natural Degradation	0.00	1.00	1.00	1.00	1.00
UA: Use of Absorbents	1.00	0.25	0.00	0.00	0.00
VC: Vacuum Cleaning	1.00	0.00	0.00	0.00	0.00
CL: Cold, Low Pressure Cleaning	1.00	0.00	0.00	0.25	0.25
CH: Cold, High Pressure Cleaning	1.00	0.25	0.25	0.25	0.25
HL: Hot, Low Pressure Cleaning	1.00	1.00	0.50	0.50	0.50
HH: Hot, High Pressure Cleaning	1.00	1.00	0.50	0.50	0.50
PC: Vapor Cleaning	1.00	1.00	0.75	0.75	0.75

This very simple example illustrates two general flexibilization mechanisms. First, the user implicitly resorted to presuppositions about the accidental scenario when he selected Type II as the default for oil type. Second, he used a form of component substitution when he chose an alternative cleaning procedure.

The following piece of OWL-S code shows the `CoastalAreaOilCleaning` service definition. It provides a name to the service and clearly references the process model and grounding:

```
<!--    CoastalAreaOilCleaning SERVICE    -->
<service:Service rdf:ID="CoastalAreaOilCleaningService">
      <!-- Reference to the Profile -->
    <service:presents
            rdf:resource="#CoastalAreaOilCleaningProfile"/>
    <!-- Reference to the Process Model -->
    <service:describedBy
            rdf:resource="#CoastalAreaOilCleaning"/>
    <!-- Reference to the Grounding -->
    <service:supports>
      <grounding:WsdlGrounding rdf:ID="EmptyGrounding"/>
    </service:supports>
</service:Service>
```

We depict below the `CoastalAreaOilCleaning` class, which is a subclass of the `ServiceProfile` class (see Section 7.3.2). Note that it references the service using the `presentedBy` property and a process, the `CoastalAreaOilCleaning`. The text description provides a natural language (free) description of the service in question.

```
<!--    CoastalAreaOilCleaning PROFILE    -->

<profile:Profile rdf:ID="CoastalAreaOilCleaningProfile">

    <!-- Reference to the service specification -->
    <service:presentedBy
            rdf:resource="#CoastalAreaOilCleaningService"/>
    <profile:has_process
            rdf:resource="#CoastalAreaOilCleaning"/>
    <profile:serviceName>Coastal Area Oil Cleaning Service
    </profile:serviceName>
    <profile:textDescription> This service provides a means
          to clean coastal areas affected by an oil spill.
    </profile:textDescription>

    <process:hasOutput rdf:resource="#CAOCOutput"/>
    <profile:hasResult rdf:resource="#CAOCPositiveResult"/>
    <profile:hasResult
    rdf:resource="#CAOCNegativeResultConditionsUndetermined"/>

</profile:Profile>
```

7.4.2 Informal Process Definition

We provide an informal explanation of the CoastalAreaOilCleaning process, referenced by the service profile description in the last section. To avoid long names, we refer to this process simply as process p.

As illustrated in Fig. 7.6, process p has the following structure.

- p is the sequential composition of p_1 and p'_1
- p_1 is the parallel composition of p_2 and p_3 defined through the OWL-S Split-Join constructor
- p_2 is the subprocess responsible for determining the coastal areas affected by the oil spill. This process is also responsible for estimating the length, width, and quantity of spilled oil. The result of the process is a list L of the coastal areas affected
- p_3 is the subprocess responsible for determining the type of oil that was spilled
- p'_1 is defined by the If-Then-Else constructor. It conditionally executes p_4, after the affected areas and the type of spilled oil are clearly identified
- p_4 is the subprocess defined by the ForAll constructor applied to list L (Vieira 2005b). The body of this subprocess is p_5
- p_5 is an abstract process responsible for the cleaning of affected areas. It represents the existing cleaning procedures described in Table 7.1. During execution, the conditions of the accident are evaluated so that the best cleaning procedure is chosen. Note that the final procedure may be either atomic or the composition of two or more procedures. Process p_5 should be invoked as many times as there are affected coastal areas in list L, which is indicated by the feedback loop arrow in process p_5 in Fig. 7.6

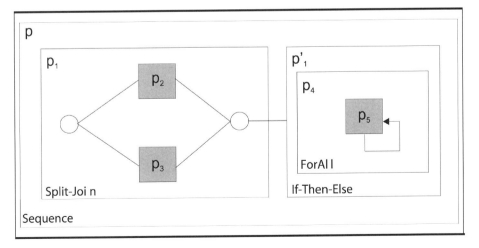

Fig. 7.6 Structure of process p.

7.4.3 OWL-S Process Definition

We outline the OWL-S definition of the `CoastalAreaOilCleaning` process (labeled process p in Fig. 7.6) and detailed in the previous section. To define a process we only need the `ServiceModel` ontology (see Section 7.3.2).

To model the `CoastalAreaOilCleaning` process, it is necessary to create a set of classes, properties, and auxiliary instances. We detail and exemplify some of these in what follows.

The `CoastalArea` class represents all existing coastal areas. With this class we associate properties that indicate its name, length, width, and quantity of spilled oil. The names of the areas are restricted to a list of known names (from `Area A` to `Area E`). The quantity of spilled oil is determined using a three-valued range: "high," "medium," and "reduced to nil." The following OWL-S code fragment shows part of the implementation of the `CoastalArea` class and its properties.

```
<owl:Class rdf:ID="CoastalArea">
  <rdfs:subClassOf>
    <!--    Restriction on Area names:    -->
    <owl:Restriction>
      <owl:onProperty rdf:resource="#name"/>
      <owl:allValuesFrom>
        <owl:DataRange>
          <owl:oneOf rdf:parseType="Resource">
            <rdf:first rdf:datatype="&xsd;string">
                Area A
            </rdf:first>
            <rdf:rest rdf:parseType="Resource">
              <rdf:first rdf:datatype="&xsd;string">
                  Area B
              </rdf:first>
              <rdf:rest rdf:parseType="Resource">
                <rdf:first rdf:datatype="&xsd;string">
                    Area C
                </rdf:first>
                <rdf:rest rdf:parseType="Resource">
                  <rdf:first rdf:datatype="&xsd;string">
                      Area D
                  </rdf:first>
                  <rdf:rest rdf:parseType="Resource">
                    <rdf:first rdf:datatype="&xsd;string">
                        Area E
                    </rdf:first>
                    <rdf:rest rdf:resource="&rdf;nil"/>
          </rdf:rest></rdf:rest></rdf:rest></rdf:rest>
          </owl:oneOf>
        </owl:DataRange>
      </owl:allValuesFrom>
    </owl:Restriction>
  </rdfs:subClassOf>
```

```
<--Restriction on the quantity of spilt oil
   (note the range values)
-->
  <rdfs:subClassOf>
    <owl:Restriction>
      <owl:onProperty rdf:resource="#oilQuantity"/>
      <owl:allValuesFrom>
        <owl:DataRange>
          <owl:oneOf rdf:parseType="Resource">
            <rdf:first rdf:datatype="&xsd;string"> high
            </rdf:first>
            <rdf:rest rdf:parseType="Resource">
              <rdf:first rdf:datatype="&xsd;string"> medium
              </rdf:first>
              <rdf:rest rdf:parseType="Resource">
                <rdf:first rdf:datatype="&xsd;string">
                 reduced to nil
                </rdf:first>
                <rdf:rest rdf:resource="&rdf;nil"/>
              </rdf:rest>
            </rdf:rest>
          </owl:oneOf>
        </owl:DataRange>
      </owl:allValuesFrom>
    </owl:Restriction>
  </rdfs:subClassOf>
</owl:Class>

<--    Properties:    -->

<owl:DatatypeProperty rdf:ID="name">
  <rdfs:domain rdf:resource="#CoastalArea"/>
  <rdfs:range  rdf:resource="&xsd;string"/>
</owl:DatatypeProperty>

<owl:DatatypeProperty rdf:ID="length">
  <rdfs:domain rdf:resource="#CoastalArea"/>
  <rdfs:range  rdf:resource="&xsd;float"/>
</owl:DatatypeProperty>

<owl:DatatypeProperty rdf:ID="width">
  <rdfs:domain rdf:resource="#CoastalArea"/>
  <rdfs:range  rdf:resource="&xsd;float"/>
</owl:DatatypeProperty>

<owl:DatatypeProperty rdf:ID="oilQuantity">
  <rdfs:domain rdf:resource="#CoastalArea"/>
  <rdfs:range  rdf:resource="&xsd;string"/>
</owl:DatatypeProperty>
```

The OilType class represents the oil types and has cardinality equal to 1. The class KnownOilType is an enumeration of the oil types depicted in Table 10.1. We show the code for these classes below.

```
<owl:Class rdf:ID="OilType">
  <rdfs:subClassOf>
    <owl:Restriction>
      <owl:onProperty rdf:resource="#type"/>
      <owl:cardinality rdf:datatype="&xsd;integer"> 1
      </owl:cardinality>
    </owl:Restriction>
  </rdfs:subClassOf>
 </owl:Class>

<owl:Class rdf:ID="KnownOilType">
  <rdfs:subClassOf rdf:resource="#OilType"/>
  <rdfs:subClassOf>
    <owl:Restriction>
      <owl:onProperty rdf:resource="#type"/>
      <owl:allValuesFrom>
        <owl:DataRange>
          <owl:oneOf rdf:parseType="Resource">
            <rdf:first rdf:datatype="&xsd;string">
                Oil type I
            </rdf:first>
             <rdf:rest rdf:parseType="Resource">
              <rdf:first rdf:datatype="&xsd;string">
                  Oil type II
              </rdf:first>
              <rdf:rest rdf:parseType="Resource">
                <rdf:first rdf:datatype="&xsd;string">
                    Oil type III
                </rdf:first>
                <rdf:rest rdf:parseType="Resource">
                  <rdf:first rdf:datatype="&xsd;string">
                      Oil type IV
                  </rdf:first>
                  <rdf:rest rdf:parseType="Resource">
                    <rdf:first rdf:datatype="&xsd;string">
                        Oil type V
                    </rdf:first>
                    <rdf:rest rdf:resource="&rdf;nil"/>
              </rdf:rest></rdf:rest></rdf:rest></rdf:rest>
          </owl:oneOf>
        </owl:DataRange>
      </owl:allValuesFrom>
    </owl:Restriction>
  </rdfs:subClassOf>
</owl:Class>
```

Because more than one coastal area can be affected by the spilled oil, we created a list to accommodate all affected areas. The following code fragment illustrates this list (`objList` is the namespace used to define a OWL-S list).

```
<owl:Class rdf:ID="KnownAffectedAreaList">
  <rdfs:subClassOf rdf:resource="&objList;List"/>
  <rdfs:subClassOf>
    <owl:Restriction>
      <owl:onProperty rdf:resource="&objList;first"/>
      <owl:allValuesFrom rdf:resource="#CoastalArea"/>
    </owl:Restriction>
  </rdfs:subClassOf>
  <rdfs:subClassOf>
    <owl:Restriction>
      <owl:onProperty rdf:resource="&objList;rest"/>
      <owl:allValuesFrom
              rdf:resource="#KnownAffectedAreaList"/>
    </owl:Restriction>
  </rdfs:subClassOf>
</owl:Class>
```

The `CoastalAreaOilCleaning` process is a sequence of two composite processes, `DetermineSpillFeatures` and `CleanAllAreas`, invoked when an oil spill occurs. When successful, it results in cleaning all affected coastal areas listed in the `KnownAffectedAreaList` class.

```
<process:CompositeProcess rdf:ID="CoastalAreaOilCleaning">
  <process:name>Coastal Area Cleaning Process</process:name>
  <service:describes
              rdf:resource="#CoastalAreaOilCleaningService"/>
  <objList:first>
    <process:Perform rdf:ID="DetermineSpillFeaturesPerform">
     <process:process rdf:resource="#DetermineSpillFeatures"/>
    </process:Perform>
  </objList:first>
  <objList:rest>
   <process:ControlConstructList>
    <objList:first>
     <process:Sequence>
      <process:components>
        <process:ControlConstructList>
          <objList:first>
            <process:Perform
                    rdf:ID="DetermineSpillFeaturesPerform">
              <process:process
                    rdf:resource="#DetermineSpillFeatures"/>
            </process:Perform>
          </objList:first>
          <objList:rest>
            <process:ControlConstructList>
              <objList:first>
```

```
                    <process:If-Then-Else>
                        <process:ifCondition
    rdf:resource="#DetermineSpillFeaturesPositiveCondition"/>
                        <process:then>
                          <process:Perform
                           rdf:ID="CleanAllAreasPerform">
                            <process:process
                             rdf:resource="#CleanAllAreas"/>
                            <process:hasDataFrom>
                              <process:InputBinding>
                                <process:toParam
    rdf:resource="#CleanAllAreasAreasList"/>
                                    <process:valueSource>
                                      <process:ValueOf>
                                        <process:theVar
    rdf:resource="#DetermineSpillFeaturesAffectedAreasOutput"/>
                                        <process:fromProcess
    rdf:resource="#DetermineSpillFeaturesPerform"/>
                                      </process:ValueOf>
                                    </process:valueSource>
                              </process:InputBinding>
                            </process:hasDataFrom>
                            <process:hasDataFrom>
                              <process:InputBinding>
                                <process:toParam
    rdf:resource="#CleanAllAreasOilType"/>
                                    <process:valueSource>
                                      <process:ValueOf>
                                        <process:theVar
    rdf:resource="#DetermineSpillFeaturesOilSpilledTypeOutput"/>
                                        <process:fromProcess
    rdf:resource="#DetermineSpillFeaturesPerform"/>
                                      </process:ValueOf>
                                    </process:valueSource>
                              </process:InputBinding>
                            </process:hasDataFrom>
                          </process:Perform>
                        </process:then>
                    </process:If-Then-Else>
                </objList:first>
                <objList:rest rdf:resource="&objList;nil"/>
              </process:ControlConstructList>
            </objList:rest>
          </process:ControlConstructList>
        </process:components>
      </process:Sequence>
    </objList:first>
   </process:ControlConstructList>
  </objList:rest>
</process:CompositeProcess>
```

Finally, the output of the `CoastalAreaCleaning` process is of type `CAOCOutpuType`. It may be that the affected coastal areas were successfully cleaned or that it was not possible to determine the spill conditions, that is, the affected areas or the oil type. We show the OWL-S code that implements the output of the process as follows.

```
<process:hasOutput>
  <process:Output rdf:ID="CAOCOutput">
    <process:parameterType  rdf:datatype="&xsd;anyURI">
      &THIS;CAOCOutputType
    </process:parameterType>
  </process:Output>
</process:hasOutput>
```

We refer the reader to Vieira (2005b) for the full OWL-S example.

References

Adams, H.; Gisolfi, D.; Snell, J.; Varadan, R. (2002) Best practices for Web services: Part 1. IBM DeveloperWorks Library. Available at: http://www-128.ibm.com/developerworks/webservices/library/ws-best1/.

Andrews, T. et al. (2003) BPEL4WS specification: Business process execution language for web services version 1.1. Available at: http://www-106.ibm.com/developerworks/library/ws-bpel/.

Booth, D.; Haas, H.; McCabe, F.; Newcomer, E.; Champion, M.; Ferris, C.; Orchard, D. (2004) Web Services Architecture. W3C Working Group Note 11, February 2004. Available at: http://www.w3.org/TR/ws-arch/.

Broberg, J. (2002) Glossary for the OASIS WebService Interactive Applications (WSIA/WSRP). OASIS Consortium. Available at: http://www.oasis-open.org/committees/wsia/glossary/wsia-draft-glossary-03.htm.

Christensen, E.; Curbera, F.; Meredith, G.; Weerawarana, S. (2001) Web Services Description Language (WSDL) 1.1. W3C Note 15 March 2001. Available at: http://www.w3.org/TR/wsdl.

Farrell, J.; Lausen, H. (2002) Semantic Annotations for WSDL. W3C Consortium. Available at: http://www.w3.org/2002/ws/sawsdl/spec/SAWSDL.html.

Gudgin, M.; Hadley, M.; Mendelsohn, N.; Moreau, J. J.; Frystyk Nielsen, H.F. (2003) SOAP Version 1.2 Part 1: Messaging framework. W3C Recommendation 24 June 2003. Available at: http://www.w3.org/TR/soap12-part1/.

Haas, H.; Brown, A. (2004) Web services glossary. W3C Working Group Note 11 February 2004. Available at http://www.w3.org/TR/ws-gloss/.

Martin, D.; Burstein, M.; Hobbs, J,; Lassila, O.; McDermott, D.; McIlraith, S.; Narayanan, S.; Paolucci, M.; Parsia, B.; Payne, T.; Sirin, E.; Srinivasan, N.; Sycara, K. (2006) OWL-S: Semantic markup for Web services. Available at: http://www.daml.org/services/owl-s/1.2/Service.owl.

Mishra, P.; Lockhart, H.; Maler, E.; Philpott, R.; Anderson, S.; Hodges, J. (2006) OASIS security services (SAML) overview. Available at: http://www.oasis-open.org/committees/tc_home.php?wg_abbrev=security#overview.

Rouault, J. (2002) Liberty bindings and profiles specification Version 1.0. Available at: http://xml.coverpages.org/liberty-architecture-bindings-and-profiles-v10.pdf.

Siddiqui, B. (2002) Exploring XML encryption: Demonstrating the secure exchange of structured data. IBM DeveloperWorks Library. Available at: http://www-128.ibm.com/developerworks/xml/library/x-encrypt/.

Simon, E.; Madsen, P.; Adams, C. (2001) An Introduction to XML Digital Signatures. O'Reilly XML.com. Available at: http://www.xml.com/pub/a/2001/08/08/xmldsig.html.

Thompson, S. (2003) Implementing WS-Security: A case study. IBM DeveloperWorks Library. Available at: http://www-128.ibm.com/developerworks/webservices/library/ws-security.html.

Vieira, T.A.S.C.; Casanova, M.A.; Ferrão, L.G. (2005a) On the design of ontology-driven workflow flexibilization mechanisms. *Journal of the Brazilian Computer Society*. Special Issue: Ontology Issues and Applications, Vol. 10, No. 4, pp. 33-43.

Vieira, T.A.S.C. (2005b) Execução Flexível de Workflows. Doctoral Dissertation. Pontifícia Universidade Católica do Rio de Janeiro, Departamento de Informática. Rio de Janeiro, Brasil.

Part III — Technologies

8

Methods for Ontology Development

8.1 Introduction

Ontology, as defined by Gruber, is an "explicit specification of a conceptualization." This definition is enough to convey an understanding of what ontologies are and for what they are. The main reasons to build an ontology are information sharing and the possibility of reusing knowledge about specific domains (Goméz-Peréz et al. 2004). Understanding what ontologies are for, however, does not provide much help in building them. According to Guarino and Welty (2002), "the ontology discipline is evolving into a discipline of its own and in this process the need for a methodology is clearly arising."

Therefore, several research groups are looking for adequate Semantic Web ontology development methods. However, the variables are so many that it may well be impossible to come up with a single method that is adequate for all situations. Probably, the best solution will be a choice among different possibilities or a composition of different ontology development methods.

With that in mind, researchers are engaged in the development of an ontology engineering discipline. Differently from other applied disciplines, engineering has distinct goals, as put in Sowa (1999):

Engineers have a more modest goal. Instead of searching for the best possible theory for all problems, they are satisfied with a theory that is good enough for the specific problem at hand. When they are assigned a new problem, they look for a new theory that can solve it to an acceptable approximation within the constraints of available tools, budgets, and deadlines. Although no one has ever found a theory that can solve all problems, people everywhere have been successful in finding more or less adequate theories that can deal with the routine problems of daily life. As science progresses, the engineering techniques advance with it, but the engineers do not have to wait for a perfect theory before they can do their work.

It is in this spirit that we present various ontology construction methods. None is the most adequate. Each has its use, depending on the application's specificity. Therefore, in this chapter, we discuss different methods as a way to understand the difficulties involved in the ontology elicitation, modeling, and construction processes.

8.2 Uschold and King Ontology Development Method

The importance of ontology as a conceptual model for capturing and reusing information is well understood in academic circles. Based on the experience that resulted from the construction of the Enterprise upper ontology, the research group at Edinburgh University proposed the first ontology construction method per se, also known as the "skeletal method" (Uschold and King 1995).

The ontology construction process, according to Uschold and King (1995), should be guided by motivating scenarios. The scenario technique, first introduced in Carroll (2000) for the design of human-computer interfaces, is largely used in software development today: as use cases in object-oriented development, as user stories in agile methodologies, or as a means to benchmark different design solutions (Alexander and Maiden 2004). Scenarios are useful in communicating, modeling, and validating information with users. Briefly, the main benefits provided by the use of scenarios in software development are (Leite and Breitman 2001):

- Ease of understanding
- Written in natural language
- Use the language of the problem and not that of requirements engineers
- Help unify criteria
- Stimulate thinking
- Gain user/client compromise
- Organize information
- Train new participants
- Help trace requirements
- Help the identification of nonfunctional requirements

In software development, scenarios are used to describe system functionality. In the case of ontology development, motivational scenarios are used to describe questioning, or kinds of questioning, that help determine the purpose of the ontology: "One excellent way to get a clear picture of the scope of the ontology is to create detailed scenarios that arise in the applications. These correspond to the story problems and the scenarios should include possible solutions to the problem" (Uschold 1996).

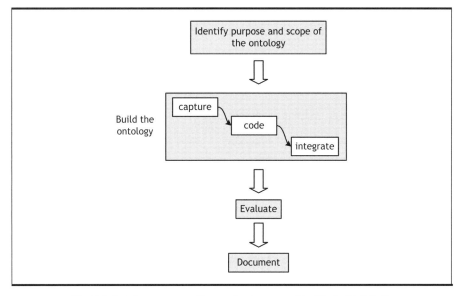

Fig. 8.1 Ontology construction method proposed by Uschold (1996).

As illustrated in Fig. 8.1, the construction process proposed in Uschold and King (1995) is composed of four distinct stages: identification, construction, evaluation, and documentation. In more detail, the stages are as follows

1. *Identify purpose and scope of the ontology:*
   Define why the ontology is being built and for what it is going to be used. An ontology may be designed with the intention of knowledge sharing, knowledge reusing, or as part of an existing knowledge base.

2. *Build the ontology:*
   2.1 *Capture:* Define concepts and relationships textually. Note that textual descriptions should not use the traditional dictionary approach, but rather they must maximize the use of other concepts present in the description. By doing so, the relationships between key concepts will be made explicit.
   2.2 *Code:* Formalize the concepts and relationships defined in Step 2.1.
   2.3 *Integrate:* Question the possibility of reusing existing ontologies. This activity can, and should, be made in parallel with the others.

3. *Evaluate the ontology:*
   Use technical criteria to verify the specification, using competency questions and real-world validations.

4. *Document the ontology:*
   Describe the ontology construction process. The final format may vary according to the type of ontology in question. Users may determine their own conventions, such as representing class names in capital letters and relationships in italics.

This method has been criticized for offering little support in identifying ontology classes and relationships. The concept elicitation process lacks formality and, as a result, there is a large gap between the elicitation and coding stages. An intermediate representation should be proposed, along with heuristics to help users decide which concepts should be included in the ontology and how they should be classified.

8.3 Toronto Virtual Enterprise Method

Gruninger and Fox (1995) proposed the Toronto Virtual Enterprise Method (TOVE). This method was derived from the authors' own experience in developing ontologies for business and corporate processes. The authors used motivating scenarios to describe problems and examples that were not addressed by existing ontologies, as proposed by Uschold (see Section 8.3). Once the motivating scenarios are ready, the developer should elaborate competency questions for the ontology, that is, the questions the ontology should answer. Those are elaborated with the purpose of helping the validation of the ontology (Gruninger and Fox 1995):

The development of ontologies is motivated by scenarios that arise in the application... often have the form of story problems or examples which are not adequately addressed by existing ontologies. A motivating scenario also provides a set of intuitively possible solutions to the scenario problems. These solutions provide a first idea of the informal intended semantics for the objects and relations that will later be included in the ontology.

Given the motivating scenario, a set of queries will arise which place demands on an underlying ontology. We can consider these queries to be requirements that are in the forms of questions that an ontology must be able to answer. These are the informal competency questions, since they are not yet expressed in the formal language of the ontology.

As illustrated in Fig. 8.2, the stages of the TOVE method are as follows

1. *Description of motivating scenarios:*
   Motivating scenarios are descriptions of problems or examples that are not adequately addressed by existing ontologies. These scenarios help develop possible solutions that carry the informal semantics of the concepts and relations to be included in the ontology.

2. *Formulation of informal competency questions:*
   Based on the motivating scenarios, competency questions are elaborated, for which the ontology to be built must provide valid answers.

3. *Specification of ontology terms using a formal representation:*
   Define a set of concepts from the competency questions. These concepts are the basis of a formal specification, developed using a knowledge representation language, such as first-order logic or the Knowledge Interchange Format (KIF).

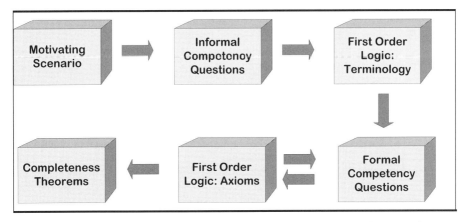

Fig. **8.2** Procedure for ontology design and evaluation (Gruninger and Fox 1995).

4. *Formulation of formal competency questions:*
   Describe the competency questions using a formal language.

5. *Axiom specification:*
   Formally describe rules that capture the semantics associated with the ontology concepts and relations.

6. *Verification of ontology completeness:*
   Establish conditions to characterize the ontology as complete, based on the formal competency questions.

   In our opinion, this approach has a major problem for it supposes that the concepts of an ontology can be derived from motivating scenarios alone. In fact, the scenario technique is best used to observe dynamical aspects of a given environment, rather than to identify static entities.

8.4 Methontology

The Methontology framework, developed in the Artificial Intelligence Lab of the Politécnico de Madrid, provides automated support for ontology development and is based on the IEEE standard for software development. This method is essentially descriptive, as it suggests which activities should be accomplished when building ontologies, but it does not provide guidance as to how they should be carried out. According to Fernandéz-Lopéz et al. (1997), it is fundamental to reach an agreement about the activities that will be instantiated, especially when the ontology is being developed by geographically dispersed groups. Activities are classified into:

1. *Ontology management activities:* include the identification, scheduling, control and quality assurance of the tasks to be performed.

2. *Ontology development-oriented activities:* include a predevelopment stage where environmental and feasibility studies are conducted. Once the ontology development is in place, typical activities include: specification, formalization, implementation, and management.

3. *Ontology support activities:* include essential activities related to knowledge acquisition, alignment, documentation, evaluation, integration, merging, and configuration management. These activities should be performed in parallel with the development-oriented activities.

The Ontology Development Environment (ODE) and WebODE applications provide semi-automated support to the ontology development process. We note that the elicitation techniques the authors use are very similar to those requirements engineers adopt when eliciting software requirements, such as structured interviews, questionnaires, and document analysis.

We detail the Methontology development process as follows

1. *Plan:*
   Develop a plan containing all activities that will be performed. The plan must include an estimation of the number of hours, resources, and tools that will be necessary.

2. *Specification:*
   Define the scope and goals of the ontology. The following questions should be addressed at this stage: (1) Why is this ontology being built? (2) Who are its users? Answers to these questions should be included in a written document, which will serve as the specification for the ontology. The level of formalism of this document is determined by the developers.

3. *Conceptualization:*
   Elicit the relevant domain concepts to be included in the ontology. Traditional elicitation techniques, such as those used in requirements engineering, can be adopted for this purpose. Table 8.1 shows a comparison among various elicitation techniques. Once the necessary information is elicited, it should be organized in some conceptual model. Some authors favor UML to represent classes, properties, and their relationships in this stage. We note that this is an intermediate representation, in the sense that it is more formal than a natural language description, but it is less formal than models based on logic.

4. *Formalization:*
   Formalize the conceptual model developed in the previous stage, using a formal ontology language. Description logic and frame-based models are two possibilities.

5. *Integration:*
   Integrate the ontology under development into existing ontologies. Methontology supports the reuse of concepts from other ontologies.

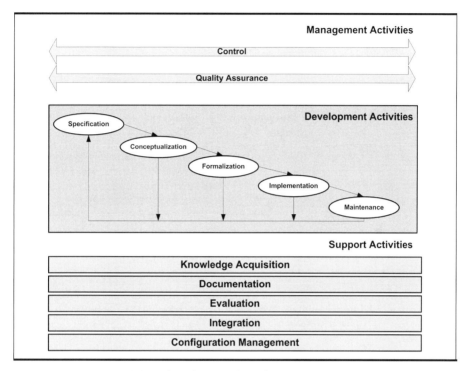

Fig.8.3 Methontology ontology development process
(adapted from Goméz-Pérez et al. (2004b)).

6. *Implementation:*
   Write the ontology in a machine-processable ontology language, such as OWL.

7. *Evaluation:*
   Carefully verify and validate the ontology so as to ensure its quality and conformance to standards. In particular, verify the adherence of the ontology under development to the upper ontologies used as reference in the development process.

8. *Documentation:*
   Similarly to other software artifacts, adequately document the ontology to facilitate maintenance and reuse.

9. *Maintenance:*
   Maintain the ontology to avoid obsolescence. Indeed, ontologies are theories about the world or a part of the world (a domain). Just as the world is in constant evolution, so are ontologies. Therefore, they should be constantly maintained so as not to become obsolete (some authors refer to this process as evolution).

Table 8.1 Comparison among techniques used in software requirement elicitation (Leite 2003).

Technique	Advantages	Disadvantages
Interviews	Direct contact with actors Immediate validation	Tacit knowledge Cultural differences
Dynamic document reading	Easy access to information sources Large volumes of information	Information dispersion Large effort required
Questionnaires	Standard statistical treatment	Answer limitation Little interaction
Requirements workshops	Multiple opinions Collective creation	Dispersion Cost
Observation	Low cost Low complexity	Dependency on the person making the observation Little exposition to the universe of information (superficiality)
Protocol analysis	Identification of nonobservable facts Better understanding of facts and events	Focus on performance what we say is not what we do
Anthropology	Inside/outside vision Contextualization	Requires a long time Little systematization
Nonfunctional requirement repositories	Knowledge reuse Anticipation of implementation issues Conflict identification	High cost to build the repository False impression of completeness

8.5 KACTUS Project Ontology Development Method

The goal of the KACTUS European ESPRIT project is to investigate knowledge reuse in computer systems and the role of ontologies in this process. The ontology construction process proposed by the project is strongly influenced by the possibility of reusing concepts defined in existing ontologies. This process is thus conditioned to the analysis and adaptation of concepts from other ontologies.

The KACTUS ontology development process consists of the following stages:

1. *Specification of the application:*
   The context of the application is captured through a list of domain-related terms.

2. *Preliminary ontology design:*
   Based on the evaluation of available upper ontologies, relevant top level categories are chosen, refined, extended to, and incorporated into the new ontology (that is, reused in the new ontology).

3. *Refinement and structuring:*
   The ontology is refactored to reorganize its structure and to achieve a more modular design that "follows the modularization and hierarchical organization principles."

In fact, the heuristics the method provides are too general to offer significant support to ontology development. Documentation, evaluation, and evolution processes are missing. The importance of the KACTUS project was to point out the necessity of considering concept reuse before "reinventing the wheel." Besides the economy of effort, the reuse of existing ontologies also offers the following advantages:

- Reduce development time
- Reduce development risk, as the concepts being reused were already tested;
- Induce vocabulary consistency
- Use of upper ontologies
- Incentive continuous update and the addition of new concepts to existing upper ontologies
- Provide information traceability
- Provide quality seal, if a "*pedigree*" ontology is adopted
- Foster a user community familiar with the concepts present in the upper ontology adopted

8.6 Lexicon-Based Ontology Development Method

Most ontology construction methods concentrate on modeling aspects, rather than on how domain concepts and relationships are to be elicited from the macro-system. Based on their research background in requirements engineering (RE), Breitman and Leite (2003) proposed an ontology construction process centered on an established requirements elicitation strategy, whose focus is on application languages. The last is rooted in a representation scheme, called the *Language Extended Lexicon* (LEL).

The LEL technique has long been incorporated into the authors' requirements engineering practice and focuses on using the language of the problem to describe the problem (Leite 1993). The lexicon provides a systematization for the elicitation, modeling, and analysis of ontology concepts. The underlying philosophy of the lexicon is contextualism, according to which particularities of a context of use of a system must be understood in detail before requirements can be derived. This approach is new to ontology building, which traditionally associates generalization and abstraction approaches to the organization of information.

LEL is a representation of the symbols in the application language (Leite 1993), anchored on a very simple idea: to understand the language of the problem without worrying about understanding the problem. Each term in the lexicon has two types of description: *notion* is the denotation of the term or phrase; *behavioral response* describes the connotation of the term or phrase, that is, provides extra information about the context at hand. In addition, the lexicon terms are classified into four categories: *object*, *subject*, *verb*, and *state*.

Central to LEL are two principles. The *principle of closure* says to maximize the use of other lexicon terms when describing the notions and behavioral responses of a new term. The *principle of minimal vocabulary* is to minimize the use of terms, external to the Universe of Discourse (UofD). If unavoidable, make sure they belong to the basic vocabulary of the natural language in use, and, as much as possible, have a clear mathematical representation.

The process of building a language-extended lexicon comprises six steps. First, we have to identify the main information sources of the UofD. The most reliable sources are usually people and documents. Second, we must identify a list of terms relevant to the UofD, using a set of elicitation techniques, such as those described in Table 8.1. The central heuristic is to list each term or expression that seems to have a special meaning in a particular environment (context).

The next step is to classify the terms. They can be: *object*, *subject*, *verb*, or *state*. The terms are described next. In this step, the objective is to elicit the meaning of each term. Each lexicon term is a set of notions, or *denotations*, and behavioral responses, or *connotations*, for that term. When describing the terms in the lexicon, one should enforce the principles of closure and minimal vocabulary. The lexicon is verified using an inspection strategy. Validation is performed by actors of the UofD using proof reading techniques.

Based on the LEL technique, Breitman and Leite (2003) proposed a construction process where LEL terms and their classification are the main knowledge source for building the ontology. The lexicon has a quality-oriented construction process systematized by subprocesses for elicitation, modeling, and analysis, and the proposed ontology construction process preserves this characteristic. The process is independent of the ontology language used in the implementation.

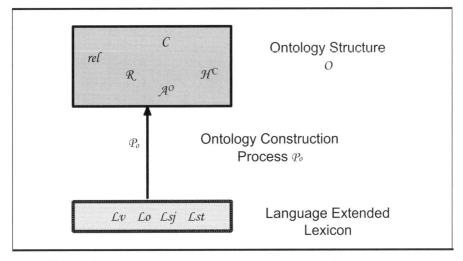

Fig. 8.4 Ontology construction process $\mathcal{P}o$ (inspired in the layered ontology engineering approach proposed by Maedche (2002)).

The resulting ontology is expressed by a five-tuple (C, $\mathcal{R}$, $C\mathcal{H}$, rel, $O\mathcal{A}$), where (see Section 2.1):

- C and $\mathcal{R}$ are disjoint sets, called the set of *concepts* and the set of *relations*
- $C\mathcal{H} \subseteq C \times C$ is a *concept hierarchy* or *taxonomy*
- $rel: \mathcal{R} \to C \times C$ is a function that relates the concepts nontaxonomically
- $O\mathcal{A}$ is a set of *ontology axioms*, expressed in an appropriate logical language

Figure 8.4 shows the role of the lexicon in the ontology structure. At the bottom layer, we have the LEL, composed of terms classified into verb ($\mathcal{L}v$), objects ($\mathcal{L}o$), subject ($\mathcal{L}sj$), and state ($\mathcal{L}st$). At the top layer, we have the ontology structure O. Process $\mathcal{P}o$ maps the lexicon terms into ontology elements. We detail process $\mathcal{P}o$ as follows (see Fig. 8.5).

1. List lexicon terms alphabetically according to their type (verb, object, subject, and state).

2. Make three lists: concepts (C), relations ($\mathcal{R}$), and axioms ($\mathcal{A}^o$). In the concept list, each entry will have a name, a description, and a list of zero, one, or more *rel* entries (that relate the present concept to others, nontaxonomically). The entries in the relation and axiom lists will have labels only.

3. Using the list of lexicon terms classified as either object or subject, for each term:
   3.1 Add a new concept to the concept list. The concept name is the lexicon term itself. The concept description is the notion of the term.

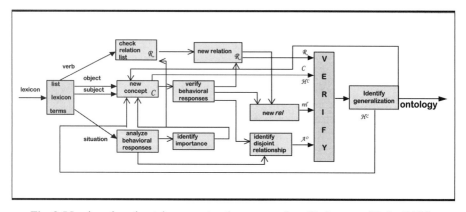

Fig. 8.5 Lexicon-based ontology construction process from Breitman and Leite (2003).

      3.1.1   For each behavioral response,
              3.1.1.1 Check the relation list for a relation that expresses it.
              3.1.1.2 If there is none, add a new relation to the relation list. The relation name is based on the verb of this behavioral response.
                  3.1.1.2.1   Verify consistency
              3.1.1.3 In the concept list, add a new *rel* to the concept in question. The *rel* is formed by the concept in question, the relation (defined in 3.1.1.1), and the concept to which it relates. (The concept is the direct/indirect object of the verb in the behavioral response. It is usually a term in the lexicon and appears underlined.)
              3.1.1.4 Check for negation indicators in the minimal vocabulary that relate the term to other terms. Analyze the pair of terms in order to identify a possible disjoint relationship.
                  3.1.1.4.1   If true, add the disjoint relationship to the axiom list.
   3.2 Verify consistency.

4. Using the list of lexicon terms classified as type verb, for each term:
   4.1 Check the relation list for a relation that expresses it.
      4.1.1   If there is none, add a new relation to the relation list. The relation name is the lexicon term itself.
   4.2 Verify consistency.

5. Using the list of lexicon terms classified as type state, for each term:
   5.1 For each behavioral response
      5.1.1   Try to identify the importance of the term to the ontology. This strategy is equivalent to the use of competency questions proposed in Gruninger and Fox (1995). The questions could be obtained from rephrasing the behavioral responses of the term into questions of type when, what, who, where, why, and how.

5.1.2 Check for negation indicators in the minimal vocabulary that relate the term to other terms. Analyze the pair of terms in order to identify a possible disjoint relationship. If true, add the disjoint relationship to the axiom list.

5.1.3 If the term is central to the ontology, classify it as a concept (C).

5.1.4 If the term is not central to the ontology, classify it as a relation ($\mathcal{R}$).

5.2 Verify consistency.

6. When all terms are added to the ontology:

    6.1 Check the ontology looking for sets of concepts that share identical *ref*.

    6.1.1 For each set of concepts that share identical *ref*, build a separate concept list.

    6.1.2 Search the ontology for a concept that refers to all members of this list. If such a concept is not found, search the notion and behavioral response of each member of the concept list trying to identify a common term from the minimal vocabulary.

    6.1.3 Build a concept hierarchy where every member of the concept list is a subconcept of that found in 6.1.2.

    6.2 Verify consistency.

The proposed ontology construction process is naturally bottom-up. It begins with a concept (a lexicon term) from the lexicon and systematically builds new properties and classes around it. The result is a web of interconnected concepts. In this approach, the authors emphasize the "putting together as opposed to dividing up" concept, which helps the identification of commonalities among concepts (Uschold 1996). The identification of common aspects shared by two or more concepts in an ontology may suggest the creation of a generalization for those concepts (Item 6.1 of the process), provided that there is either an ontology concept (6.1.2) or a term of the minimal vocabulary of the lexicon can be found (6.1.2.1) to represent the generalization. The authors make a point in not introducing new concepts for the sake of generalization alone, for they would rather avoid the introduction of artificial concepts that may be foreign to the Universe of Discourse.

We note that every time a new element is added to the ontology, consistency verification is needed. Ideally, the verification task is done with the aid of automated tools, such as FaCT and RACER (see Chapter 11). Typical reasoning services provided include finding concept inconsistency and determining subsumption relationships.

8.7 Simplified Methods

8.7.1 Ontology Development 101

This method was proposed in Noy and McGuiness (2001) as a guide to help users create their first ontology. In this method, in fact a set of heuristics, the authors summarize their experiences with the development of the Protégé2000, Ontolingua and Chimaera tools. According to the authors, developing an ontology encompasses:

- Defining classes in the ontology
- Arranging the classes in a taxonomic (subclass–superclass) hierarchy
- Defining slots and describing allowed values for these slots
- Filling in the values for slots for instances

We should always keep in mind, however, that there is no single way to correctly model a domain. The best solution depends on the model application and its possible extensions. The ontology development process is not linear. We should leave room for a number of interactions and refinements in the process of finding an adequate model. At the end of each interaction, it is desirable to conduct a validation process with domain experts and analysts. This process can also be responsible for retrofitting new information and modifications into the ontology, which requires returning to previous stages. In Fig. 8.6, we illustrate the method.

Briefly, the major steps of the method are:

1. *Determine the domain and scope of the ontology:*
   The user should start by providing answers to the following questions.

   - What is the domain that the ontology will cover?
   - For what are we going to use the ontology?
   - For what types of questions should the information in the ontology provide answers?
   - Who will use and maintain the ontology?

   We note that the questions proposed are no other than informal versions of the competency questions proposed by Gruninger (see Section 8.4). These questions will be useful when evaluating the finished ontology. At the end of Step 1, the user must ask himself or herself if the future ontology will suffice to answer the above questions.

2. *Consider reusing existing ontologies:*
   It is always a good practice to verify if others have not implemented some of the terms in another ontology, or if it is possible to extend an existing ontology to serve our needs. Model reuse may very well be a prerequisite, if the ontology to be built will have to interact with other existing ontologies.

   A good number of high-quality ontologies are available for download, sometimes ready to be imported to ontology development tools. The native ontology language is not a drawback to this process, as many ontology editors can import and export to different formats and languages (please bear in mind that some of those operations will incur on expression loss).

   Today, there are a significant number of public ontology libraries that provide reference ontologies for reuse. The Ontolingua project library (www.ksl.stanford.edu/software/ontolingua) and the DAML public library (www.daml.org/ontologies) are just two examples. The site of the KACTUS project (see Section 8.5) also offers a large number of ontologies for immediate reuse.

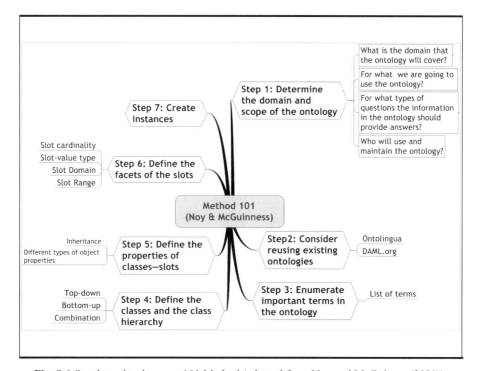

Fig. 8.6 Ontology development 101 Method (adapted from Noy and McGuiness (2001)).

3. *Enumerate important terms in the ontology:*
   It is paramount to make a list of terms that require definitions or explanations. Such a list can be obtained using traditional elicitation techniques, such as those surveyed in Table 8.1.

4. *Define classes and the class hierarchy:*
   Steps 4 and 5 should be executed in parallel; that is, classes and properties should be defined together. In practice, after defining a class, one goes on to describe its properties. There are at least three approaches to define the class hierarchy.

   The Top-Down Approach: this familiar approach, also known as functional decomposition, or as the *Divide et Impera*, has been in use for centuries as an effective problem-solving technique. In computer science, the canonical examples are structured and essential analysis.

   In the top-down approach, the most general classes are first defined and then successively decomposed into more specialized classes. A class and its specializations are connected by the specialization (or subsumption) relationship.

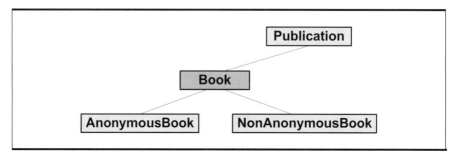

Fig. 8.7 Book taxonomy.

The Bottom-Up Approach: in this approach, the most specific classes are first defined, then successively grouped, according to some generalization criteria, and, for each group, a more generic class is chosen as a superclass of the more specific classes. This approach favors listing the entire set of classes before deciding on its organization. It also drastically reduces the risks associated with making a bad decomposition decision early in the process (Jackson 1995). In general, the bottom-up approach results in more balanced ontologies than the top-down approach.

The Mixed Approach: as the name implies, this approach combines the previous two approaches. The more salient classes are first identified and included in the ontology, and then the generalization/decomposition process is recursively applied to this initial set of classes.

Despite the fact that no approach is better than the other, the mixed approach is typically adopted by novice users. Their justification, according to Rosch, is that the concepts more frequently used in the real world tend to occupy an intermediate position in an ontology, being neither the more general nor the more specific ones (Lakoff 1987).

Classes should be organized in a taxonomic hierarchy guided by the following property: if a class A is the superclass of a class B, then every instance of B is also an instance of A. In other words, B represents a concept that is a *kind of* A. For example, imagine the class hierarchy depicted in Fig. 8.7. The class NonAnonymousBook is a subclass of the Book class, so that every instance of the NonAnonymousBook class is also an instance of the Book Class. For example, Karin's battered copy of *Principia Mathematica*, an instance of NonAnonymousBook, is also an instance of Book. In other words, Karin's battered copy of *Principia Mathematica* is a *kind of* Book.

5. *Define class properties (or slots):*
   Classes alone do not provide the necessary semantics to define the domain, as well as the use of the ontology. In other words, a class hierarchy does not convey all the information required to answer the competency questions stated in Step 1.

   In ontologies, differently from object models, properties exist independently of the classes; that is, they do not need to be associated with any class to justify their existence. Of course, most properties will be related to one or more classes, otherwise there will not be much sense in keeping them in the ontology.

A subclass inherits all properties of its superclass. For instance, in the example depicted in Fig. 8.7, if the class Book has a `publishedIn` property, every subclass will necessarily inherit this property. It means that all `NonAnonymousBooks` will inherit this property and, therefore, Karin's battered copy of *Principia Mathematica* will have a `publishedIn` value of its own (even if the property is associated with its "grandfather" class; inheritance is transitive).

6. *Define the facets of the properties:*
Depending on the expressiveness of the ontology language in use, property values may be constrained in different ways. The cardinality constraint is a good example. Some languages, such as OWL, allow properties to assume a single value or multiple values. For example, the license plate property of a car should be single valued, whereas the allowed drivers property should be multiple valued. Other systems allow for more precision by accepting minimum and maximum cardinality values.

7. *Create instances:*
The last step in this method is to create individual instances for the classes. According to its authors, this step requires: (1) choosing a class; (2) creating an individual instance of that class, and (3) filling in the property values.

8.7.2 Horrocks Ontology Development Method

The Manchester research group, lead by Ian Horrocks and responsible for the development of the OilEd Ontology Editing tool and the CO-Ode project among others, has a long tradition in teaching and training in ontology development. Horrocks (2003) proposed a simplified, but very useful method to help users in the development and editing of simple OWL ontologies, summarized as follows

1. *Determine how the world (domain) should work:*

- Determine the classes and properties in the domain
- Determine domains and ranges for properties
- Determine characteristics of classes
- Add individuals and relationships as necessary
- Some individuals belong here
- Iterate until the current ontology is good enough
- Package all this into an ontology

2. *Build the OWL ontology:*

- Ask whether the ontology is consistent
- Ask whether the classes are coherent

Recommended Reading

The guiding reference for this chapter is the book by Gómez-Pérez et al. (2004). We also recommend the survey on ontology learning methods, that is, how to build an ontology from scratch, enriching or adapting existing ones (Gómez-Pérez and Manzano-Macho 2004). The authors review ontology learning methods from texts, dictionaries, knowledge bases, structured, semi-, and unstructured data.

References

Alexander, I.; Maiden, N. (2004) *Scenarios, Stories, Use Cases*. John Wiley and Sons, New York, USA.

Breitman, K.; Leite, J.C.S. (2003) Ontology as a requirement engineering product. In: *Proceedings of the Eleventh IEEE International Requirements Engineering Conference*. 8-12 Sept. 2003, Monterey Bay, California, USA, pp. 309–319.

Carroll, J.M. (2000) Making Use: Scenario-Based Design of Human-Computer Interactions. MIT Press, Cambridge, MA, USA.

Fernandéz-Lopéz, M.; Goméz-Peréz, A.; Juristo, N. (1997) METHONTOLOGY: From ontological arts towards ontological engineering. In: *Proceedings of the AAAI97 Spring Symposium Series on Ontological Engineering*, Stanford, CA, USA, pp. 33–40.

Fernández-López M, Gómez-Pérez A, Pazos A, Pazos J (1999) Building a chemical ontology using methontology and the ontology design environment. *IEEE Intelligent Systems & their applications* 4(1), pp. 37–46.

Gómez-Pérez, A. (1998) Knowledge sharing and reuse. In: *The Handbook of Applied Expert Systems*. CRC, Boca Raton, FL, USA.

Gómez-Pérez, A.; Fernadéz-Peréz, M.; Corcho, O. (2004) *Ontological Engineering*. Springer Verlag, London, UK.

Gómez-Pérez, A.; Manzano-Macho, D. (2004) An overview of methods and tools for ontology learning from texts. *The Knowledge Engineering Review*. 19(3), pp. 187–212.

Gruninger, M.; Fox, M. (1995) Methodology for the design and evaluation of ontologies. In: *Proceedings of the Workshop on Basic Ontological Issues in Knowledge Sharing*, in IJCAI-95, Canada.

Guarino, N.; Welty, C. (2002) Evaluating ontological decisions with Ontoclean. *Communications of the ACM*, Vol. 45, No. 2, pp. 61–65.

Horridge, M.; Knublauch, H.; Rector, A.; Stevens, A.; Wroe, C. (2004) A practical guide to building OWL ontologies using the Protégé - OWL plugin and CO-ODE Tools Edition 1.0. University of Manchester. Available at: www.co-ode.org.

Horrocks, I. (2003) An example OWL ontology. (Foils from the ISCW 2003 tutorial). Available at: www.cs.man.ac.uk/~horrocks/ISWC2003/Tutorial/examples.pdf.

Jackson, M. (1995) *Software Requirements Specification: A Lexicon of Practice, Principles and Prejudices*. Addison-Wesley, Reading, MA, USA.

Jacobson, I. et al (1992) *Object Oriented Software Engineering: A Use Case Driven Approach*. Addison-Wesley/ACM Press, Reading, MA, USA.

Lakoff, G. (1987) Women, Fire and Dangerous Things – What Categories Reveal about the Mind. Chicago University Press, Chicago, USA.

Leite, J.C.S.P. (2003) Requirements engineering class notes, Dept. Informática, Pontifícia Universidade Católica do Rio de Janeiro.

Leite, J.C.S.P.; Breitman, K.K. (2001) Slides from the requirements elicitation through scenarios tutorial, presented at RE01, Toronto, Canada.

Leite, J.C.S.P.; Franco, A.P.M. (1993) A strategy for conceptual model acquisition. In: *Proceedings of the IEEE International Symposium on Requirements Engineering*, San Diego, CA, USA, IEEE Computer Society Press, pp. 243–246.

Maedche, A. (2002) *Ontology Learning for the Semantic Web.* Kluwer Academic, Hingham, MA, USA.

Matuszek, C.; Cabral, J.; Witbrock, M.; DeOliveira, J. (2006) An Introduction to the Syntax and Content of Cyc. In: *Proceedings of the 2006 AAAI Spring Symposium on Formalizing and Compiling Background Knowledge and its Applications to Knowledge Representation and Question Answering*, Stanford, CA, March 2006.

Noy, N.; McGuiness, D. (2001) Ontology Development 101 – A guide to creating your first ontology. KSL Technical Report, Stanford University, Stanford, CA, USA.

Sowa, J.F. (1999) Knowledge Representation: Logical, Philosophical and Computational Foundations. Brooks/Cole, Pacific Grove, CA, USA.

Sure, Y.; Studer, R. (2003) A methodology for ontology-based knowledge management. In: Davies, J., Fensel, D.; Harmelen, F.V. (Eds.) *Towards the Semantic Web: Ontology Driven Knowledge management*. Wiley and Sons, New York, USA, pp. 33–46.

Uschold, M. (1996) Building ontologies: Towards a unified methodology. Artificial Intelligence Application Institute. AIAI-TR-183.

Ushold, M.; Gruninger, M. (1996) Ontologies: Principles, methods and applications. *Knowledge Engineering Review*, Vol. 11, No. 2, pp. 93–136.

Uschold, M.; King, M. (1995) Towards a Methodology for Building Ontologies. In: Skuce, D. (Ed.) IJCAI'95 Workshop on Basic Ontological Issues in Knowledge Sharing. Montreal, Canada, pp 6.1–6.10.

Uschold, M.; King, M.; Moralee, S.; Zorgios, Y. (1998) The Enterprise ontology. In: Uschold, M. and Tate, A (Eds.) *Special Issue on Putting Ontologies to Use. The Knowledge Engineering Review*, Vol. 13.

9

Ontology Sources

9.1 Introduction

For many, the greatest benefit of the Web is to allow a growing number of services to be accessed from offices and homes. Today's Web grants direct access to financial, travel, commercial, and trading information at the same time that it facilitates buying and selling books, electronic equipment, stocks, bonds, and airline tickets, just to mention a few among myriad other options. The possibilities seem infinite, but the underlying Web technology falls short at a crucial point: there is no information about information. Any ordinary search will typically bring, together with the desired results, a large amount of worthless information. This situation, known to database experts as the "low precision, high recall" scenario, is hindering the usability of search engines. To ameliorate this situation, it is paramount to properly index Web resources, in other words, to add annotation elements that explain what the Web resources are about.

In this chapter, we discuss metadata standards, upper ontologies, and ontology libraries that are relevant to the indexing of resources in the Semantic Web. In Section 9.2, we address metadata standards, including the Dublin Core, the Warwick Framework, and some RDF-based representations. By design, we left out other representations, such as the MAchine-Readable-Cataloguing (MARC), the Record Export for Art and Cultural Heritage (REACH), the Text Encoding Initiative (TEI), and the Summary Object Interchange Format (SOIF), as they do not have a direct impact on the Semantic Web.

In Section 9.3, we discuss upper ontologies, which are complex knowledge representation models built with the aim of capturing human knowledge for future reference. We survey the Suggested Upper Merged Ontology (SUMO), developed by IEEE's Standard Upper Ontology (SUO) Working Group; John Sowa's KR ontology; CYC, the largest effort ever devoted to writing an upper ontology; and WordNet, a lexical database that provides the meaning of over 120,000 words in English, developed at Princeton University, in a project coordinated by Professor George Miller.

Finally, in Sections 9.4 and 9.5, we list other ontologies of interest and indicate a few ontology libraries, which facilitate and support the sharing of ontologies developed by geographically dispersed groups.

9.2 Metadata

9.2.1 What is Metadata?

Metadata is data about data, that is, information about a given document, such as date, author, and publisher. The International Federation of Library Associations (IFLA) defines: "Metadata is data about data. The term refers to any data used to aid the identification, description and location of networked electronic resources. Many different metadata formats exist, some quite simple in their description, others quite complex and rich" (IFLA 2006).

Berners-Lee (1997) introduces a metadata definition that better serves the Semantic Web purposes: "(in Web design)… Metadata is machine understandable information about Web resources or other things". This is a restrictive definition as it limits the scope of metadata to the Internet world. The truth is that this definition could be applied to any artifact. In this light, the traditional library card is metadata, by the same rule that an item in the *Victoria's Secret Swimsuit Catalogue*, represented by the product ID number, also is.

In fact, there is no universal definition for the term metadata, and the theme is still under discussion in many communities. However, we note that metadata is neither new nor peculiar to the Semantic Web community, but a practice that has been in use for centuries by librarians, museum curators, archive experts, and book editors. Ironically, once considered an archaic discipline, metadata studies are now at the forefront of research in information science.

We must also note that the Semantic Web poses new challenges to metadata research and application. Metadata was never before employed at such a large scale, nor used to catalogue such a wide range of artifacts. The global use of metadata is pushing the adoption of controlled vocabularies, left aside for decades, as a means to provide shared understanding across different user groups and applications. According to Gill (1998), new tools and skills will be required to implement the use of metadata on the Semantic Web scale.

In Table 9.1, we present UCLA's Department of Library and Information Science classification of the different types of metadata and their functions.

Table 9.1 Metadata types and functions (Gilliland-Swetland 1998).

Type	Definition	Examples
Administrative	Metadata used in managing information resources	Acquisition information Rights and reproduction tracking Documentation of legal access requirements Location information Selection criteria for digitalization Vision control
Descriptive	Metadata used to describe or identify information resources	Cataloguing resources Finding aids Specialized indexes Hyperlinked relationships between resources Annotation by users
Preservation	Metadata related to the preservation management of information resources	Documentation of physical condition of resources Documentation of actions taken to preserve physical and digital versions of resources, e.g., data refreshing and migration
Technical	Metadata related to how a system functions or metadata behaves	Hardware and software documentation Digitalization information, e.g., compression ratios, scaling routines Tracking system response times Authentication and security data, e.g., encryption keys, passwords
Use	Metadata related to the level and type of use of information resources	Exhibition records Use and user track Content reuse and multiversioning information

9.2.2 Dublin Core

In October 1994, during one of the first conferences about the Web, the need for semantics to describe Web resources was brought to discussion. From a librarian's point of view, it would be sufficient to create some sort of "virtual card," similar to its paper counterpart used to catalogue books. The card would contain information describing the resource in question in a way that helped users find that for which they were looking.

A first representation, known as the *Dublin Core* (DC) standard, was proposed some time later in a workshop held at Dublin, Ohio (hence the name). During the workshop, it became clear that a set of descriptors that were easy to create and understand was on call. The greatest appeal of the Dublin Core standard is providing a simplified set of elements that can be used to describe resources across many disciplines. The Dublin Core quickly became a standard for metadata descriptions. Indeed, today, it is an ANSI standard (ANSI/NISO Z39.85), as well as an ISO standard (ISO 15836:2003). Table 9.2 lists the elements of the Dublin Core.

The users of the DC standard organized themselves in the Dublin Core Metadata Initiative (DCMI) (URL: www.dublincore.org). This organization is dedicated to the dissemination and adoption of metadata standards and to the development of specialized vocabularies to describe resources so as to facilitate intelligent data retrieval.

Table 9.2 Elements of the Dublin Core.

Element	Definition
Title	object name
Creator	person/people responsible for the intellectual property of the object
Subject	main topic
Description	description of the object contents
Publisher	agent or agency responsible for making the object available
Contributor	person/people that made significant contributions to the object
Date	publication date
Type	object type, e.g., fiction, reference, novel, poem
Format	physical manifestation of the object, e.g., executable file, PDF
Identifier	an unambiguous reference to the resource within a given context
Relation	reference to a related resource
Source	a Reference to a resource from which the present resource is derived
Language	language of the intellectual content
Coverage	spatial location and temporal duration of the object
Legal rights	legal rights information about the object in question

Table 9.3 Goddard Core element set (Hodge et al. 2005).

Element	Definition
Controlled Subject	terms that characterize the subject of the expression specified in the Identifier element
Code	contains a Goddard organizational code under which the expression originated in whole or in part
Contract	contains a value that identifies the project under which the expression originated in whole or in part
Organization	contains a value that identifies the organization under whose auspices the expression was produced in whole or in part
Project Phase	specifies the phase that the project specified in the Project element was in when the expression was completed
Instrument	contains a value that identifies a piece of equipment to which the expression pertains

The Dublin Core is a very simple standard, as can be observed from the core set of elements. It has been adapted by different communities to better serve specific needs. One example is the NASA Goddard Space Flight Center extended Dublin Core set of elements, the *Goddard Core*, depicted in Table 9.3.

The NASA/Goddard Space Flight Center carries out extensive programs of research on earth and space sciences. In addition to producing spacecraft, the center also produces very large amounts of data, collected during space missions, and gathered from the processes of designing, implementing, launching, and maintaining spacecraft. These data are stored in several repositories. Because of the specificity of the data in question, an additional set of descriptive metadata was defined to facilitate the indexing and retrieval of data (Hodge et al. 2005).

In summary, the simplicity of the Dublin Core is its greatest strength, for it is a widely disseminated and easy to use standard, but it is also a weakness because the standard does not accommodate more expressive semantics. In fact, the specification of the Dublin Core favored ease of use (visibility) over expression power.

9.2.3 Warwick Framework

One year after the Dublin workshop, during another event, a new metadata standard was proposed. This new standard, named the *Warwick Framework*, sprung from the necessity to extend the original Dublin Core, considered too simple because it only provided one format to describe resources. Other types of metadata, such as terms, conditions, and responsibilities, also needed to be accommodated. A new architecture was then created, based on the notion of a container, that would aggregate different types of metadata in separate packages.

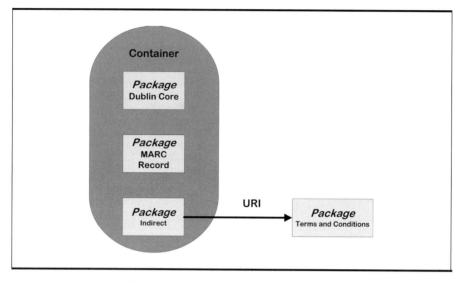

Fig. 9.1 Warwick Framework (Lagoze 1996).

We illustrate the Warwick Framework architectural model in Fig 9.1. Note that the Dublin Core is just one of the packages. In fact, the Warwick Framework left the original Dublin Core standard unaltered, and introduced additional packages that contain:

- Document domain-specific descriptions (object)
- Terms and conditions
- Labels and gradations
- Security, authenticity and signatures
- Supplier source
- Container set, for composite documents
- Pointers to every manifestation, instance or version of the document in question
- Person or group responsible for storing the document
- Dublin Core descriptors for the document

A container may not contain all packages, but it must contain at least the Dublin Core element set. One should be able to encrypt, compact, and address the container (that includes every instance package). The packages should be made publicly available. At Web site level, it is expected that each package represents a large number of documents, for example, the package that contains the selling and exchanging policies of a commercial Web site is also shared by all pages related to selling and exchanging activity. Search services, mediators, and catalogues should be the major users of this kind of metadata.

Despite having a very well-defined architecture, the Warwick Framework leaves some open questions. The first is syntax independence: each of the packages is allowed to use a different syntax. Although it augments the flexibility of the framework, it does not guarantee that two packages can exchange information. Because packages are independent of one another, it is possible that two or more packages use the same concept with different semantics. As a means to address such problems, another standard emerged, the Resource Definition Framework (RDF), discussed in depth in Chapter 4.

9.2.4 PICS

The *Platform for Internet Content Selection* (PICS) is a metadata notation, developed in 1995 by W3C, as a response to various society groups that were concerned with child and adolescent free access to undesirable Web content. PICS is a specification that allows people to distribute digital files labeled with metadata. Computer applications will therefore be able to filter or veto labeled files according to predefined user preference settings.

PICS is a classical metadata schema, in the sense that it is a mechanism to communicate Web page classification from a server to a client. Resource classification is communicated through metadata labels, which contain information about the contents of the resource in question. PICS does not have preestablished classification criteria, (e.g., nudity or violence), but value-neutral labels whose meaning is defined at server level. Instead of simply censoring Web sites, as was first suggested by parents and other groups, PICS provides the necessary controls so that users may make their own decisions about which sites should be allowed by their browsers. The original idea was that different organizations would have their own classification schemas and users would filter the content they judged inadequate for their families. Because the labels are value-neutral, they can be interpreted in different ways, depending on the client; for example, the label "Ti2WCVF78FYji8" may signify "sexual content" for some, whereas it may mean "feline reproduction" for others.

PICS presented many problems, the most serious one being its dependence on the classification made by external entities. As a response, W3C opted for developing another language, the Resource Definition Framework (RDF), discussed in depth in Chapter 4, which caters to the emerging metadata needs of other communities.

PICS remains a W3C recommendation and is available at the W3C Web site. Its technical documentation consists of:

- PICS label distribution, label syntax, and communication protocols
- PICS rating services and rating systems recommendation
- PICS rules recommendation (to specify profiles for information filters)
- PICS signed labels recommendation

9.2.5 vCards

The *vCard file format* was proposed by the Versit consortium (Apple, IBM, AT&T, and Siemens) as a standard for e-business cards in 1995. The standard was accepted by the International Mail Consortium and made a MIME standard by the IETF. A vCard is a series of typed elements that describe the attributes that may be found on a business card, for example, name, position, business address, fax, and phone numbers. A vCard may be expressed in RDF with the help of the namespace http://imc.org/vCard3/3.0#.

The following example is a full vCard written in RDF/XML (adapted from Ianella (2001)):

```
<?xml version="1.0"?
  <!ENTITY vc "http://www.w3.org/2001/vcard-rdf/3.0#">]>
  <rdf:RDF
    xmlns:rdf="http://www.w3.org/1999/02/22-rdf-syntax-ns#"
    xmlns:vCard="http://www.w3.org/2001/vcard-rdf/3.0#">
    <rdf:Description
      rdf:about="http://qqqfoo.com/staff/breitman" >
      <vCard:FN>Corky Crystal</vCard:FN>
      <vCard:N rdf:parseType="Resource">
        <vCard:Family>Breitman</vCard:Family>
        <vCard:Given>Karin</vCard:Given>
        <vCard:Prefix>Dr</vCard:Prefix>
      </vCard:N>
      <vCard:BDAY>1969-04-18</vCard:BDAY>
      <vCard:TITLE>Researcher PRO SET</vCard:TITLE>
      <vCard:ROLE>Programmer</vCard:ROLE>
      <vCard:TEL rdf:parseType="Resource">
        <rdf:value>+55 21 3257 31500</rdf:value>
        <rdf:type
        rdf:resource="http://www.inf.puc-rio.br/~karin"/>
        <rdf:type rdf:resource="&vc;voice"/>
      </vCard:TEL>
      <vCard:EMAIL rdf:parseType="Resource">
        <rdf:value>breitman@qqqfoo.com</rdf:value>
        <rdf:type rdf:resource="&vc;internet"/>
      </vCard:EMAIL>
      <vCard:ADR rdf:parseType="Resource">
        <vCard:Street>M. Sao Vicente 225</vCard:Street>
        <vCard:Locality>Rio de Janeiro</vCard:Locality>
        <vCard:Pcode>22457-900</vCard:Pcode>
        <vCard:Country>BRAZIL</vCard:Country>
      </vCard:ADR>
    </rdf:Description>
  </rdf:RDF>
```

9.2.6 FOAF

The *Friend of a Friend* (FOAF) vocabulary enables sharing personal information about people, describing basic facts, such as "married to," "cousin of," and so on. The principle that underlines FOAF is that of the "six degrees of separation" in which any person on the planet would be connected to any other human being by, at most, six nodes (Barabási 2002).

Table 9.4 Example of some attributes of the FOAF vocabulary.

Property	Value
Nick	Character string that provides the nickname by which the person wants to be called
Homepage	Personal home page URL
Workplacehomepage	Workplace URL
Depiction	Photo URL
Phone	Telephone number

The attributes of a person are specified as RDF triples, using the FOAF vocabulary, as exemplified in Table 9.4.

The following code fragment exemplifies a possible FOAF identification. Note that the tag foaf:knows, in the last portion of the code, provides an indication of a known person.

```
<rdf:RDF
   xmlns:rdf="http://www.w3.org/1999/02/22-rdf-syntax-ns#"
   xmlns:foaf="http://xmlns.com/foaf/0.1/">
   <foaf:Person>
      <foaf:name>Karin Breitman</foaf:name>
      <foaf:mbox rdf:resource=
        "mailto:karin@inf.puc-rio.br" />
      <foaf:nick >edd</foaf:nick>
      <foaf:workplacehomepage rdf:resource=
        "http://www.inf.puc-rio.br/~karin" />
      <foaf:depiction rdf:resource=
      "http://www.inf.puc-rio.br/~karin/foto/karin.jpg" />
      <foaf:knows>
         <foaf:Person>
            <foaf:mbox
              rdf:resource="mailto:daniel@waterloo.edu" />
            <foaf:name>Prof. Daniel M. Berry</foaf:name>
         </foaf:Person>
      </foaf:knows>
   </foaf:Person>
</rdf:RDF>
```

FOAF allows other vocabularies to be imported, such as the vCard vocabulary, through RDF namespaces. The FOAF experiment shows that data dispersed in a world scale could be used in a practical way without requiring complex technology and elaborated data schemas (Dumbill 2002).

9.3 Upper Ontologies

An *upper ontology* is a complex knowledge representation model, defined with the purpose of capturing human knowledge for future reference. According to the IEEE Upper Ontology Working Group (Schoening 2003), an upper ontology

> *... is limited to concepts that are meta, generic, abstract and philosophical, and therefore are general enough to address (at a high level) a broad range of domain areas. Concepts specific to given domains will not be included; however, this standard will provide a structure and a set of general concepts upon which domain ontologies (e.g. medical, financial, engineering, etc.) could be constructed.*

In this section, we survey our upper ontologies: SUMO, the KR ontology, CYC, and WordNet.

9.3.1 SUMO

The *Suggested Upper Merged Ontology* (SUMO) is an upper ontology developed by IEEE's Standard Upper Ontology (SUO) Working Group as an open source initiative with the purpose of creating a public standard, accessible through the Web. The idea is to use SUMO as a source for general-purpose definitions and as the foundation for the construction of middle-level and domain-specific ontologies.

SUMO will promote data interoperability, information retrieval, automated inference, and natural language processing. Indeed, SUMO serves many goals, among which we list:

- Project knowledge and databases: based on SUMO, developers will be able to articulate new facts and define data elements in terms of a common ontology, thus allowing interoperability with other systems based on this standard
- Reuse/Integration of legacy databases: data elements from existing systems need to be mapped to SUMO only once
- Domain ontology integration: domain ontologies will be interoperable as long as they share SUMO-based terminology and definitions

SUMO was first developed as a way to synthesize content from several available formal ontologies, including the Enterprise ontology (Uschold et al. 1998) and John Sowa's upper ontology (Sowa 1999). It consists of approximately 4000 assertions (including over 800 rules) and 1000 concepts.

Some of the general topics covered in SUMO include (Niles and Pease 2001):

- Structural concepts such as instance and subclass
- General types of objects and processes
- Abstractions including set theory, attributes, and relations
- Numbers and measures

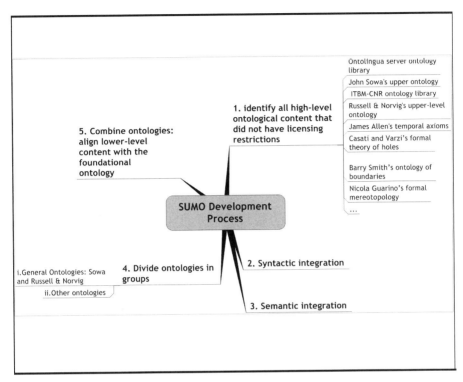

Fig. 9.2 SUMO ontology construction process.

- Temporal concepts, such as duration
- Parts and wholes
- Basic semiotic relations
- Agency and intentionality

SUMO was developed by the Teknowledge Corporation from input received from the Standard Upper Ontology (SUO) Working Group. The ontology is being progressively created through the integration of public content. SUMO is written in a simplified version of KIF (Knowledge Interchange Format), called SUO-KIF, widely accepted by the knowledge representation community (Genesereth 1991). Today, SUMO is also available in OWL, LOOM, and Protégé formats.

Figure 9.2 illustrates SUMO's incremental construction process (Niles and Pease 2001). Briefly, the major steps of SUMO's incremental construction process are:

1. *Identify upper ontologies that do not have licensing restrictions:*

In this step, online library content and independent ontologies (even anonymous ones) are considered. Ontologies posted on the Ontolingua server, John Sowa's upper ontology, TIBM-CNR ontologies (Unrestricted-Time, Representation,

Anatomy, Biologic-Functions, and Biologic-Substances), Russell and Novig's upper ontology, the Enterprise ontology, Fike's product ontology, portions of the frame-ontology authored by Ontolingua user Mribiere and the okbc-ontology authored by Ontolingua user Xpetard and mereotopological axioms from the Theory of Holes are just a few examples of the representation models that were merged into SUMO.

2. *Syntactic integration:*

    In this step, ontologies are translated from their native languages into SUO-KIF, SUMO's knowledge representation language.

3. *Semantic integration:*

    In this step, ontologies are combined into a single consistent framework. This step, according to SUMO leading researchers, Ian Niles and Adam Pease, is the most difficult one (Niles and Pease 2001).

4. *Divide ontologies into groups:*

    To achieve the goals of step 3, it was necessary to divide ontologies into two distinct groups. The first group contains the most general ontologies, for example, Sowa's and the ontology proposed by Russell and Norvig. The second group contains the other representations.

5. *Combine ontologies:*

    The ontologies proposed by Sowa and Russell and Norvig were amalgamated into a unique conceptual structure, that was compared to the remaining ontologies. During the combination process, the following scenarios were identified:

    Scenario 1: A new concept or axiom was not present in the ontology. If deemed important, the concept or axiom was included in SUMO.
    Scenario 2: A new concept or axiom was judged out of place in a generic ontology, that is, an all-purpose ontology. The concept or axiom was either too specific or restrictive. In this case, the new concept or axiom was left out of the ontology.
    Scenario 3: Total superposition of a new concept or axiom with others already in SUMO was detected. In this case, the new concept or axiom was not included to avoid redundancy.
    Scenario 4: Partial superposition of a new concept or axiom with others already in SUMO was detected. In this case, the new concept or axiom was carefully analyzed and individually discussed; the decision to include it was taken case by case.

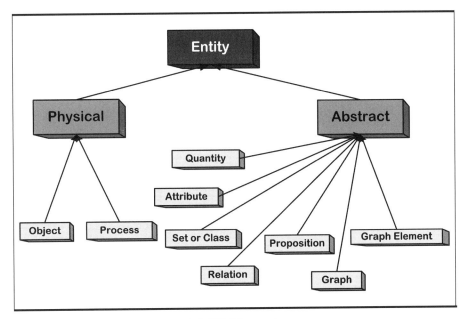

Fig. 9.3 SUMO's top classes.

Figure 9.3 illustrates SUMO's top classes, where:

- The topmost class is Entity
- The Entity class is specialized into the Physical and Abstract classes
- The Physical class is further specialized into the Object or Process classes, which are disjoint
- The Abstract class is specialized into the Quantity, Relation, SetOrClass, Graph, Proposition, GraphElement, and Attribute classes

To illustrate the SUO-KIF knowledge representation language, we show below an axiom written in this language, which states that every instance of the class `SefConnectedObject` will necessarily be a composition of `connected` object parts:

```
(<=>
    (instance-of ?OBJ SelfConnectedObject)
    (forall (?PART1 ?PART2)
        (<=> (and
                    (part-of   ?PART1 ?OBJ)
                    (part-of   ?PART2 ?OBJ))
              (connected   ?PART1   ?PART2) ))
```

Figure 9.4 shows the representation of the concept of book, using the SUMO ontology browser (available at http://sigma.ontologyportal.org:4010/sigma/Browse.jsp?kb=SUMO).

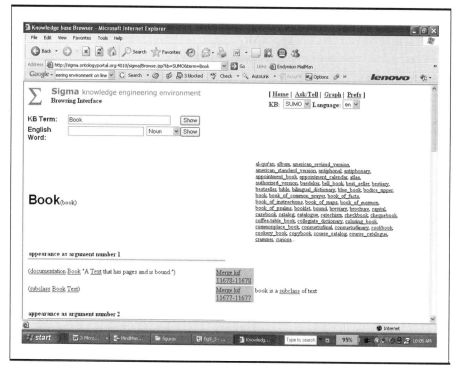

Fig. 9.4 Book concept in the SUMO upper ontology.

9.3.2 KR Ontology

The *Knowledge Representation* (KR) ontology, proposed in Sowa (1999), is based on a variety of sources, but primarily Peirce's semiotic and Whitehead's categories of existence.

As illustrated in Fig. 9.5, the KR ontology is composed of seven primitive categories: Independent, Relative, Mediating, Physical, Abstract, Continuant or Occurrent. The topmost category, known as Universal and represented by T, is divided in three primitive combination sets:

• Physical, Abstract (P, A)
• Independent, Relative, Mediating (I, R, M)
• Continuant or Occurrent (C, O)

In the center of the KR ontology, there are 12 categories, derived by combinations of primitive categories, for example, Nexus is a combination of Physical and Mediating. At the bottom is the Absurd category, represented by the ⊥ symbol. Formally, it is also a primitive category that satisfies two axioms: (1) nothing is an instance of ⊥; (2) every category is a supercategory of ⊥.

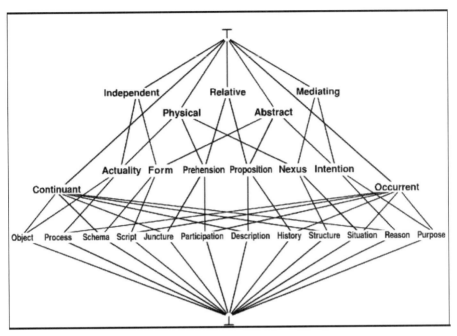

Fig. 9.5 The KR ontology.

Table 9.5 Matrix representation for the 12 KR center categories.

	Physical		Abstract	
	Continuant	Occurrent	Continuant	Occurrent
Independent	Object	Process	Schema	Script
Relative	Juncture	Participation	Description	History
Mediating	Structure	Situation	Reason	Purpose

The 12 categories displayed in the center of the lattice of Fig. 9.5, and the primitives from which they are generated, can also be arranged as the matrix shown in Table 9.5.

Following Sowa (1999), we reproduce, in what follows, the definitions of the primitive categories. The definitions of the remaining categories can be found in Sowa (1999). Nine primitive categories are axiomatized: T, ⊥, Independent, Relative, Mediating, Physical, Abstract, Continuant, and Occurrent. Each subcategory is defined as the *infimum* (greatest common subcategory, represented by the symbol ∩) of two supercategories, whose axioms it inherits. For example, the category Form is defined as Independent∩Abstract. It therefore inherits the axioms of Independent and Abstract, and it is abbreviated IA to indicate its two supercategories.

⊤ ( )

The Universal category, which has no differentiae, that is, properties that distinguish it from other categories. Formally, ⊤ is a primitive category that satisfies the following axioms.

(1)   There exists something: $(\exists x)\top(x)$
(2)   Everything is an instance of ⊤: $(\forall x)\top(x)$
(3)   Every category is a subcategory of ⊤: $(\forall t{:}\text{Class})t{\le}\top$

All other categories are defined by adding differentiae to ⊤ to show how they are distinguished from ⊤ and from one another. The category Entity is a pronounceable synonym for ⊤.

⊥ (IRMPACO)

The Absurd category inherits all differentiae. Formally, ⊥ is a primitive that satisfies the following axioms.

(1)   Nothing is an instance of ⊥: $\sim(\exists x)\bot(x)$
(2)   Every category is a supercategory of ⊥: $(\forall t{:}\text{Type})\bot{\le}t$

Because ⊥ is the inconsistent conjunction of all differentiae, it is not possible for any existing entity to be an instance of ⊥. Two categories, s and t, are said to be *incompatible* if and only if their only common subtype $s{\cap}t$ is ⊥. For example, Dog∩Cat = ⊥ because it is not possible for anything to be both a dog and a cat at the same time.

Abstract (A)

Pure information, as distinguished from any particular encoding of the information in a physical medium. Formally, Abstract is a primitive that satisfies the following axioms.

(1)   No abstraction has a location in space:
        $\sim(\exists x{:}\text{Abstract})(\exists y{:}\text{Place})\text{loc}(x,y)$
(2)   No abstraction occurs at a point in time:
        $\sim(\exists x{:}\text{Abstract})(\exists t{:}\text{Time})\text{pTim}(x,t)$

As an example, the information you are now reading is encoded on a physical object in front of your eyes, but it is also encoded on paper, magnetic spots, and electrical currents at several other locations. Each physical encoding is said to represent the *same* abstract information.

Absurdity (IRMPACO) = ⊥

A pronounceable synonym for ⊥. It cannot be the category of anything that exists.

Continuant (C)

An entity whose identity continues to be recognizable over some extended interval of time. Formally, Continuant is a primitive that satisfies the following axioms.

(1)   A continuant x has only spatial parts and no temporal parts.

(2)   At any time t when x exists, all of x exists at the same time t.

(3)   New parts of a continuant x may be acquired and old parts may be lost, as when a snake sheds its skin.

(4)   Parts that have been lost may cease to exist, but everything that remains a part of x continues to exist at the same time as x.

The identity conditions, that is, conditions that determine whether two different appearances of an object represent the same individual for a continuant are independent of time. If c is a subtype of Continuant, then the identity predicate $Id_c(x,y)$ for identifying two instances x and y of type c does not depend on time.

A physical continuant is an object, and an abstract continuant is a schema that may be used to characterize some object.

Independent (I)

An entity characterized by some inherent Firstness, independent of any relationships it may have to other entities. Formally, Independent is a primitive for which the *has*-test need not apply (Sowa 1999). If x is an independent entity, it is not necessary that there exist an entity y such that x has y or y has x:

$$(\forall x : Independent) \sim \Box (\exists y)(has(x,y) \vee has(y,x))$$

Mediating (M)

An entity characterized by some Thirdness that brings other entities into a relationship. An independent entity need not have any relationship to anything else, a relative entity must have some relationship to something else, and a mediating entity creates a relationship between two other entities. An example of a mediating entity is a marriage, which creates a relationship between a husband and a wife.

According to Peirce, the defining aspect of Thirdness is "the conception of mediation, whereby a first and a second are brought into relation." That property could be expressed in second-order logic:

(1) $(\forall m : Mediating)(\forall x,y : Entity)$

(2) $((\exists R,S : Relation)(R(m,x) \wedge S(m,y))) \supset \Box (\exists T : Relation)T(x,y)$

This formula says that for any mediating entity m and any other entities x and y, if there exist relations R and S that relate m to x and m to y, then it is necessarily true that there exists some relation T that relates x to y. For example, if m is a marriage, R relates m to a husband x, S relates m to a wife y, then T relates the husband to the wife (or the wife to the husband).

Instead of a second-order formula, an equivalent first-order axiom could be stated in terms of the primitive *has* relation (discussed in Section 2.4 of Sowa (1999)):

(1) $(\forall m{:}\text{Mediating})(\forall x,y{:}\text{Entity})$

(2) $((has(m,x) \wedge has(m,y)) \supset \Box(has(x,y) \vee has(y,x))$

This formula says that for any mediating entity m and any other entities x and y, if m *has* x and m *has* y, then it is necessary that x *has* y or y *has* x. In effect, the *has* relation in this formula is a generalization of the relations R, S, and T in the second-order formula. For example, if m is a marriage that *has* a husband x and a wife y, then the husband *has* the wife or the wife *has* the husband (or both).

Occurrent (O)

An entity that does not have a stable identity during any interval of time. Formally, Occurrent is a primitive that satisfies the following axioms.

(1)   The temporal parts of an occurrent, which are called *stages*, exist at different times.

(2)   The spatial parts of an occurrent, which are called *participants*, may exist at the same time, but an occurrent may have different participants at different stages.

(3)   There are no identity conditions that can be used to identify two occurrents that are observed in nonoverlapping space time regions.

A person's lifetime, for example, is an occurrent. Different stages of a life cannot be reliably identified unless some continuant, such as the person's fingerprints or DNA, is recognized by suitable identity conditions at each stage. Even then, the identification depends on an inference that presupposes the uniqueness of the identity conditions.

Physical (P)

An entity that has a location in space time. Formally, Physical is a primitive that satisfies the following axioms.

(1)   Anything physical is located in some place:

$\forall x{:}\text{Physical})(\exists y{:}\text{Place})loc(x,y)$

(2)   Anything physical occurs at some point in time:

$(\forall x{:}\text{Physical})(\exists t{:}\text{Time})pTim(x,t)$

More detailed axioms that relate physical entities to space, time, matter, and energy would involve a great deal of physical theory, which is beyond the scope of the KR book.

Relative (R)

An entity in a relationship to some other entity. Formally, Relative is a primitive for which the *has*-test must apply:

$(\forall x{:}\text{Relative})\Box(\exists y)(has(x,y) \vee has(y,x))$

For any relative x, there must exist some y such that x *has* y or y *has* x.

9.3.3 CYC

The CYC project is responsible for the largest effort ever devoted to writing an upper ontology. Its goal is to develop a large-scope upper ontology that contains definitions for most concepts. In terms of effort, the estimates are that over 900 person-years were already spent in CYC's construction over the last 20 years. The model is indeed very large, it contains over 2.2 million assertions, facts, and rules, describing more than 250,000 terms (Matuszek et al. 2006). We note that CYC is not a frame-based system, but rather a very large collection of assertions. The CYC knowledge base is divided into many (currently thousands of) *microtheories*, each of which is essentially a collection of assertions that share a common set of assumptions; some microtheories are focused on a specific knowledge domain, a particular level of detail, a particular interval in time, and so on. The microtheory mechanism allows CYC to independently maintain assertions that are *prima facie* contradictory; it also enhances the performance of the CYC system by focusing the inferencing process. Contrasting with SUMO, CYC is proprietary and its use restricted. Cycorp is the corporation that detains the rights to the CYC ontology.

The CYC ontology was designed to accommodate the totality of human knowledge so far. The name of the ontology itself stands for enCYClopedia. CYC topmost classes cover over circa 3000 concepts and are organized into 43 categories, such as time, dates, and space. The root of the ontology is the *Thing* class, which represents the Universal.

The 3000 top concepts are those that satisfy the following criteria:

- *Universal:* any imaginable concept must be correctly related to any of those 3000 concepts, independently of its nature (general or specific, arcane or prosaic, context, time, and language).

- *Articulated:* the distinctions made by the ontology should be necessary and sufficient for most purposes. By necessity, Cycorp means that all distinctions are worth being made, that is, for each there should be both pragmatic and theoretical argumentation to support it. By sufficient, Cycorp means that sufficient distinctions have been made so as to make shared support available, to disambiguate terms, among many others.

CYC may be used as a basis to construct domain ontologies. In this process, ontology engineers relate new classes (from the domain in question) to others from CYC's upper ontology, using a specialization relationship, called genls, in CycL, Cycorp trademarked ontology construction language.

In addition to helping construct domain ontologies, CYC can also be used for the following purposes:

- Online brokering of goods and services
- "Smart" interfaces
- Intelligent character simulation for games
- Enhanced virtual reality

- Improved machine translation
- Improved speech recognition
- Sophisticated user modeling
- Semantic data mining
- Advice services: e-shopping assistant

A subset of CYC is available in an open source format, OpenCYC. It contains 6000 concepts, which are defined and elaborated using 60,000 assertions.

Cycorp offers its users several tools to help manipulate the OpenCYC ontology. These include hypertext tools, which allow for navigation and visualizations of specific portions of the ontology, an inference machine, and a visualization tool.

In Fig 9.6, we illustrate the top categories in OpenCyc. Cycorp has also demonstrated a large interest in the Semantic Web by developing ontologies and making them publicly available through the DAML Ontology Library.

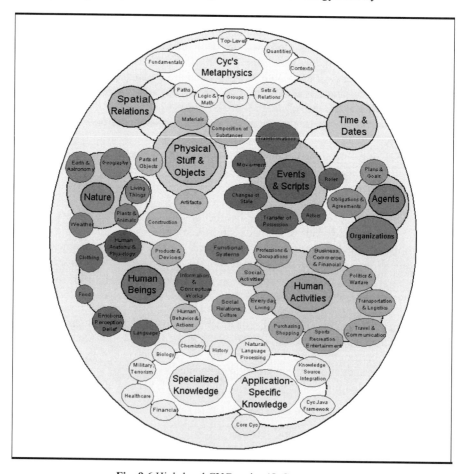

Fig. 9.6 High-level CYC topics (© Cycorp, Inc.).

Table 9.6 WordNet semantic relationships (George Miller 1995).

Semantic Relationship	Syntactic Category	Examples
Synonym (similar)	N, Aj, V, Av	Go up, ascend Sad, unhappy Fast, quick
Antonym (opposite)	Aj, Av (S,V)	Wet, dry High, low
Hyponym (subordinated)	N	Apple tree, tree Tree, plant
Hypernym (superordinate)	N	Tree, Apple Tree Plant, Tree
Meronym (part-of)	N	Ship, fleet Sleeve, shirt
Connection/Consequence	V	Drive, get ride Divorce, marry

Legend: N = noun, Aj = adjective, V = verb, Av = adverb

9.3.4 WordNet

WordNet is a lexical database that provides the meaning of over 120,000 words in English, organized in sets of synonyms, called *synsets*. WordNet was developed at Princeton University, in a project coordinated by Prof. George Miller (Miller 1995).

Computer applications that process natural language are very much dependent on the senses of the words that are being processed. If a word has more than one sense, a dictionary can be used to identify the correct sense of the word in a given context or situation. Dictionaries, however, were developed to serve humans and very few can actually be processed by computers. WordNet was developed to cover this gap. Its goal is to provide a lexical framework that can be used by computer programs. Nouns, verbs, adverbs, and adjectives in WordNet are organized in synonym sets, each representing a lexical concept. Semantic relationships link synsets. Table 9.6 illustrates the semantic relationships WordNet supports.

9.4 Other Ontologies of Interest

GUM (Generalized Upper Model)
purl.org/net/gum2

GUM is a linguistic ontology oriented toward grammatical elements, developed by the Information Sciences Institute (USA), GMD (Germany), and CNR (Italy). As opposed to WordNet, which focuses on the semantics of the terms, GUM describes the semantics of the grammatical constructs of phrases.

SENSUS

http://www.isi.edu/natural-language/projects/ONTOLOGIES.html

SENSUS is a term ontology that is very popular among natural language applications. It was developed at the University of Southern California and contains over 70,000 terms. The upper part of the SENSUS ontology contains circa 400 terms, which are referenced as the Ontology Base. The information sources used to build this ontology were electronically available information and WordNet.

EDR (Electronic Dictionary Research)

http:///www.iijnet.or.jp/edr/

EDR is a dictionary with over 400,000 concepts, developed in the context of a Japanese project. It contains mappings from Japanese terms and expressions to English to help translating text between the two languages. Although EDR contains more terms than WordNet, it does not provide much detail for each individual term.

Euro WordNet

Euro WordNet is a database with WordNet translated to several European languages. The European versions are structured similarly to the original WordNet, using synsets. Versions for Portuguese, Danish, Swedish, Greek, Basque, Romanian, Lithuanian, Russian, and Bulgarian are among the many available.

Open Directory Project (ODP)

http://dmoz.org/

The Open Directory Project (ODP), similarly to SUO, is a public initiative that relies on voluntary work from collaborators around the world. The initiative's goal is to build a huge thesaurus of RDF terms. Each person (editor) organizes a small portion of the Web and presents it to the community, which discards undesirable parts and adds the contents deemed valuable to the ODP body. Today, the Open Directory contains over 8000 terms and has many registered Web sites as clients, such as Google.

North American Industry Classification System (NAICS)

http://www.census.gov/epcd/www/naics.html

The North American Industry Classification System (NAICS) was created in collaboration with Canadian and Mexican authorities. NAICS classifies products and services in general. NAICS was developed based on a standard that dates back to the 1930s, the Standard Industrial Classification (SIC). In today's NAICS catalogue, products are classified using a six-digit code, differently from the old SIC classification, which adopted a four-digit classification code. This specification contains standards for several sectors of the economy, including agriculture, mining, construction, food, and real estate, among many others.

GALEN
http://www.opengale.org/

Developed by the OpenGalen organization, this ontology contains medical and clinical terminology. GALEN was developed to specify restrictions that apply to the medical domains. Among others, GALEN's goals are to support patient integration and information reuse demands, support data transmission, and provide a standard to facilitate the calculus of medical statistics.

Gartner
http://www.gartner.com

The Gartner group made its topic index available to the public. It is divided into 11 categories, which are used to classify the research conducted by the Gartner group. The original categories are expanded to over 500 subtopics.

9.5 Ontology Libraries

The ability to reuse existing ontologies is becoming increasingly important for the integration and development of new Semantic Web ontologies. Ontology library management services are available to facilitate and support the sharing of ontologies developed by geographically dispersed groups, by

- Providing an infrastructure for storing, searching and retrieving ontologies
- Supporting ontology reuse
- Supporting different languages
- Offering translation mechanisms that help map ontologies written in one language to another
- Supporting ontology editing

In this section, we list a few ontology libraries, indicating to what extent they provide the above services.

Ontolingua
http://www-ksl-svc.stanford.edu:5915/doc/ontology-server-projects.html

The Ontolingua server was developed at Stanford University in the beginning of the 1990s. It functions as an ontology repository and a representation language. The server supports translating, testing, and integrating ontologies, and offers sophisticated search mechanisms.

The server makes ontologies available basically to help the construction and refinement of new ontologies. Among many others, the Enterprise and InterMed ontologies are housed in this server.

WebOnto

http://eldora.open.ac.uk:3000/Webonto

WebOnto is a library service developed at the Knowledge Media Institute of the London Open University. It supports visualization and collaborative editing of ontologies through an interactive graphical interface. Search is restricted to the ontologies stored in the server.

DAML Library

http://www.daml.org/ontologies/

This library is maintained by DARPA as part of the DAML Project, whose broad goal is to contribute to the Semantic Web vision by developing languages and tools. The DAML Library contains ontologies in XML, HTML, DAML, and OWL. Ontology submission is public and open, without refereeing. Today, the library houses almost 300 ontologies ready for download.

SchemaWeb

http://www.schemaWeb.info/

SchemaWeb is a large model repository, which includes ontologies, dedicated to developers of RDF applications and, in particular, to those that use software agent technologies. It supports RDF, OWL, and DAML+OIL, but the schemas are stored as RDF triples.

SchemaWeb offers support to humans as well as Semantic Web applications, which may browse through the repository using Web services, for it supports SOAP and REST.

References

Barabási, A-L. (2002) Linked: The New Science of Networks. Perseus.

Berners-Lee, T. (1997) Axioms of Web architecture: Metadata. Available at: http://www.w3.org/DesignIssues/Metadata.html

Dumbill, E. (2002) Finding friends with XML and RDF: The friend-of-a-friend vocabulary can make it easier to manage online communities. IBM Developer Works. Available at: http://www-128.ibm.com/developerworks/xml/library/x-foaf.html.

Genesereth, M.R. (1991) Knowledge interchange format. In: J. Allen, R. Fikes, and E. Sandewall (Eds.) *Principles of Knowledge Representation and Reasoning: Proceedings of the Second International Conference (KR'91)*. Morgan Kaufmann, San Francisco, CA, USA.

Gill, T. (1998) Metadata and the World Wide Web. In: Baca, M. (ed.) *Metadata: Pathways to Digital Information*. Getty Information Institute, pp. 9–18.

Gilliland-Sweland, A. (1998) Defining metadata. In: Baca, M. (ed.) *Metadata: Pathways to Digital Information*. Getty Information Institute.

Hodge, G.; Clay, T.; Allen, R. (2005) A metadata element set for project documentation. *Science & Technology Libraries Journal*, Vol. 25, Issue 4, pp. 5–23.

Ianella, R. (2001) Representing vCard Objects in RDF/XML. W3C Note 22 February 2001. Available at: http://www.w3.org/TR/vcard-rdf.

IFLA (2006) Digital Libraries: Metadata Resources. Available at: http://www.ifla.org/II/metadata.htm.

Lagoze, C. (1996) The Warwick Framework: A container architecture for diverse sets of metadata. *D-Lib Magazine*, July/August.

Matuszek, C.; Cabral, J.; Witbrock, M.; Oliveira, J. (2006) An introduction to the syntax and content of Cyc. In: *Proceedings of the 2006 AAAI Spring Symposium on Formalizing and Compiling Background Knowledge and Its Applications to Knowledge Representation and Question Answering*. Stanford, CA, USA.

Miller, G. (1995) WordNet: A lexical database for English. *Communications of the ACM*, Vol. 38, Issue 11, pp. 39–41.

Niles, I., and Pease, A. (2001) Towards a standard upper ontology. In: Welty, C. and Smith, B. (Eds.) *Proceedings of the Second International Conference on Formal Ontology in Information Systems (FOIS-2001)*, Ogunquit, Maine, October 17-19, 2001. (See also http://www.ontologyportal.org)

Schoening, J. (2003) Standard Upper Ontology Working Group (SUO WG). IEEE P1600.1, 2003. Available at: http://suo.ieee.org/.

Sowa, J.F. (1999) Knowledge Representation: Logical, Philosophical and Computational Foundations. Brooks/Cole, Pacific Grove, CA, USA.

Uschold, M.; King, M.; Moralee, S.; Zorgios, Y. (1998) The Enterprise ontology. In: Uschold. M. and Tate. A. (Eds) *Special Issue on Putting Ontologies to Use. The Knowledge Engineering Review*, Vol. 13.

10

Semantic Web Software Tools

10.1 Introduction

Semantic Web tools are getting better every day. New companies are starting to form. Big companies are starting to move.

(Hendler 2001)

Today, there is a series of available tools that support the Semantic Web. Such tools can be classified into three major groups: ontology and metadata editors, plugins and APIs, and inference mechanisms. The last group contains software tools with the ability to derive new facts or associations from other facts. There is a myth that such tools are capable of emulating how humans think and derive conclusions on their own. In fact, they do not implement magical artificial intelligence capabilities, but rather straightforward data-processing strategies. Inferences are as good as the quality of the data available for processing. In the case of the Semantic Web, inference mechanisms have a very restricted set of primitives, that is, classes and properties, which are essentially what can be described using OWL or RDF. Examples of inference mechanisms for the Semantic Web are JESS, FaCT, Pellet, and RACER.

In this chapter, we discuss a small selection of Semantic Web tools that we judged relevant to this book, with no intention to produce a complete survey, which would represent an enormous task.

10.2 Metadata and Ontology Editors

10.2.1 Dublin Core Metadata Editor

http://www.ukoln.ac.uk/metadata/dcdot/

The metadata annotation process for any given document can be performed at the moment the artifact is created or later on in the artifact's lifecycle. The Semantic Web supporting claim is that most of the information available on the Web today lacks associated metadata. As a result, there is an ongoing effort to develop tools that are able to recognize and add metadata annotations *a posteriori*.

Some tools receive HTML pages as input and generate a suggested annotation. For text pages, information about the author, date of creation, title, language, and subject are the usual targets. The Dublin Core Metadata Editor (DC-Dot) is one such tool. This service retrieves a Web page and automatically generates Dublin Core metadata for it, either as HTML <meta> tags or as RDF/XML, suitable for embedding in the <head>...</head> section of the page. It uses the tags proposed by the Dublin Core Element Set discussed in Chapter 9.

In Fig. 10.1, we show the result of sending Karin Breitman's home page, www.inf.puc-rio.br/~karin, to the DC-Dot editor.

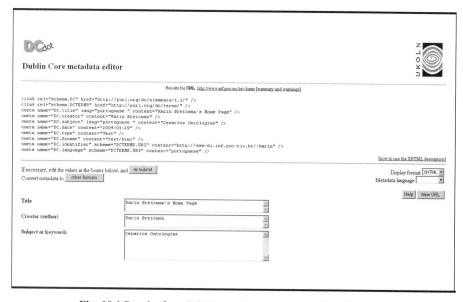

Fig. 10.1 Results from DC-Dot automatic metadata identification.

10.2.2 OilEd

http://oiled.man.ac.uk

One of the first Semantic Web software tools, OilEd is an editor for DAML+OIL, developed at the University of Manchester and distributed under the GPL license. In fact, in the developers' own words, OilEd was meant to be the "NotePad" of ontology editors (Bechofer et al. 2001).

OilEd does not provide support to any specific ontology method. It also does not support either integration or ontology versioning. Consistency checking is done with the help of FaCT, an inference mechanism. Class hierarchy visualization and navigation are enabled through the OilViz plugin.

Although the original developers continue to maintain the editor, the group is now responsible for the development of Protégé-OWL. As a result, for example, the OilViz plugin is now available for the Protégé environment. Similarly, FaCT^{++} is now available as the new version of the FaCT reasoner.

10.2.3 OntoEdit

OntoEdit is an ontology editor developed by the On-To-Knowledge project effort, whose goal was to "develop methods and tools and employ the full power of the ontological approach to facilitate knowledge management" (Davies et al. 2002).

OntoEdit implements an ontology construction process, which consists of three stages — requirement specification, refinement, and evaluation — very similar to the ontology development methodologies discussed in Chapter 8.

The editor stores the ontology conceptual model in the SESAME repository, thereby producing RDF concrete representations.

10.2.4 Protégé Ontology Editor

http://protege.stanford.edu/

The Protégé project started in 1987, when Mark Musen built a metatool for knowledge-based systems in the medical domain (Gennari et al. 2003). Protégé was developed by the Stanford Medical Informatics at the Stanford University School of Medicine, with support from a number of government agencies and private institutions.

The goal of Protégé I was to facilitate the knowledge acquisition process by helping engineers build custom-tailored tools that would help experts in knowledge acquisition processes. Protégé II extended the original project and included support for ontologies, problem-solving components (users could decide among alternative problem-solving strategies), and mappings between different ontologies. Protégé II ran on the NeXTStep operating system. Protégé/Win, a Windows version of Protégé, was developed as a means to expand the Protégé user group. Protégé 2000, the current version and often referred to as just Protégé, is the result of re-engineering Protégé/Win, a process triggered by user feedback.

Protégé is by far the most popular Semantic Web ontology editor in use today, with nearly 50,000 registered users at the time this book was written. A great deal of the success may be attributed to the increasing numbers of tutorials and materials available online (Noy and McGuiness 2001; Horridge et al. 2004; Horridge 2005; Drummond et al. 2005). Protégé is supported by a strong community of developers in more than 100 countries worldwide. The Stanford Medical Informatics hosts annual Protégé conferences and maintains the Protégé Community Wiki, a relation of nearly 200 projects that are using Protégé for knowledge solutions in areas as diverse as biomedicine, intelligence gathering, and corporate modeling.

The most significant change from Protégé/Win to Protégé 2000 was the migration to an underlying knowledge model influenced by frame-based systems and based on the OKBC (Open Knowledge Base Connectivity). A salient characteristic of the OKBC model is the lack of distinction between classes and instances (Chaudhri et al. 1998). In addition to the possibility of creating metaclasses (classes whose instances are other classes), Protégé 2000 blurs the distinction between classes and instances, providing more flexibility than its previous versions.

Protégé features a plugin architecture, which facilitates dividing the development effort among different groups, testing and maintaining separate functionality, and catering to specific group needs. Protégé is in fact extensible, allowing users to program new plugins based on their specific needs.

Protégé supports two major ways of modeling ontologies: via Protégé-Frames and via Protégé-OWL editors. In Fig. 10.2, we depict the Protégé frames interface. The Protégé-OWL plugin extends Protégé to provide a graphical software development environment that supports the authoring of OWL ontologies (Knublauch et al. 2004). The development of this plugin is under the responsibility of the Collaborative Open Ontology Development Environment Project of the Medical Informatics Group at the University of Manchester (CO-ODE).

In Protégé-OWL, properties are entered using the properties panel. In Fig.10.3, we depict the placeOfPublication object property. Please note that this property is also declared to be functional (see the ticked box in the bottom right panel of the screen). A functional property can have at most one value for a particular subject individual. If, for example, we were to use the placeOfPublication as a functional object property from the confPaper class to the city class, the placeOfPublication property would associate each individual of the confPaper class with at most one (unique) individual of the city class.

Classes are organized and displayed in a hierarchical way, as depicted in the left panel of Fig. 10.4. We observe that the JournalPaper class is a subclass of the Publication class, which in turn is a subclass of the owl:Thing class. The panels to the right show information about the highlighted class, JournalPaper in this case. Note that there is also room for adding documentation, annotations (owl:AnnotationProperty, a special type of property to describe a construct), a list of properties (both datatype and object), restrictions (owl:Restriction), and disjoints (owl:disjointWith) for the class in question. In Fig. 10.4, we depict how to describe, using Protégé-OWL, the OWL example in Section 5.4 (lines 1-42).

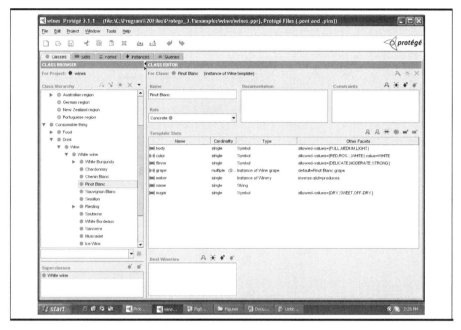

Fig. **10.2** Protégé frames 3.1.1 interface.

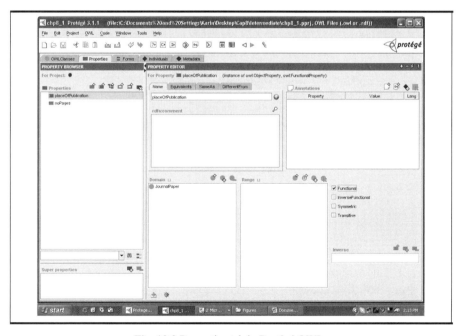

Fig. **10.3** Properties tab in Protégé OWL.

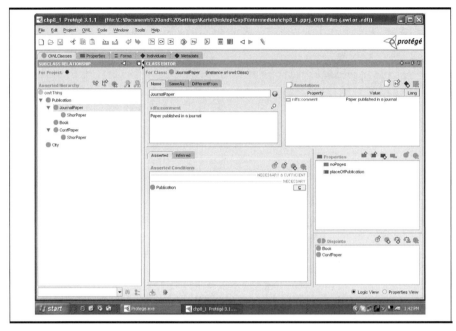

Fig. 10.4 Class hierarchy in Protégé-OWL.

The Protégé–OWL restriction editor allows users to write class restrictions in a notation very similar to that of description logic. For example, consider the restriction, borrowed from Section 5.4.1, defining the class `EuropeanConf`:

```
10.   <owl:Class rdf:about="EuropeanConf"/>
11.     <rdfs:subClassOf rdf:resource="Conf"/>
12.     <rdfs:subClassOf>
13.       <owl:Restriction>
14.         <owl:onProperty rdf:resource="heldIn">
15.         <owl:allValuesFrom rdf:resource="EuropeanCity">
16.       </owl:Restriction>
17.     </rdfs:subClassOf>
18.   </owl:Class>
```

Set Theory: EuropeanConf ⊆
                   Conf ∩ { x / $\forall y$ (heldIn (x, y) ⟹ $y\in$ EuropeanCity) }

Description Logic: EuropeanConf ⊑ Conf ⊓ $\forall$heldIn.EuropeanCity

In Table 10.1, we show the Manchester OWL syntax used by Protégé (URI: http://www.co-ode.org/resources/reference/manchester_syntax/). In Fig. 10.5, we depict how to describe, using Protégé-OWL, the above restriction. Note how similar the description logic and the Protégé syntaxes are.

Table 10.1 Manchester OWL syntax used by Protégé.

OWL	DL Symbol	Manchester OWL Syntax Keyword	Example
someValuesFrom	∃	some	hasChild **some** Man
allValuesFrom	∀	only	hasSibling **only** Woman
hasValue	∋	has	hasCountryOfOrigin **has** England
minCardinality	≥	min	hasChild **min** 3
cardinality	=	exactly	hasChild **exactly** 3
maxCardinality	≤	max	hasChild **max** 3
intersectionOf	⊓	and	Doctor **and** Female
unionOf	⊔	or	Man **or** Woman
complementOf	¬	not	**not** Child

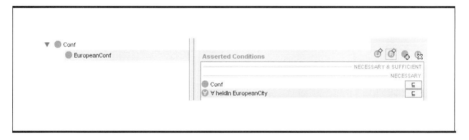

Fig. 10.5 Definition of the `EuropeanConf` class in Protégé-OWL.

10.2.5 Protégé Plugins and APIs

Protégé is written in Java, thus providing a plug-and-play extensible environment that makes it a flexible base for rapid prototyping and application development. The official Protégé site provides over 50 plugin downloads, whose topics range from biomedical informatics to natural language processing, including plugins for visualization, import/export, inference/validation, software engineering, and specific Semantic Web plugins to be used with the Protégé-OWL editor. Some of these plugins are already bundled with the full Protégé download. We discuss a small sample in what follows.

Protégé OWLViz Plugin
http://www.co-ode.org/downloads/owlviz/co-ode-index.php

OWLViz is one of the official Protégé plugins developed by the CO-ODE group. It permits visualizing and navigating through the class hierarchy of an OWL Ontology.

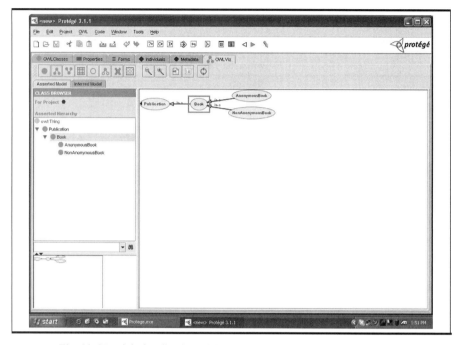

Fig. 10.6 Partial visualization of the Publication ontology using OWLViz.

The major attribute of this tool is that it allows the visual distinction between the asserted class hierarchy and the inferred class hierarchy. The use of a consistent color code helps the user to distinguish between primitive and defined classes and to identify mistakes. Such views can be saved in a variety of formats that include PNG, JPEG, and SVG. Figure 10.6 shows a graphical representation of the Publication ontology created using OWLViz.

Other popular visualization tools include OntoViz, based on the AT&T Graphviz graph visualization software, the TGViz Tab Widget, that uses the TouchGraph library to provide different ways to display the ontology, and the Jambalaya editor, that uses the Simple Hierarchical Multi-Perspective (SHrIMP) tool to display ontologies.

Protégé Prompt Tab Plug- in
http://protege.stanford.edu/plugins/prompt/prompt.html

Prompt is a tool to help users in ontology maintenance. It supports ontology merging and comparison (i.e., it allows comparison of different versions of the same ontology), merging two ontologies into one (merging more than two ontologies has to be done in two-by-two incremental steps), and extracting parts of an existing ontology (useful when knowledge reuse is being considered).

Protégé WordNet Tab Plugin

http://protege.stanford.edu/plugins/wordnettab/wordnet_tab.html

This plugin allows users to annotate their Protégé ontologies directly with information from WordNet (see Section 9.3.4).

Protégé OWL API

http://protege.stanford.edu/plugins/owl/api/index.html

The Protégé OWL API was developed to support the manipulation of RDF/OWL ontology elements. It provides classes and methods that implement save, load and query tasks over OWL models, as well as reasoning based on description logic inference engines. This API is designed to support the development of ontology components within Protégé, as well as standalone applications. It is implemented as a Java open source library.

Protégé OWL Reasoning API

http://protege.stanford.edu/plugins/owl/api/ReasonerAPIExamples.html

This API enables the communication of Protégé with any external DIG compliant reasoner. OWL-DL ontologies can be directly translated into description logic, thus allowing for reasoning over the ontology.

10.3 Reasoners

Because writing a Description Logic reasoner is a non-trival task, and highly optimised 3rd party Description Logic reasoners have been developed, it would not make sense to write a reasoner for a specific application. Fortunately, a standard exists that provides a specification for a common way of connecting to 3rd party DL reasoners. This standard is called DIG. A DIG compliant reasoner is a Description Logic reasoner that provides a standard access interface (known as a DIG interface), which enables the reasoner to be accessed over HTTP, using the DIG language. The DIG language is an XML based representation of ontological entities such as classes, properties and individuals, and also axioms such as subclass axioms, disjoint axioms and equivalent class axioms. The DIG language contains constructs that allow clients to tell a reasoner about an ontology (i.e. describe an ontology to a reasoner), and also ask a reasoner about what it has inferred, such as subclass relationships, type relationships.

(Horridge 2006)

DIG stands for the DL Implementation Group, a group devoted to the implementation of description logic systems. Their key contribution is the development of the DIG interface, which provides a common interface for DL reasoners thus allowing a variety of ontology tools, such as Protégé and OilEd, to make use of reasoners. We review some reasoners in what follows.

Pellet

http://www.mindswap.org/2003/pellet/

Pellet is an open source Java OWL DL inference mechanism that can be used with the JENA API. Pellet implements tableau algorithms that manipulate description logic expressions. It can be used online by submitting a valid ontology URI. Pellet is part of a Semantic Web tool suite made available by the MindSwap Group at the University of Maryland. Besides the inference mechanism, MindSwap also makes an ontology editor (SWOOP) and an OWL photo annotation tool (PhotoStuff) publicly available.

FaCT++

http://owl.man.ac.uk/factplusplus/

FaCT ++ is the evolution of the OilEd companion inference mechanism, FaCT (Fast Classification of Terminologies). Programmed in C++ for higher efficiency, this reasoner is released under a GNU public license and is available for download both as a binary file and as source code. FaCT++ supports SHOIQ with simple datatypes (i.e., for OWL-DL with qualifying cardinality restrictions). It implements a tableau-based decision procedure for general TBoxes (subsumption, satisfiability, classification) and incomplete support of ABoxes (retrieval) (Satler 2005).

KAON2

http://kaon2.semanticWeb.org/

KAON2 is the result of a joint effort between the Research Center for Information Technologies, the University of Karlsruhe and the University of Manchester. An evolution of KAON1, an infrastructure to support ontology management in the business domain that used a proprietary format based on RDFS, KAON2 is a completely new system based on the OWL-DL, SWRL, and F-Logic standards. KAON2 provides ontology management, access, querying, inference, and instance extraction capabilities (Motik et al. 2004).

Cerebra Engine

http://www.cerebra.com/

Cerebra Engine is a commercial C++-based reasoner. It implements a tableau-based decision procedure for general TBoxes (subsumption, satisfiability, classification) and ABoxes (retrieval, tree-conjunctive query answering using an XQuery-like syntax). It supports the OWL-API, as well as other features (Satler 2005).

Racer

http://www.racer-systems.com/

RacerPro was the first OWL reasoner available. Its first (freeware) version is known as Racer and was released in 2002. Today's commercial 1.9 version provides many features over the original Racer engine, including: an expressive query language nRQL; support for OWL DL (almost completely), not employing the unique name assumption, as required by OWL DL; and a rule engine that provides for efficient and application-controlled ABox augmentation based on rules. A model-checking facility is integrated with nRQL as well.

10.4 Other Tools

OWL Validator
http://owl.bbn.com/validator/

This online tool validates OWL code. It inspects an input file comparing it with a list of potential problems. At the end of the process, a list of errors and recommendations is produced. The tool also identifies compilation problems.

JENA API
http://jena.sourceforge.net

JENA is a Java API whose goal is to support the development of Semantic Web applications. JENA is open source, and it was originally developed at the HP Labs Semantic Web Programme. It supports RDF, RDF Schema, and OWL, and includes an inference mechanism.

The JENA API transforms an ontology into an object-oriented abstract data model, and allows its primitives (classes and relationships) to be treated as objects thereafter. Therefore, JENA allows ontology elements to be manipulated by object-oriented programming languages.

Oracle Spatial Resource Description Framework (RDF) 10g
http://www.oracle.com/technology/tech/semantic_technologies/index.html

Oracle 10g is the first commercial database management system to offer facilities to store, query, and retrieve RDF triples. It provides a platform for semantic data management that scales to billions of triples, thereby meeting the needs of the most demanding RDF applications.

The RDF-specific functionality includes:

- Full support for RDF statements and RDF schema
- SQL search and retrieval of RDF models using graph patterns
- Full support for RDF datatypes (URIs, blank nodes, plain literals, typed literals, long literals, collection types)
- Inferencing of RDF schema
- Reification of assertions (statements)
- Support for `subClassOf` and `subPropertyOf`
- Visualization of RDF data

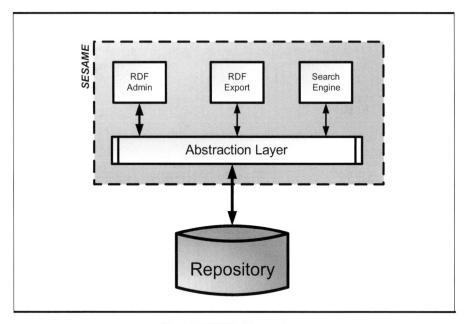

Fig. 10.7 SESAME repository.

SESAME
http://www.ontoknowledge.org/

Sesame is a platform-independent data repository and search mechanism for data in RDF format. It was developed in the scope of the On-To-Knowledge project, which also delivered the OntoEdit (see Section 10.2.3), QuizRDF, OntoShare, and Spectacle tools. An abstraction layer intermediates access to the data repository, which can be a relational database, a data structure, or an RDF repository. This abstraction layer, therefore, hides repository implementation details from the rest of Sesame's implementation. Sesame offers an export mechanism and a search mechanism, supporting the RQL, RDQL, and SeRQL query languages. Communication with other applications uses this layer, as depicted in Fig. 10.7.

IBM Integrated Ontology Development Toolkit
http://www.alphaworks.ibm.com/tech/semanticstk

Formerly called SNOBASE (Semantic Network Ontology Base), the Integrated Ontology Development Toolkit is a tool suite for ontology-driven development. This toolkit includes: the Eclipse's Ontology Definition Metamodel (EODM), a runtime library that allows the application to read and serialize an RDFS/OWL ontology in RDF/XML format; the EODM workbench, an Eclipse-based, integrated, ontology-engineering environment that supports ontology building, management, and visualization; and Minerva, an OWL Ontology Repository.

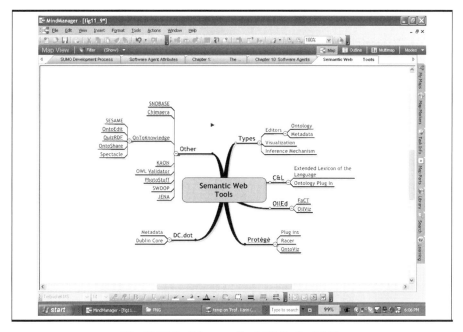

Fig. 10.8 MindManager Tool (©Mindjet LLC).

Mind Map Tools — Mind Manager, Free Mind, and NovaMind
http://www.mindjet.com/us/
http://freemind.sourceforge.net/wiki/index.php/Main_Page
http://www.nova-mind.com/

Although not exactly Semantic Web tools, Mind Map Tools, Mind Manager, Free Mind, and NovaMind support Mind Mapping, which is a very effective strategy for the elicitation of concepts and their relationships.

The Mind Map concept is thoroughly described in Buzan (1993). Essentially, a Mind Map is a diagram that depicts a central concept surrounded by related concepts distributed in a concentric radius around the original concept. All concepts are related by relationships (labeling is optional). In Fig. 10.8, we show an example of a Mind Map.

PhotoStuff
http://www.mindswap.org/2003/PhotoStuff/

PhotoStuff is an image annotation application. Intended as a semantic markup tool for photos, it provides users with the ability to annotate regions of images with respect to an ontology, and publish the automatically generated metadata to the Web. This tool was produced in the context of the MindSwap project at the University of Maryland, College Park.

Adobe Extensible Metadata Platform
http://www.adobe.com/products/xmp/index.html

This commercial tool is responsible for creating annotation that can be attached to files as metadata. It provides a unified method for capturing, annotating, and sharing metadata. According to Adobe, with the Extensible Metadata Platform they have "taken the 'heavy lifting' out of metadata integration, offering content creators an easy way to embed meaningful information about their projects and providing industry partners with standards-based building blocks to develop optimized workflow solutions."

References

Bechhofer, S.; Horrocks, I.; Goble, C.; Stevens, R. (2001) OILEd: A reason-able ontology editor for the Semantic Web. In: *Proceedings of the KI2001, Joint German/Austrian conference on Artificial Intelligence*, September 19-21, Vienna. Springer-Verlag LNAI, Vol. 2174, pp. 396–408.

Buzan, T. (1993) The Mind Map Book: How to Use Radiant Thinking to Maximize Your Brain's Untapped Potential. Plume.

Chaudhri, V.K.; Farquhar, F.R.; Karp, P.D.; Rice, J.P. (1998) Open knowledge base connectivity 2.0.3. Knowledge Systems Laboratory, Stanford.

Davies, J.; Fensel, D.; Harmelen, F.V. (Eds) (2002) *Towards the Semantic Web: Ontology-driven Knowledge Management*. John Wiley & Sons, New York, USA.

Drummond, N.; Horridge, M.; Knublauch, H. (2005) Protégé-OWL tutorial. In: *Proceedings of the Eighth International Protégé Conference*, Madrid, July 2005. Available at: http://protege.stanford.edu/conference/2005/slides/T2_OWLTutorialI_Drummond_final.pdf.

Erdmann, M.; Angele, J.; Staab, S.; Studer, R. (2002) OntoEdit: Collaborative ontology development for the Semantic Web. In: *Proceedings of the First International Semantic Web Conference (ISWC 2002)*, June 9–12, 2002, Sardinia, Italy.

Fellbaum, C. (1998) WordNet – An Electronic Lexical Database. MIT Press. Cambridge, MA, USA.

Gennari, F. Musen M., Fergerson, Grosso, W.; Crubezy, M.; Eriksson, H.; Noy, N.; Tu, S.W. (2003) The evolution of Protégé: An environment for knowledge-based systems development. *International Journal of Human Computer Studies*, Vol. 58, No. 1, pp. 89–123.

Gómez-Pérez, A.; Fernadéz-Peréz, M.; Corcho, O. (2004) *Ontological Engineering*. Springer-Verlag New York, USA

Hendler, J. (2001) Agents and the Semantic Web. *IEEE Intelligent Systems*, March/April 2001, pp.30–37.

Horridge, M. (2005) The Manchester OWL syntax editor guide. The University of Manchester. Available at: http://www.co-ode.org/downloads/Manchesterowlsyntaxeditor/EditorGuide.pdf.

Horridge, M. (2006) Using the Protege-OWL reasoning API. Medical Informatics Group, at The University of Manchester. Available at: http://protege.stanford.edu/plugins/owl/api/ReasonerAPIExamples.html.

Horridge, M.; Knublauch, H.; Rector, A.; Stevens, R.; Wroe, C. (2004) A practical guide to building OWL ontologies using the Protégé-OWL plugin and CO-ODE tools edition 1.0. The University Of Manchester and Stanford University, August 27, 2004. Available at: http://www.co-ode.org/resources/tutorials/ProtegeOWLTutorial.pdf.

Knublauch, H.; Fergerson, R.; Noy, N.; Musen, M. (2004) The Protégé OWL plugin: An open development environment for Semantic Web applications. In: *Proceedings of the Third International Semantic Web Conference (ISWC 2004)*, Hiroshima, Japan.

McGuiness, D.; Fikes, R..; Rice, J.; Wilder, S. (2002) An environment for merging and testing large ontologies. In: *Proceedings of the Seventh International Conference on Principles of Knowledge Representation and Reasoning (KR-2000)*, Breckenridge, Colorado, April 12-15. Morgan Kaufmann, San Francisco, USA, pp. 483–493.

Miller, G. (1995) WordNet: A lexical database for English. *Communications of the ACM*, Vol. 38, Issue 11, pp. 39–41.

Motik, B.; Sattler, U.; Studer, U. (2004) Query answering for OWL-DL with rules. In: *Proceedings of the Third International Semantic Web Conference (ISWC 2004)*, Hiroshima, Japan, November, 2004, pp. 549–563.

Noy, N.; McGuinness, D. (2001) Ontology development 101: A guide to creating your first ontology. Technical Report KSL-01-05, Stanford Knowledge Systems Laboratory.

Noy, N.; Sintek, M.; Decker, S.; Crubezy, R.; Fergerson, R.; Musen, A. (2001) Creating Semantic Web contents with Protégé 2000. *IEEE Intelligent Systems*, Vol. 16, No. 2, pp. 60–71.

Oberle, D.; Volz, R.; Motik, B.; Staab, S. (2004) An extensible ontology software environment. In: Staab, S.; Studer, R. (Eds) *Handbook on Ontologies*, Chap. III. Springer, New York, USA, pp. 310–333.

Sattler, U. (2005) Description Logic Reasoners. Information Management Group, School of Computer Science, University of Manchester. Available at: http://www.cs.man.ac.uk/~sattler/reasoners.html.

W3C (2006) The Semantic Web Best Practices and Development Work Group Semantic Web Tutorial Page. Available at: http://www.w3.org/2001/sw/BestPractices/Tutorials.

Part IV — Applications

11

Software Agents

11.1 Introduction

Technological advance, allied with a consistent reduction in hardware costs, is accelerating the automatization of society as a whole. Hand in hand with this process, we are faced with the problem of coping with the rapidly growing complexity of the processes of integrating, managing, and operating computer-based systems (Sterritt and Hinchey 2005). Today's distributed systems demand software applications that do more than simply coping with service demands; they must also be able to anticipate, predict, and adapt themselves to respond to user needs. Indeed, researchers from both industry and academia are investigating the development of autonomous software agents that may take over tasks once conducted by humans. The development of autonomic (i.e., self-managing) systems is only part of this effort (Rouff 2006). According to the Software Agents Group of the MIT Media Laboratory, software agents are very different from conventional software because they are semi-autonomous, pro-active, adaptive, and long-lived.

Software agents will play a fundamental role in building the Semantic Web (Hendler 2001). According to Tim Berners-Lee, software agents will be responsible for coordinating searches, comparing and negotiating on the Web, and greatly reducing user effort (Berners-Lee et al. 2001). An important distinction is that agents on the Semantic Web will not act in a completely autonomous way, but rather they will take care of the "heavier load" for their users. They will be responsible for conducting the investigation, with the obligation to present the results to the user, so that he or she can make his or her own decisions.

The most adequate metaphor to illustrate the presence of software agents is that of an assistant. Antoniou and Harmelen (2004) define software agents as follows:

Agents are pieces of software that work autonomously and proactively. Conceptually they evolved out of the concepts of object-oriented programming and component-based software development. A personal agent on the Semantic Web will receive some tasks and preferences from the person, seek information from Web sources, communicate with other agents, compare information about user requirements and preferences, select certain choices, and give answers to the user.

James Hendler, author of the seminal *Nature* paper "Is There an Intelligent Agent in Your Future?" created an analogy between software agents and human agents (Hendler 1999). His vision of intelligent software agents is that:

...rather than doing everything for a user, the agents would find possible ways to meet user needs, and offer the user choices for their achievement. Much as a travel agent might give you a list of several flights you could take, or a choice of flying vs. taking a train, a Web agent should offer a slate of possible ways to get you what you need on the Web.

Most available software agent definitions use a set of attributes to characterize the Agent entity. In Fig. 11.1, we list the attributes that are most frequently found in the literature. It is important to note that a software agent is defined by a combination of some of those attributes, rather than by their totality. The attribute set of each software agent depends on the task(s) the agent is intended to perform, that is, the type of agent in question.

In Section 11.2, we discuss software agents in the context of information technology systems and present the taxonomy of software agent forms proposed by the Object Management Group. In Section 11.3, we discuss the Goddard Agent Architecture, which is highly component-based and supports most agent development methodologies. Finally, in Section 11.4, we discuss agents and the role that ontologies play in the context of the Semantic Web.

11.2 Agent Forms

The Agent Special Interest Group of the Object Management Group (OMG) identified and organized several forms of software agents in the context of Information Technology (IT) systems (OMG 2000). According to the group, "agents found in IT systems have special requirements: they must execute as software, hardware, robotics, or a combination of these." The group has identified eight general-purpose agent forms that can be considered in any agent-based system, and several specific, context-dependent forms. In the rest of this section, we briefly discuss OMG's top eight agent forms (OMG 2000).

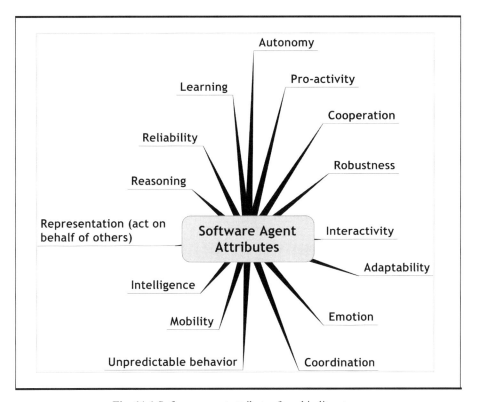

Fig. 11.1 Software agent attributes found in literature.

Software Agents

A *software agent* is an autonomous software entity that can interact with its environment. Such agents are designed to interact with humans and other software applications. There are no restrictions on the implementation techniques used for developing a software agent. Possibilities range from generic object-oriented tools to specific agent-based tools, not leaving out any tool in which autonomous behavior could be effectively implemented.

Autonomous Agents

Autonomy is the degree of independence that an agent has from external control. Autonomy guarantees that the agent operates independently of external invocation or intervention. Agents can react not only to specific method invocations, but also to observable events within the environment. Proactive agents will actually poll the environment for events and other messages to determine what action they should take. Without autonomy, an agent would be a passive entity. Therefore, autonomy is considered by FIPA, the Foundation for Intelligent Physical Agents, and by the OMG Agent Special Interest Group a required property of agents.

Autonomy has two independent aspects: *dynamic autonomy* and *unpredictable autonomy*. Agents are dynamic because they can exercise some degree of activity. Agents may also exhibit some degree of unpredictable (or nondeterministic) behavior.

Interactive Agents

Interactivity is the ability of an agent to communicate with other agents (entities) and its environment. Interaction among agents goes from simple message exchange to coordinating the action of heterogeneous agents (either cooperatively or competitively). The latter requires very sophisticated skills such as monitoring, interpretation, negotiation, estimation, and planning. Interaction is considered by FIPA and by the OMG Agent Special Interest Group a required property of agents.

Adaptive Agents

Adaptability is the ability of an agent to respond to other agents or its environment. Minimal adaptability skills are measured by the degree to which an agent is able to react to a simple stimulus. More sophisticated agents are able to reason, learn, and evolve.

An agent that cannot respond to its environment or to other agents is not very useful. Therefore, adaptation is considered by FIPA and by the OMG Agent Special Interest Group a required property of agents.

Mobile Agents

Mobility is measured by the ability of an agent to transport itself from one environment to another, that is, to move its code to a new host where it can resume executing. Conceptually, mobile agents can also be regarded as itinerant, dynamic, wandering, roaming, or migrant. The rationale for mobility is the improved performance that can sometimes be achieved by moving the agent closer to the services available on the new host. Mobility is not considered by FIPA and by the OMG Agent SIG a requirement for agenthood.

Coordinative Agents

Coordination is the ability of an agent to organize a population of heterogeneous agents so that they are able, similarly to human organizations, to interact, negotiate, exchange information, delegate, manage, cooperate, and compete around a single goal. Without some degree of coordination, complex agent systems are not viable.

Intelligent Agents

Intelligence is vaguely defined by a basic set of attributes an agent must have. This set must include the ability of formalizing the agent's state (assumptions, goals, plans, and others) and the ability to interact with other agents using symbolic language. Neither FIPA nor the OMG Agent Special Interest Group provides a standard definition for an intelligent agent.

Wrapper Agents

Wrapping is the ability to connect to a nonagent software system or to a service uniquely identified by a software description. Wrapper agents are specially built to help other agents relay to external, nonagent software applications. They provide a bridge to legacy code and facilitate code reuse. A wrapper transforms a static piece of code into an active processing entity.

11.3 Agent Architecture

In this section, we briefly discuss the Goddard Agent Architecture. This architecture is highly component-based and supports most agent development methodologies such as GAIA (Zambonelli et al. 2003), AUML — Agent Unified Modeling Language (Bauer et al. 2002), MaSE — Multiagent Systems Engineering (DeLoach 2006), and TROPOS (Castro et al. 2002). A lengthier discussion on the Goddard Agent Architecture can be found in Truszkowski (2006).

A component is a software module that performs a defined task. Components, when combined with other software components, may constitute more robust pieces of software, which are easily maintained and upgraded. Components interact with one another through various communication mechanisms. Each component, in our agent architecture, can communicate information to/from all other components as needed through, for example, a publish/subscribe communication mechanism. Components may be implemented with a degree of intelligence through the addition of, for example, reasoning and learning functions. Furthermore, the use of components facilitates maintaining and upgrading agent systems.

The use of components also gives a great deal of flexibility to the designer of agents. A simple agent can be designed using a minimum number of simple components that would receive percepts from the environment and react to those percepts. A robust agent may be designed to use many components that allow the agent to do what a simple agent does and, in addition, reason, plan, schedule, model the environment, and learn.

Figure 11.2 details the agent architecture, showing the components required to allow an agent to act with a high degree of intelligence. Note that it contains components for reasoning, modeling, and planning.

The Perceptor component receives percepts through sensors and communication with external software/systems and agents. These percepts are passed from the perceptor to the Modeling and State component where a model's state is updated as needed.

A special perceptor, the Agent Communication Perceptor/Effector, sends messages to and receives messages from other agents. Incoming Agent Communication Language (ACL) messages are formatted and passed to the Agent Reasoning component.

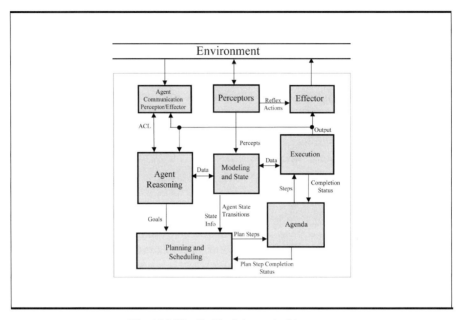

Fig. 11.2 The Goddard Agent Architecture.

The Agent Reasoning component reasons with the facts contained in the ACL messages received and those acquired from the Modeling and State component to formulate goals for the agent, when necessary.

Goals are then acquired by the Planning component along with state and state transition information. The Planning component formulates a plan for the agent to achieve the desired goals.

When a plan has been developed, the Agenda keeps track of the execution of the plan's steps. Steps are marked when they are ready for execution and the completion status of each step is also tracked by the Agenda.

The Execution component manages the execution of steps and determines the success or failure of each step's execution. Output produced during a step's execution can be passed to an Effector or the Reasoning component.

State changes will be recorded by the Modeling and State component. When a plan is finished executing, a completion status is passed to the Planning component for evaluation of the plan for future use.

The Goddard Agent Architecture incorporates a distributed knowledgebase. Each component that creates or stores a kind of information is responsible for keeping that information current. Distributing responsibility for knowledge is advantageous when compared to a central, shared knowledgebase. With a central, shared knowledgebase, the knowledgebase component needs to understand the content of all data it keeps in order to update the data appropriately. Centralizing responsibility for knowledge therefore results in a complex component. By adopting a distributed data storage strategy, data can be updated more efficiently, accurately, and in an overall simpler fashion.

11.4 Agents in the Semantic Web Context

11.4.1 The Role of Ontologies

In the context of the Semantic Web, software agents will communicate by sharing domain ontologies. The role of ontologies, more than making explicit domain theories, is to serve as a framework that will enable information sharing among software agents (Hendler 2001).

Although agent communication would be greatly facilitated by the adoption of a single reference ontology, we cannot guarantee that this will always be the case. James Hendler, one of the Semantic Web visionaries, predicts that in the future each Web site, organization, or business on the Web will have its own ontology. As a result, the Web of the future will be composed of myriad small, highly contextualized ontologies, or a "great number of small ontological components consisting largely of pointers to each other" (Hendler 2001). Such ontologies, rather than being developed by knowledge engineering experts, will be created by local software engineers. With the widespread distributed use of ontologies, different parties will inevitably develop ontologies with overlapping content.

This scenario will have a significant impact, because future implementations will have to take into consideration the following questions:

- How will agents determine if shared concepts are semantically equivalent?
- How will agents determine that different concepts have the same meaning?
- How will agents determine if different ontologies belong to the same domain?

11.4.2 Software Agent Communication in the Semantic Web

Software agents acting autonomously in an open-ended environment will often require collaboration with other agents to fulfill their goals. Because different software agents are likely to provide separate ontologies, the ability to integrate the ontologies into a single representation is paramount to ensure communication among agents. This operation, referred to as ontology integration, aims at finding an intermediate representation that can be shared by both agents to ensure communication, also known as semantic interoperability. Thus, the ability to integrate different ontologies meaningfully is critical to assure coordinated action in multiagent environments.

To exemplify this scenario, suppose that two different agents, from different application sites, want to negotiate. The first agent belongs to a Fast Food application domain and the second agent belongs to the Beverage application domain. In the Fast Food application domain, only nonalcoholic drinks are available, as illustrated in Fig. 11.3. In the Beverage application domain, however, both alcoholic and nonalcoholic beverages are available. These are illustrated by the beer mug, wine glass and soft-drink bottle in the right oval in Fig 11.3. The ontology alignment process, which will try to identify the concepts that are shared between the two ontologies, must guarantee that no alcoholic beverages will be included in the final result, nor should any food. The result should only display the concepts that

Fig. 11.3 Intersection of concepts from the Fast Food and Beverage Domains.

are shared between the two ontologies, illustrated by the intersection of the two ovals, depicted in the center of Fig. 11.3.

Semantic interoperability and ontology integration have been on the research agenda of knowledge engineers for a while now. A few approaches to help deal with the ontology integration problem have been proposed. Note that we use the term ontology integration as an abstraction that encapsulates all different treatments. The most prominent ones are:

- *Ontology merging* (Noy and Musen 1999) results in a unique model that contains the union of the concepts from the original ontologies, without indicating their provenance.

- *Ontology alignment* (Noy and Musen 2003; Stoilos et al. 2005; Ehrig et al. 2005) is the identification of the links that hold between concepts from two different inputs. Such links provide the shared semantics of both representations. Alignment is usually done in pairs. The result of the alignment of two input ontologies can be presented either in the form of an intermediate representation (the third "*aligned*" ontology), or extra markup added to the original ontologies, also known as an *ontology mapping* (Noy and Musen 2003).

- *Ontology integration* (Pinto et al. 1999; Zhang and Lee 2005) results in a unique ontology created by assemblage, extension, specialization, or adaptation of ontologies from different subject areas. When integrating ontologies, it is possible to identify the relationships with the original ontology.

For example, the CATO tool provides a fast, reliable, user-independent process that allows for autonomous online ontology alignment. This approach combines well-known algorithmic solutions, such as natural language processing and tree comparison. CATO is implemented in Java and is publicly available on the Web. It is distributed as an Eclipse plugin, and works with any pair of OWL ontologies (Felicíssimo and Breitman 2004).

Bailin and Truszkowski (2001) propose ontology negotiation as a means for communication between information agents. They propose an ontology negotiation protocol and implement a framework that supports software agents that use this protocol. Using the framework, software agents are able to discover ontology conflicts and then, through incremental interpretation, clarification, and explanation establish a common basis for communicating with one another. Their agent framework was implemented based on the Java Remote Method Invocation (RMI). The protocol state machine and negotiation functions (e.g., interpretation, clarification, and explanation) were implemented in Java combined with JESS — Java Expert System Shell (Bailin and Truszkowski 2001).

There are several semi-automatic ontology merging tools available. The GLUE system (Doan et al. 2003) uses multiple learning strategies to help find mappings between two ontologies. Given any two ontologies and their instances, the system is able to find nodes that are similar, given a predefined similarity measurement. It is an automated tool that feeds its result to a semantic interoperability tool that can interpret and use its results. IPrompt provides guidance to the ontology merge process by describing the sequence of steps and helping identify possible inconsistencies and potential problems. AnchorPROMPT (Noy and Musen 2003), an ontology alignment tool, automatically identifies semantically similar terms. It uses a set of anchors (pairs of terms) as input and treats the ontology as a directed graph. In this graph, the nodes are the ontology classes and the links, the properties. It uses similarity measurements and equivalence groups to help detect similar terms. The Protégé PROMPT plugin implements most of the original AnchorPROMPT functionalities. We refer the reader to Chapter 10 for a more detailed discussion on the Protégé plugins.

The Chimaera environment (McGuinness et al. 2000) provides a tool that merges ontologies based on their structural relationships. Instead of investigating terms that are directly related to one another, Chimaera uses the super- and subclass relationships, central to concept hierarchies, to find possible matches. Their implementation is based on the Ontolingua editor (Farquhar et al 1996).

References

Antoniou, G.; Harmelen, F.V. (2004) *A Semantic Web Primer*. MIT Press, Cambridge MA, USA.

Bailin, S.; Truszkowski, W. (2001) Ontology negotiation between scientific archives. In: *Proceedings of the Thirteenth International Conference on Scientific and Statistical Database Management*, IEEE Computer Society, Washington, DC, USA, pp. 245–250.

Bauer, B. and Odell, J. (2002) UML 2.0 and agents: How to build agent-based systems with the new UML standard. *Journal of Engineering Applications of AI*, 18(2), pp. 141–157.

Berners-Lee, T.; Lassila, O.; Hendler, J. (2001) The Semantic Web: A new form of Web content that is meaningful to computers will unleash a revolution of new possibilities. *Scientific American*, 284(5), pp. 34–43. Available at: http://www.scientificamerican.com/2001/0501issue/0501berners-lee.html.

Castro, J.; Kolp, M., Mylopoulos, J. (2002) Towards requirements-driven information systems engineering: The Tropos project. *Information Systems Journal*, Vol. 27, pp. 365–89.

DeLoach, S. (2006) Engineering organization-based multiagent systems. In: *Proceedings of the Fourth International Workshop on Software Engineering for Large-Scale Multi-Agent Systems (SELMAS'05)*, Saint Louis, EUA, pp. 1–7.

Doan, A. et. al (2003) Learning to match ontologies on the Semantic Web. *The International Journal on Very Large Data Bases*, Vol. 12, Issue 4, pp. 303–319.

Ehrig, M.; Staab, S.; Sure, Y. (2005) Bootstrapping ontology alignment methods with APFEL. In: *Proceedings of the Fourth International Semantic Web Conference (ISWC 2005)*, Galway, Ireland, Nov. 2005, pp. 186–200.

Farquhar, A. Fikes, R.; Rice, J. (1996) The Ontolingua server: A tool for collaborative ontology construction. In: *Proceedings of the Tenth Knowledge Acquisition for Knowledge Base Systems Workshop*, Banff, Canada.

Felicíssimo, C.H.; Breitman, K.K. (2004) Taxonomic ontology alignment - An implementation. In: *Proceedings of the Seventh Workshop on Requirements Engineering*, Tandil, Argentina, Dec. 9–10.

Hendler, J. (1999) Is there an intelligent agent in your future? In: *Nature Web Matters*, 11 March 1999. Available at: http://www.nature.com/nature/webmatters/agents/agents.html.

Hendler, J. (2001) Agents and the Semantic Web. *IEEE Intelligent Systems*, March/April 2001, pp.30–37.

McGuinness, D.; Fikes, R.; Rice, J.; Wilder, S. (2000) The Chimaera ontology environment. In: *Proceedings of the Seventeenth National Conference on Artificial Intelligence*.

Noy, N.F.; Musen, M.A. (1999) SMART: Automated support for ontology merging and alignment. In: *Workshop on Knowledge Acquisition, Modeling, and Management*, Banff, Alberta, Canada.

Noy, N.F.; Musen, M.A. (2003) The PROMPT suite: Interactive tools for ontology merging and mapping. *International Journal of Human-Computer Studies*.

OMG. (2000) Object Management Group – Agent Platform Special Interest Group: Agent Technology – Green Paper, Version 1.0. Available at: http://www.objs.com/agent/agents_Green_Paper_v100.doc.

Pinto, S.H.; Goméz-Peréz, A.; Martins, J.P. (1999) Some issues on ontology integration. In: *Proceedings of the Workshop on Ontologies and Problem Solving Methods: Lessons Learned and Future Trends*, in conjunction with IJCAI99.

Rouff, C. (2006) *Autonomous and Autonomic Systems: With Applications to NASA Intelligent Spacecraft Operations and Exploration Systems*. NASA Monographs in Systems and Software Engineering Series. Springer Verlag, London.

Sterritt, R.; Hinchey, M. (2005) Autonomic computing – Panacea or poppycock? In: *Proceedings of the Twelfth IEEE International Conference and Workshops on the Engineering of Computer-Based Systems (ECBS'05)*, IEEE Computer Society Press, Los Alamitos, CA, USA, pp. 535–539.

Stoilos, G.; Stamou, G.; Kollias, S. (2005) A string metric for ontology alignment. In: *Proceedings of the Fourth International Semantic Web Conference (ISWC 2005)*, Galway, Ireland, Nov. 2005, pp. 624–637.

Truszkowski, W. (2006) What is an agent? And what is an agent community? In: Rouff, C.A., Hinchey, M., Rash, J. (Eds.) *Agent Technology from a Formal Perspective*. NASA Monographs in Systems and Software Engineering. Springer Verlag, London, UK.

Wooldridge, M.J. (2002) *An Introduction to Multiagent Systems*. John Wiley & Sons, New York, USA.

Zambonelli, F.; Jennings, N.; Wooldridge, M. (2003) Developing multiagent systems: The Gaia methodology. *ACM Transactions on Software Engineering and Methodology*, 12(3), pp. 317–370.

Zhang, D.; Lee, W.S. (2005) Learning to integrate Web taxonomies. *Journal of Web Semantics*, Vol. 2, Issue 2.

12

Semantic Desktop

12.1 Introduction

In this chapter, we exemplify the use of Semantic Web technologies in personal computing applications called semantic desktops. These applications combine ontologies, taxonomies, and metadata in general to enhance personal information management, software application usage, and collaboration. According to the semantic desktop community (URL: semanticdesktop.org):

The use of ontologies, metadata annotations, and semantic Web protocols on desktop computers will allow the integration of desktop applications and the Web, enabling a much more focused and integrated personal information management as well as focused information distribution and collaboration on the Web beyond sending e-mails. The vision of the Semantic Desktop for personal information management and collaboration has been around for a long time: visionaries like Vannevar Bush and Doug Engelbart have formulated and partially realized these ideas.

We explore a semantic desktop implementation focused on the automation of otherwise tedious and repetitive tasks. We argue that it is possible to semi-automate the information-update process with the use of software agent technology (Breitman et al. 2006; Williams 2004; Pazzani and Billsus 2002; Wooldridge et al. 1999; Sycara 1998). Our goal is to provide a desktop application that behaves proactively in providing user-centered services and updating their posted information. Among others, this application automates the update of CVs, agenda, contact information, travel information (directions, hotel names and locations, airplane ticketing information), displays automatic update/alerts on what colleagues/partners are doing at present (articles published, books in print, presentations they gave, etc.), automatically changes Web pages, includes new links of interest, and provides an understandable model of the user profile in the format of a user ontology.

In this ontology-driven software agent implementation of the semantic desktop, two major issues stand out: system architecture and update processes. The system architecture issue addresses the current static nature of information. In order to achieve the level of proactivity desired, we have to be able to identify, classify, and code important bits of information in a way that can be automatically manipulated by machines. The second issue is related to the strategies used to dynamically update information. Because of the variety of actions required to effectively update information on a personal computer system, for example, monitoring changes to personal information (phone numbers, addresses, hobbies, etc.), maintaining a knowledge of institutional information, reacting to external events, reacting to political and environmental changes, and so on, we argue that no single strategy for maintaining dynamic information-awareness is sufficient, but rather a variety of strategies needs to be put into practice.

12.2 Semantic Desktop Metadata

The information relevant to the implementation of the semantic desktop is a composition of multimedia elements — text, image, sound, or video — interrelated and organized in some coherent, however, domain-dependent fashion. For example, in a personal Web page, we expect to find information about an individual at the top of the Web page, whereas in a product Web page, we would expect the specification of the product to appear before the manufacturer's contact data.

A first step in the preparation of the information for automated processing is to identify a taxonomy of information types, such as research area, technology used, contact information, or institutional policies. That is not a trivial task, for the relevant information is presented in different degrees of abstraction, for example:

- *High level (general):* what the person is (researcher, vendor, businessperson, etc.)
- *Medium level:* if researcher, what areas he or she works in, what types of events he or she is interested in, what standards and rules he or she must abide by, and so on
- *Low level (specific):* what are his or hers specific interests, who are the colleagues he or she works with, what institutions he or she is connected with, what special interest groups and associations he or she belongs to, and so on

Once we identify and classify the existing information types, it is possible to associate adequate metadata with them (see Section 9.2). In the research and academic context, most types of information are already organized by some existing taxonomy, such as IEEE's list of computer science areas, which may, however, have to be rewritten into some metadata-compatible language. Other examples are:

- People: Friend of a Friend (FOAF)
- Publications: Dublin Core
- Projects: RDF taxonomy, structured as the NFS list of research areas
- Areas: RDF taxonomy, structured as the Societies lists of topics
- Physical Location and Contact information: RDF version of the university directory, floor plan, vCard taxonomy
- Academic Courses: RDF version of the university catalogue

We call *information chunks* each of these pieces of information. In Fig. 12.1, we illustrate the variety of information chunks that can be concomitantly present in a resource, in this case a Web page.

Available Information Chunks:

Bio, Bibliographical Production (Conference Proceedings, Tech Reports, Books, chapters), People (Colleagues, Students, Fellow Research Project Members), Research areas(Requirements Engineering, Semantic Web, Formal Systems) Events and Conferences she is organizing, Consulting, Activity in Scientific Societies.

Fig. 12.1 Researcher's home page.

For each item present in the page, some annotation describing its provenance, ownership, and categorization is required. To exemplify, we consider one of the many links to bibliographical references, in this case an article in a conference:

Breitman, K.K.; Casanova, M.A.; Truszkowski, W. — Extreme Infrared Explorer to Explorer Platform Interface Control Specification Document — NASA/GSFC document ID doi:10.1000/4575- 2006. 325 pp.

Possibly, the best way to describe this item would be to adopt the NASA Goddard extension of the Dublin Core Metadata Schema, the Goddard Core (see Section 9.2.2), as illustrated in Table 12.1.

Table 12.1 Goddard Core metadata annotation for a bibliographical reference (adapted from Hodge et al. 2005).

Title: Extreme Infrared Explorer to Explorer Platform Interface Control Specification Document
Creator: Karin K. Breitman
Creator: Marco Antonio Casanova
Creator: Walter Truszkowski
Contributor: Michael G. Hinchey

Subject: Spacecraft
Subject: Science Payload Module
Subject: Mission Equipment Deck
Subject: Interface Control
Subject: Astrophysics
Subject: Extreme Infrared
Subject: Astronomy
Subject: Electromagnetic Spectrum
Subject: Radiation

Description: defines the interfaces between the Mission Equipment Deck (MED) of the explorer platform and the Extreme Infrared Explorer (EUVE) payload

Type: Project Document.Specification
Format: PDF
Identifier: doi:10.1000/4575
Relation: doi:10.1000/6734
Relation: doi:10.1000/9812
Rights: unrestricted/uncopyrighted
Code: 588

Project: XYZ
Organization: NASA/GSFC
Organization: Center for Extreme Infrared Astrophysics

Project Phase: Formulation

In this case, there is a hierarchy of other information nested within this reference. The co-author of the article, a colleague named "Walt Truszkowski" is an information chunk in its own right and needs to be unambiguously referenced. A possible metadata representation for it would use the FOAF (see Section 9.2.6), as follows

```
<rdf:RDF
     xmlns:rdf="http://www.w3.org/1999/02/22-rdf-syntax-ns#"
     xmlns:foaf="http://xmlns.com/foaf/0.1/">
  <foaf:Person>
     <foaf:name>Walter Truszkowski</foaf:name>
     <foaf:mbox
        rdf:resource="mailto: walt@ultraproject.nasa.gov"/>
     <foaf:nick >Walt</foaf:nick>
     <foaf:workplacehomepage
        rdf:resource="http://www.gsfc.nasa.gov/"/>
  </foaf:Person>
</rdf:RDF>
```

12.3 Semantic Desktop Ontologies

Metadata markup will be very useful in referencing and storing information chunks. However, in addition to the information provided about the information objects themselves, we also want to represent properties, rules, and relationships that hold between information chunks. For that purpose, we have to resort to domain ontologies.

In the case of the Researcher Home Page example, we can easily identify different sources that could serve for composing the information chunks concept subtrees. In Table 12.2, we summarize some possibilities (see Chapter 9 for a fuller discussion).

In practice most of the top nodes of the ontology (that is, those that represent more general concepts), can be reused from existing ontologies. As we navigate down, specializing the concepts, we identify the need for incorporating information specific to that particular ontology. Most of the construction effort will be spent on the identification and incorporation of specialized (leaf) concepts and their instances to the ontology.

In Fig. 12.2, we illustrate part of the Researcher Home Page ontology. We can identify three zones. The top level contains concepts so general that they could be used in the creation of any personal home page. These concepts can be reused in the spirit of upper ontologies, such as CYC and WordNet (see Section 9.3), that embody consensual knowledge. The middle level corresponds to the specialization of the concepts to the computer science area. At this level, reuse is viable, but requires some adaptation effort. At the bottom level, the concepts and instances reflect specific information about the individual that owns this particular Web page. At this level, very little reuse can be accomplished. Once ready, this ontology will model the preferences of a single user, or at most a reduced number of users.

Table 12.2 Reusable information sources for ontological composition.

Information Chunk Type	Reusable Information Sources
People	FOAF taxonomy of family and work relationships
Research Area	IEEE taxonomy, NAICS
Events	University ontology, IEEE/ACM calendar of events
Projects	Subcategories of NSF and/or Esprit European projects
Physical Location and Contact information	University directory, floor plan, vCard taxonomy.
Courses	University catalogue

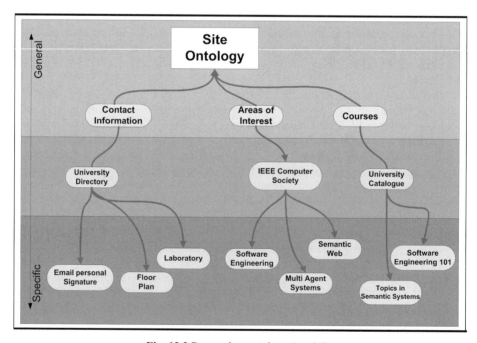

Fig. 12.2 Researcher ontology (partial).

12.4 Semantic Desktop Architecture

In the previous section, we discussed the organization that has to be imposed on the information resources in order to allow for automated computer processing. The nature of the information in question suggests that there are two possible types of sources:

- Internal (privately owned): information that comes from the user's personal computer (e-mail, recent files, articles recently written/submitted, discussion groups, directory structure itself, etc.)
- External (worldly): from syndication (Web sites) and from myriad heterogeneous distributed sources (conferences, publishers, Amazon, scientific societies, colleague home pages, etc.)

The current exponential growth of Web accessible resources has created a demand for new tools to help people cope with the volume of information. Balabanovic and Shoham et al. (1995) proposed a software agent that learns user patterns and browses the Internet on his or her behalf. Etzioni investigates the possibilities of semantic e-mail (McDowell et al. 2004) and Rucker and Polanco (1997) made SiteSeer available, a site that uses references in scientific articles that serves as a guide to other works of interest.

However, there are myriad information sources available in today's Web, ranging from static elements (written text in Web pages and files) to the results of behavioral patterns, such as navigation and user preferences. It is clear that different information mining strategies will be needed, case by case. These strategies will be incorporated in the profiles of different software agents (Jennings et al. 1998; Wooldridge and Jennings 1995; Hendler 2001). An introduction to software agents in the Semantic Web can be found in Chapter 11.

Agent-based architectures became an alternative that helps deal with complexity and increasing volumes of information. Multiagent systems are being used to build information and knowledge-sharing systems (Dignum 2003; Abecker et al. 2003; Chen 2000). The MACRON architecture, proposed by Decker et al. (1995), was designed specifically for the proactive acquisition of information in complex information-gathering environments. This architecture relies on the use of agents to find and conciliate heterogeneous information from different sources. Agent-based systems are also being used to build organization information systems, such as in the FRODO project, whose goal is to build distributed organizational memory systems. (Abecker et al. 2003).

The architecture of our semantic desktop is a composition of several software agents, that is, a community of agents or a multiagent system (MAS). Ferber (1999) defines a multiagent system as a "collection of possibly heterogeneous, computational entities, having their own problem solving capabilities and which are able to interact among them in order to reach an overall goal." Among the most distinctive characteristics of multiagent systems are the decentralization of data, lack of global control, and the fact that each individual agent has a partial view of (and capabilities of solving) the problem (Jennings et al. 1998).

There are four software agents in the semantic desktop current implementation:

- External Agents:

Syndicating Agent: This agent roams the Web, cataloguing information of interest to the semantic desktop. It was implemented using the RSS - Really Simple Syndication format - also called "feed" (XML format that allows for the update of information links on other sites). The downside is that RSS is an XML dialect, so it provides little semantics. We propose to overcome this effect by combining the use of RSS markup with ontology and metadata.

Serendipity Agent: Besides syndicating well-known Web pages, we implemented a serendipity agent, whose goal is to roam the Web in search of new interesting pieces of information. The concepts it searches for are those in the user ontology. The agent should identify important concepts and align those to the Web pages in a serendipitous manner. Strategies can use similarity ("if you like this") or (ontology-driven) semantic search.

- Internal Agents:

Indexing Agent: This agent is responsible for updating the user ontology based on the information obtained when indexing the user's computer(s). It can work in conjunction with indexing software, such as the Google Desktop Search Plugin or the Copernic desktop search. This agent will provide the information needed to update the most specialized links in the Web site ontology, files and the address book. Because it indexes personal files, e-mails, and e-mail attachments stored anywhere in the user's personal computer, the information it contains reflects the owner's personal interests and choices.

Spy Agent: The role of this agent is to monitor the semantic desktop user's activities. The behavior of the semantic desktop user can tell much about his or her preferences, among others:
  - Internet: sites he or she frequently visits, list of preferred sites, pop-ups he or she always dismisses
  - Mail: monitoring the e-mail can help identify, among others:
    - Colleagues with whom the user corresponds frequently
    - Confirmation on ticket and hotel reservations (update Outlook)
    - Notification of acceptance of papers
    - News that appeared on lists to which he or she subscribes to

Finally, we note that the services provided by the software agents are mutually independent and can be combined as needed. New software agents can be included in the architecture providing additional services in the future.

12.5 Semantic Desktop Related Applications

In the previous section, we illustrated the use of the Semantic Web technologies addressed in this book using a semantic desktop as an example. In this section, we discuss a series of other tools that implement similar environments.

IRIS

Developed by SRI International, the IRIS semantic desktop application provides users with the ability to organize their information resources in ways that suit their individual needs, while maintaining semantic interoperability with other applications. IRIS includes an ontology-based knowledge store that stores rich semantic models that capture several aspects of the user's work environment. It enables users to create a "personal map" across their office-related information objects. IRIS includes a machine-learning platform to help automate this process. IRIS serves as the knowledge store for the larger, DARPA-funded, SRI CALO (Cognitive Agent that Learns and Organizes) project whose mission is to "serve its user as a personal assistant, collaborating in all aspects of work life: organizing information; preparing information artifacts; mediating person-person interactions; organizing and scheduling in time; monitoring and managing tasks; and acquiring and allocating resources" (Cheyer et al. 2005).

Gnowsis

Developed at the Knowledge Management Lab of the DFKI (Deutsche Forschungszentrum für Künstliche Intelligenz, German Research Center for Artificial Intelligence GmbH), the Gnowsis system indexes and integrates user documents such as e-mails, addresses, photos, and calendar appointments using semantic technologies. Data from different standard applications are integrated into the server and stored in an RDF Database (Jena Model based).

In this environment, information is represented and accessed in a uniform way, enabling users to use desktop computers like a small personal semantic Web (Sauermann 2005). Gnowsis is part of the larger Nepomuk (Social Semantic Desktop) project, whose goal is to provide methods, data structures, and a set of tools for extending the personal computer into a collaborative environment (URL: http://nepomuk.semanticdesktop.org).

Longwell

Developed at MIT, Longwell is a Web application designed for browsing and searching RDF models. The most relevant feature of this tool is its ability to perform faceted browsing. A facet is a particular metadata field that is considered important for the dataset in question. Longwell lets its users select the facets of interest and then processes their values, and the number of times each facet value occurs in the dataset. Searches can be restricted by specific, user-typed strings; the results will be limited to the items that contain the searched string in their properties' values (Butler et al. 2006).

Magpie

Developed at the Open University, the Magpie browser proposed to do semantically enriched browsing. The tool identifies and filters Web pages for "concepts-of-interest," that is, concepts relevant from the perspective of a particular ontology. Magpie is a lightweight tool that does not modify the original look and feel of the visited pages. Semantic menus can be turned on and off to help users identify ontology concepts and their instances and facilitate navigation (Domingue et al. 2004).

semantExplorer

Developed at the University of Malta, the semantExplorer tool tries to bridge the gap between tools that navigate through semantic Web pages (that is, pages with associated semantics, called Semantic Web Browsers) and tools that provide semantic functionalities on top of regular Web pages (that is, augment standard Web browsers with the ability to visualize hidden metadata). It provides visualization mechanisms that display standard HTML documents, as well as RDF and OWL ontologies, RDF triple processing (both text and graphics), and filtering mechanisms (Scerri et al. 2005).

References

Abecker, A.; Bernardi, A.; van Elst. (2003) Agent technology for distributed organizational memories. In: *Proceedings of the Fifth International Conference on Enterprise Information Systems*, Vol. 2, 2003. pp. 3–10.

Balabanovic, M; Shoham, Y. (1995) Learning information retrieval agents: Experiments with automated web browsing. In: *Proceedings of the AAAI Spring Symposium on Information Gathering from Heterogenous, Distributed Resources*, pp. 13–18.

Berners-Lee, T.; Lassila, O.; Hendler, J. (2001) The Semantic Web: a new form of web content that is meaningful to computers will unleash a revolution of new possibilities. *Scientific American*, 284(5), pp. 34–43. Available at: http://www.scientificamerican.com/2001/0501issue/0501berners-lee.html.

Breitman, K.K.; Truszkowski, W.; Felicissimo, C.H. (2006) The autonomic semantic desktop: Helping users cope with information system complexity. In: *Proceedings of the Third IEEE International Workshop on Engineering of Autonomic and Autonomous Systems EASe 2006*, pp. 156–162.

Butler, M.; Huynh, D.; Hyde, B.; Lee, R.; Mazzocchi, S. (2006) Longwell site. Available at: http://simile.mit.edu/longwell/.

Cheyer, A.; Park, J.; Giuli, R. (2005) IRIS: Integrate. Relate. Infer. Share. In: *Proceedings of the Workshop on the Semantic Desktop: Next Generation Personal Information Management and Collaboration Infrastructure*, in conjunction with the *International Semantic Web Conference*, Galway, Ireland.

Decker, K.; Lesser, V.; Nagendra Prasad, M.V.; Wagner, T. (1995) MACRON: An architecture for multiagent cooperative information gathering. In: *Proceedings of the CIKM '95 Workshop on Intelligent Information Agents*.

Dignum, V. (2003) Using agent societies to support knowledge sharing. In: *AAMAS-03 Workshop on Autonomy, Delegation and Control*, Melbourne, Australia, July 14th 2003.

Domingue, J.B.; Dzbor, M.; Motta, E. (2004) Collaborative Semantic Web browsing with Magpie. In: *Proceedings of the First European Semantic Web Symposium (ESWS)*, May 2004, Greece.

Ferber, J. (1999) *Multi-Agent System: An Introduction to Distributed Artificial Intelligence*. Pearson Education.

Hendler, J. (2001) Agents and the Semantic Web. *IEEE Intelligent Systems*, March/April 2001, pp. 30–37.

Hodge, G.; Clay, T.; Allen, R. (2005) A metadata element set for project documentation. *Science & Technology Libraries Journal*, Vol. 25, Issue 4, pp. 5–23.

Jennings, N.R.; Sycara, K.; Wooldridge, M. (1998) *A Roadmap for Agent Research and Development. Autonomous and Multi-Agent Systems*, Vol. 1, pp. 7–38.

Matuszek, C.; Cabral, J.; Witbrock, M.; Oliveira, J. (2006) An introduction to the syntax and content of CYC. In: *Proceedings of the 2006 AAAI Spring Symposium on Formalizing and Compiling Background Knowledge and Its Applications to Knowledge Representation and Question Answering*, Stanford, CA, March 2006.

McDowell, L.; Etzioni, O.; Halevey, A.; Levy, A. (2004) Semantic email. In: *Proceedings of the Thirteenth International WWW Conference*.

Miller, G. (1995) WordNet: A lexical database for English. *Communications of the ACM*, Vol. 38, Issue 11, pp. 39–41.

Pazzani, M.; Billsus, D. (2002) Adaptive Web site agents. *Autonomous Agents and Multi Agent Systems* 5, pp. 205–218.

Rucker, J.; Polanco, M.J. (1997) SiteSeer: Personalized navigation for the Web. *Communications of the ACM*, Vol. 40, No. 3, pp. 73–75.

Sauermann, L. (2005) The Gnowsis semantic desktop for information integration: In: *Proceedings of the First Workshop on Intelligent Office Appliances, in conjunction with the Workshop of the Professional Knowledge Management Conference*, Kaiserslautern, 2005.

Scerri, S.; Abela, C.; Montebello, M. (2005) semantExplorer: A semantic Web browser. In: *Proceedings of the IADIS International Conference WWW/Internet 2005*, Lisbon, Portugal, October.

Sycara, K. (1998) Multiagent systems. *IA Magazine*, Vol. 19, No. 2, pp. 79–92.

Williams, A.B. (2004) Learning to share meaning in a multi-agent system. *Journal of Autonomous Agents and Multi-Agent Systems*, Vol. 8, No. 2, pp. 165–193.

Wooldridge, M.; Jennings, N. (1995) Intelligent agents: Theory and practice. *Knowledge Engineering Review*, Vol. 10, No. 2, pp. 115–152.

Wooldridge, M.; Jennings, N.R.; Kinny, D. (1999) A methodology for agent-oriented analysis and design. In: Etzioni, O.; Muller, J.P.; Bradshaw, J. (Eds.) *Agents '99: Proceedings of the Third International Conference on Autonomous Agents*, Seattle, WA, May.

13

Ontology Applications in Art

13.1 Introduction

Cataloguing our cultural heritage has naturally been a major activity of museums and other cultural institutions throughout the world. Today, almost all major museums make their collections available over the Web, often with remarkable quality, such as the Hermitage Museum Web site (Mintzer et. al. 2001).

In parallel, many organizations have been working toward the development of standards for describing and retrieving information about cultural objects. The International Committee for Documentation of the International Council of Museums (ICOM-CIDOC) published the *CIDOC Conceptual Reference Model* (CRM; CIDOC 2006), that provides definitions and a formal structure for describing the concepts and relationships used in cultural heritage documentation. The CIDOC CRM was accepted as a working draft by ISO/TC46/SC4/WG9 in September 2000 and is currently in the final stage of the ISO process as ISO/PRF 21127 (ISO 2006). Other examples of metadata schemas are the *Categories for the Description of Works of Art* (CDWA), created and maintained by The Getty Research Institute (Baca and Harpring 2005), and The *VRA Core Categories, Version 3.0* (VRA 2002), published by the Visual Resources Association.

The choice of an appropriate domain for metadata elements is of considerable importance to achieve an optimum rate of retrieval and a high level of consistency. In this respect, The Getty Research Institute has done remarkable work in developing thesauri and controlled vocabularies.

This chapter reviews these standardization efforts and describes an application that combines a metadata schema with controlled vocabularies to create semantic annotations for still images of works of art. This profitable combination — metadata schemas, controlled vocabularies, and standardization efforts — is repeated in Chapter 14 in the context of geospatial applications, setting a pattern for other application areas.

13.2 Ontologies for the Description of Works of Art

The Getty vocabulary databases, maintained by the Getty Vocabulary Program (Getty 2006a), are thesauri compliant with the ISO standard for thesaurus construction. They contain terms, names, and other information about people, places, things, and concepts relating to art, architecture, and material culture. The primary users of the Getty vocabularies include museums, art libraries, archives, visual resource collection cataloguers, bibliographic projects concerned with art, researchers in art and art history, and the information specialists who are dealing with the needs of these users.

The Getty vocabularies comprise the Art & Architecture Thesaurus (AAT), the Union List of Artist Names (ULAN) and the Getty Thesaurus of Geographic Names (TGN). The first two vocabularies are discussed in what follows, and TGN is reviewed in Section 14.14.1, in the context of geographic gazetteers.

In this section, we also introduce a visual annotation ontology, composed of a spatial annotation ontology fragment and a visual feature annotation ontology fragment, which are both useful for the semantic annotation of art images, an application discussed in detail in Section 14.4.

13.2.1 The Art & Architecture Thesaurus

The *Art & Architecture Thesaurus* (AAT) contains around 34,000 concepts, including 131,000 terms, descriptions, bibliographic citations, and other information relating to fine art, architecture, decorative arts, archival materials, and material culture (Getty 2006b). AAT contains generic terms to describe these subjects; it contains no iconographic subjects and no proper names. AAT is a compiled resource that grows through contributions. New versions are released in licensed files annually and on the Web site every month.

The AAT hierarchical structure is organized into seven major subdivisions, called *facets*, summarized in Table 13.1. AAT is polyhierarchical, in the sense that a term may have multiple broader terms. A broader term provides an immediate generalization of a concept, and serves to clarify its meaning. The narrower term is always a type of, a kind of, an example of, or a manifestation of its broader context. In addition to the hierarchical relationships, AAT supports equivalence and associative relationships.

A record in AAT describes a *concept* and contains at least a numeric ID, a term, and a position in the hierarchy. Figure 13.1 shows a sample AAT entry, and Table 13.2 contains a brief explanation of the fields shown.

Table 13.1 Facets in the AAT (© J. Paul Getty Trust).

Facet / Hierarchies	Description
Associated Concepts Hierarchy: Associated Concepts	This facet contains abstract concepts and phenomena that relate to the study and execution of a wide range of human thought and activity, including architecture and art in all media, as well as related disciplines.

Physical Attributes
 	
Hierarchies:
  Attributes and Properties;
  Conditions and Effects;
  Design Elements;
  Color
	This facet concerns the perceptible or measurable characteristics of materials and artifacts as well as features of materials and artifacts that are not separable as components. Included are characteristics such as size and shape, chemical properties of materials, qualities of texture and hardness, and features such as surface ornament and color.

Styles and Periods Hierarchy: Styles and Periods	This facet provides commonly accepted terms for stylistic groupings and distinct chronological periods that are relevant to art, architecture, and the decorative arts.

Agents
 	
Hierarchies:
  People;
  Organizations
	This facet contains terms for designations of people, groups of people, and organizations identified by occupation or activity, by physical or mental characteristics, or by social role or condition.

Activities
 	
Hierarchies:
  Disciplines;
  Functions;
  Events;
  Physical and Mental Activ.;
  Processes and Techniques
	This facet encompasses areas of endeavor, physical and mental actions, discrete occurrences, systematic sequences of actions, methods employed toward a certain end, and processes occurring in materials or objects. Activities may range from branches of learning and professional fields to specific life events, from mentally executed tasks to processes performed on or with materials and objects, from single physical actions to complex games.

Materials Hierarchy: Materials	This facet deals with physical substances, whether naturally or synthetically derived. These range from specific materials to types of materials designed by their function, such as colorants, and from raw materials to those that have been formed or processed into products that are used in fabricating structures or objects.

Objects
 	
Hierarchies:
  Object Groupings and
    Systems;
  Object Genres;
  Components
	This facet encompasses those discrete tangible or visible things that are inanimate and produced by human endeavor; that is, that are either fabricated or given form by human activity. They range, in physical form, from built works to images and written documents. They range in purpose from utilitarian to the aesthetic. Also included are landscape features that provide the context for the built environment.

ID: 300021474   **Record Type:** concept

⚏   **Modernist** (<modern European styles and movements>, <European styles and periods>, ... Styles and
     Periods)

Note: Refers to the succession of 20th-century avant-garde art and architectural movements formed in a
reaction to social modernity. Modernism was eclipsed by the Post-Modernism movement, which began in the
1970s.

Terms:
    Modernist (preferred, C,U,D,American English-P)
    Modernism (C,U,AD,American English)

Facet/Hierarchy Code: F.FL

Hierarchical Position:
    Styles and Periods Facet
    .... Styles and Periods
    .... <styles and periods by region>
    .... European
    .... <European styles and periods>
    .... <modern European styles and movements>
    .... Modernist

Related concepts:
    distinguished from ....   Modern
    .... (<styles and periods by general era>, Styles and Periods) [300264736]

Sources and Contributors:
    Modernism............ [VP]
    .... CDMARC Subjects: LCSH (1988-) **Modernism (Art)**
    .... Grove Dictionary of Art (1996) **Vol. 21, 775**
    .... Lucie-Smith, Thames & Hudson Dictionary of Art Terms (1986)
    .... RILA, Subject headings, unpub. (1975-1990)
    Modernist............ [VP Preferred]
    .... Candidate term **Candidate term - AVERY - 10/88**
    .... Lewis and Darley, Dictionary of Ornament (1986)
    .... Walker, Glossary of Art (1977)

    Subject: ..... [VP]
    .... CDMARC Subjects: LCSH (1988-) **Modernist art**
    .... RIBA, Architectural Keywords (1982) **Architecture: history: c1910-1940**
    .... RILA, Subject headings, unpub. (1975-1990) **Modernist...**

    Note: .... [VP]

Fig. 13.1 Sample AAT entry (© J. Paul Getty Trust).

Table 13.2 Selected fields of an AAT record (© J. Paul Getty Trust).

Field *Value in Fig. 13.1*	Description
Subject ID *200021474*	Each concept in the AAT database is uniquely identified by a numeric ID that serves to link the terms and all other pertinent information to the concept record.
Record Type *concept*	Type designation that characterizes the AAT record, including the following. **Concept:** refers to records in the AAT that represent concepts, which include the majority of terms. **Guide term** or **node label**: refers to records that serve as place savers to create a level in the hierarchy under which the AAT can collocate related concepts. **Hierarchy name:** refers to the top of a hierarchy. **Facet:** Refers to the top of a facet.
Label *modernist*	Brief text identification of the concept, concatenated from the preferred term (descriptor), qualifier (if applicable), and the parent string.
Note (or **Scope Note**) *(explanation of modernism)*	What the term means in the context of the AAT.
Terms *Modernist (preferred)* *Modernism*	Words or phrases referring to the concept, including a preferred term and variant terms. All terms in a record are considered synonyms.
Hierarchical Position *Styles and Periods Facet* *... Styles and Periods* *........*	Concepts in the AAT typically have a genus/species relationship (rather than whole/part relationship). For end-users, the Hierarchical Position is typically indicated in a display that shows broader contexts or *parents* of the concept.
Related concepts *distinguish from... modern*	Associative relationships to other concepts (subjects) in the AAT; they include various types of ties or connections between concepts, excluding genus/species (hierarchical) relationships.
Sources and Contributors	The institutions or projects that contributed information to the AAT record.

13.2.2 The Union List of Artist Names

The *Union List of Artist Names* (ULAN) contains close to 120,000 records, including 293,000 names and biographical and bibliographic information about artists and architects, including a wealth of variant names, pseudonyms, and language variants. ULAN is also a compiled resource that grows through contributions.

Although displayed as a list, ULAN is structured as a thesaurus, just like AAT. It currently has two published facets: *Person* and *Corporate Body*. Entries in the Person facet typically have no children. Entries in the Corporate Body facet may branch into trees. ULAN is also polyhierarchical and supports equivalence and associative relationships.

The focus of each ULAN record is an artist, and includes such fields as a unique numeric ID, names, related artists, sources for the data, and notes. Figure 13.2 shows a sample ULAN record and Table 13.4 contains a brief explanation of the fields shown.

In particular, an ULAN record may contain a term or phrase characterizing the relationship between the artist represented in the record and another artist. Relationship Types are linked to both records, and are taken from the list shown in Table 13.3.

Table 13.3 ULAN relationships.

Relationship	Property
associate of	reflexive
partner of	reflexive
parent of	inverse of *child of*
child of	inverse of *parent of*
teacher of	inverse of *student of*
student of	inverse of *teacher of*

For example, the artist Lucas van Leyden has a *child of* relationship with Hughe Jacobsz and a *student of* relationship with Cornelius Engebrechtszhis, described as in the fragment below:

Related People or Corporate Bodies:
child of .... Jacobsz., Hughe
.... (North Netherlandish painter, 1480–1538) [500017959]
student of .... Engebrechtsz., Cornelius
.... (North Netherlandish painter, ca. 1465–1527) [500003586]

ID: 500022426   Record Type: Person

⚘ **Portinari, Cândido** (Brazilian painter, ceramicist, and printmaker, 1903-1962)

Names:
    Portinari, Cândido (preferred, index, V)
    Cândido Portinari (display, V)
    Portinari, Candido (V)

Nationalities:
    Brazilian (preferred)
    South American

Roles:
    artist (preferred)
    painter
    printmaker
    ceramicist

Gender: male

Birth and Death Places:
    Died: Rio de Janeiro (Rio de Janeiro state, Sudeste region, Brazil) (inhabited place)

List/Hierarchical Position:
    ⚘ .... Person
    ⚘ .... Portinari, Cândido

Biographies:
    (Brazilian painter, ceramicist, and printmaker, 1903-1962) ..... [VP Preferred]
    (Brazilian painter, ceramist, printmaker, 1903-1962) ..... [BHA]
    (Brazilian painter 1903-1964) ..... [GRLPSC]
    (Brazilian artist, 1903-1962) ..... [WCP]

Sources and Contributors:
    Cândido Portinari ....   [VP]
    .... Getty Vocabulary Program
    Portinari, Candido ....   [BHA Preferred, GRLPSC Preferred, WCP Preferred]
    .... Vollmer, Künstler-Lexikon 20. Jahrhunderts (1953-62)
    Portinari, Cândido ....   [VP]
    .... Grove Dictionary of Art online (1999-2002) **accessed 16 October 2003**

       Subject: .... [BHA, GRLPSC, VP, WCP]
    .... Bénézit, Dictionnaire des Peintres (1976)
    .... Grove Dictionary of Art online (1999-2002) **accessed 16 October 2003**
    .... MoMA, Library Catalog (1976)
    .... Vollmer, Künstler-Lexikon 20. Jahrhunderts (1953-62)

Fig. 13.2 Sample ULAN entry (© J. Paul Getty Trust).

Table 13.4 Selected fields of an AAT record (© J. Paul Getty Trust).

Field *Value in Fig. 13.2*	Description
Subject ID *500022426*	Each artist in the ULAN database is uniquely identified by a numeric ID that serves to link the names and all other pertinent information to the artist record.
Record Type *Person*	Type designation that characterizes the ULAN record, including the following. **Person:** refers to records in the ULAN that represent a single individual, usually someone who was engaged in the design or creation of art or architecture. **Corporate Body:** refers to records in the ULAN that represent two or more people, not necessarily legally incorporated. They are generally people who worked together to collectively create art. A family of artists may also be a "corporate body." **Guide Term, Hierarchy Name, and Facet:** currently these record types are hidden from end-users.
Label *Portinari, Cândido*	Brief text identification of the artist, concatenated from the preferred Name and preferred Display Biography.
Note (or **Descriptive Note**) *(not present in the example)*	A note that describes the career of the artist, his relationship to other artists, or the usage of his names.
Names *Portinari, Cândido* (preferred) *Cândido Portinari* *Portinari, Candido*	Words or phrases referring to the concept, including a preferred term and variant terms. All terms in a record are considered synonyms.
Nationality *Brazilian* (preferred) *South American*	A reference to the nationality, culture, or ethnic group associated with the person or corporate body.
Roles *artist* (preferred) *painter* *printmaker* *ceramist*	Words or phrases describing one or more roles or characteristics of the artist. Roles are the major professional roles or activities performed by the artist throughout his or her lifetime (e.g., artist, architect, sculptor). For a corporate body, roles include the major activities or purpose of the firm, institution, or other corporate body (e.g., studio, manufactory, workshop).
List / Hierarchical Position *... Person* *......Portinari, Cândido*	For individual artists in the Person facet, the broader context is usually simply Person. In the Corporate Body facet, there may be some hierarchical depth, for example between institutions and their divisions.
Contributors	The institutions or projects that contributed information to the ULAN record.

13.2.3 A Visual Annotation Ontology for Art Images

When describing an image, users typically resort to either the absolute position of the objects depicted in the image, or to their relative position. Users also commonly introduce planes, such as the image foreground and background, to indicate the relative position of the main features depicted in the scene. A second form of annotations has to do with information about the visual features of the image, such as the dominant color and texture. Following Hollink et al. (2004a) and Hollink et al. (2005), we introduce in this section a *visual annotation ontology*, composed of a *spatial annotation ontology* fragment and a *visual features annotation ontology* fragment, that cover these aspects.

A Spatial Annotation Ontology

As for the absolute positions, the spatial annotation ontology contains the major WordNet cardinal points: `North (N)`, `South (S)`, `East (E)`, `West (W)`, `Northeast (NE)`, `Southeast (SE)`, `Northwest (NW)`, and `Southwest (SW)`. The image is then divided into nine squares, as shown in Fig. 13.3, to determine the absolute position of each object (in the image). In fact, WordNet lists 32 cardinal compass points that could have been adopted for further precision.

The spatial annotation ontology includes a simple set of relative spatial relations, taken from SUMO's PositionalAttributes: `Right`, `Left`, `Above`, `Below`, `Near`, `Far`, and `Contains`. However, the spatial relation `Far` is taken from WordNet, because SUMO does not include such concept. For each such relation, the spatial annotation ontology indicates whether it is a SymmetricRelation, or a TransitiveRelation, and what is its inverseOf, if any.

Finally, the spatial annotation ontology contains the `VisibleObject` class, the `spatialRelation`, and the `hasPosition` object properties. Figure 13.4 shows (a partial account of) the spatial annotation ontology defined thus far, indicating relationships between the properties, and following the recommendations in van Assem et al. (2005) for using WordNet terms in OWL. Thus, `wn:compass_point-n-1` indicates "compass point" refers to the first sense of the term as a noun, and similarly for `wn:center-n-1` and `wn:far-a-1`, where "a" stands for adverb.

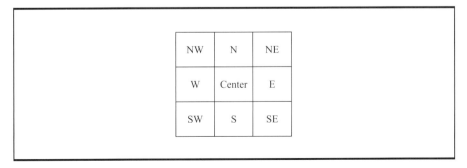

Fig. 13.3 Absolute position of an object within an image.

```xml
<?xml version="1.0"?>
<!DOCTYPE rdf:RDF [
   <!ENTITY
      sumo  "http://reliant.teknowledge.com/DAML/SUMO.owl#">
   <!ENTITY wn  "http://wordnet.princeton.edu/wn#">
   <!ENTITY owl "http://www.w3.org/2002/07/owl#">]>
<rdf:RDF
   xml:base="http://www.art.com/spatial-ontology/"
   xmlns:owl="http://www.w3.org/2002/07/owl#"
   xmlns:rdf="http://www.w3.org/1999/02/22-rdf-syntax-ns#"
   xmlns:rdfs="http://www.w3.org/2000/01/rdf-schema#">

   <owl:Ontology rdf:about="">
      <rdfs:comment> The Spatial Annotation Ontology in OWL
      </rdfs:comment>
      <rdfs:label>Spatial Annotation</rdfs:label>
   </owl:Ontology>

   <owl:Class rdf:about="visibleObject"/>

   <owl:Class rdf:about="Position"/>

   <owl:Class rdf:about="&wn;compass_point-n-1">
      <rdfs:subClassOf rdf:resource="Position"/>
   </owl:Class>

   <owl:Class rdf:about="&wn;center-n-1">
      <rdfs:subClassOf rdf:resource="Position"/>
   </owl:Class>

   <owl:ObjectTypeProperty rdf:about="spatialRelation">
      <rdfs:domain rdf:resource="visibleObject"/>
      <rdfs:range rdf:resource="visibleObject"/>
   </owl:ObjectTypeProperty>

   <owl:ObjectTypeProperty rdf:about="hasPosition">
      <rdfs:domain rdf:resource="visibleObject"/>
      <rdfs:range rdf:resource="Position"/>
   </owl:ObjectTypeProperty>

   <owl:ObjectTypeProperty rdf:about="&sumo;Contains">
      <rdfs:subPropertyOf rdf:resource="spatialRelation"/>
   </owl:ObjectTypeProperty>

   <owl:ObjectTypeProperty rdf:about="&wn;far-a-1">
      <rdfs:subPropertyOf rdf:resource="spatialRelation"/>
      <rdfs:type rdf:resource="&owl;SymmetricProperty"/>
   </owl:ObjectTypeProperty>

   <owl:ObjectTypeProperty rdf:about="&sumo;near">
      <rdfs:subPropertyOf rdf:resource="spatialRelation"/>
      <rdfs:type rdf:resource="&owl;SymmetricProperty"/>
   </owl:ObjectTypeProperty>
```

```
<owl:ObjectTypeProperty rdf:about="&sumo;Above">
   <rdfs:subPropertyOf rdf:resource="spatialRelation"/>
   <rdfs:type rdf:resource="&owl;TransitiveProperty"/>
   <owl:inverseOf rdf:resource="Below"/>
</owl:ObjectTypeProperty>

<owl:ObjectTypeProperty rdf:about="&sumo;Below">
   <rdfs:subPropertyOf rdf:resource="spatialRelation"/>
   <rdfs:type rdf:resource="&owl;TransitiveProperty"/>
   <owl:inverseOf rdf:resource="Above"/>
</owl:ObjectTypeProperty>

<owl:ObjectTypeProperty rdf:about="&sumo;Left">
   <rdfs:subPropertyOf rdf:resource="spatialRelation"/>
   <rdfs:type rdf:resource="&owl;TransitiveProperty"/>
   <owl:inverseOf rdf:resource="Right"/>
</owl:ObjectTypeProperty>

<owl:ObjectTypeProperty rdf:about="&sumo;Right">
   <rdfs:subPropertyOf rdf:resource="spatialRelation"/>
   <rdfs:type rdf:resource="&owl;TransitiveProperty"/>
   <owl:inverseOf rdf:resource="Left"/>
</owl:ObjectTypeProperty>

</rdf:RDF>
```

Fig. 13.4 The spatial annotation ontology.

A Visual Features Annotation Ontology

To describe visual features, we may resort to a fragment of the MPEG-7 Ontology introduced in Hunter (2001).

Examples of widely used visual features include color, texture, shape, and motion (which we discard, because we are interested only in still images). Table 13.5 illustrates the relationship between MPEG-7 descriptors (ISO 2001) and visual features, and Fig. 13.5 contains the OWL fragment for the descriptor Color.

Table 13.5 Visual features and their corresponding descriptors.

Feature	Descriptors
Color	DominantColor, ScalableColor, ColorLayout, ColorStructure, GoFGoPColor (extension of ColorStructure)
Texture	HomogeneousTexture, TextureBrowsing, EdgeHistogram
Shape	RegionShape, ContourShape, Shape3D

```
<rdfs:Class rdf:ID="Color">
    <rdfs:label>Color</rdfs:label>
    <rdfs:comment>Color of a visual resource</rdfs:comment>
    <rdfs:subClassOf
        rdf:resource="http://www.w3.org/2000/01/rdf-schema#Resource"/>
</rdfs:Class>
<rdfs:Class rdf:ID="DominantColor">
    <rdfs:label>DominantColor</rdfs:label>
    <rdfs:comment>The set of dominant colors in an arbitrarily-shaped
                  region.
    </rdfs:comment>
    <rdfs:subClassOf rdf:resource="#Color"/>
</rdfs:Class>
<rdfs:Class rdf:ID="ScalableColor">
    <rdfs:label>ScalableColor</rdfs:label>
    <rdfs:comment>Color histogram in the HSV color space.
    </rdfs:comment>
    <rdfs:subClassOf rdf:resource="#Color"/>
</rdfs:Class>
<rdfs:Class rdf:ID="ColorLayout">
    <rdfs:label>ColorLayout</rdfs:label>
    <rdfs:comment>Spatial distribution of colors.</rdfs:comment>
    <rdfs:subClassOf rdf:resource="#Color"/>
</rdfs:Class>
<rdfs:Class rdf:ID="ColorStructure">
    <rdfs:label>ColorStructure</rdfs:label>
    <rdfs:comment>Describes color content and the structure of this
                  content.
    </rdfs:comment>
    <rdfs:subClassOf rdf:resource="#Color"/>
</rdfs:Class>
<rdfs:Class rdf:ID="GoFGoPColor">
    <rdfs:label>GoFGoPColor</rdfs:label>
    <rdfs:comment>Group of frames/pictures color descriptor.
    </rdfs:comment>
    <rdfs:subClassOf rdf:resource="#ScalableColor"/>
</rdfs:Class>
<rdf:Property rdf:ID="color">
    <rdfs:label>color</rdfs:label>
    <rdfs:comment>The color descriptor is applicable to video
                  segments, still regions and moving regions.
    </rdfs:comment>
    <rdfs:subPropertyOf rdf:resource="#visualDescriptor"/>
    <rdfs:domain rdf:resource="#VideoSegment"/>
    <rdfs:domain rdf:resource="#StillRegion"/>
    <rdfs:domain rdf:resource="#MovingRegion"/>
    <rdfs:range rdf:resource="#Color"/>
</rdf:Property>
```

Fig. 13.5 A visual features annotation ontology (Hunter, 2001).

13.3 Metadata Schemas for the Description of Works of Art

In this section, we focus on metadata schemas for the description of works of art. We briefly address the Categories for the Description of Works of Art (CDWA), developed by The Getty Research Institute, the CIDOC Conceptual Reference Model (CIDOC CRM), which is about to be published as the ISO standard ISO/PRF 21127:2006, and the VRA Core Categories, published by the Visual Resources Association. Inasmuch as the sample application described in the next section adopts the VRA Core Categories, this is the only metadata schema we describe in some detail.

13.3.1 The Categories for the Description of Works of Art

The Categories for the Description of Works of Art (CDWA) is a metadata schema for works of art, architecture, other material culture, and groups and collections of works and related images, developed by The Getty Research Institute (Baca and Harpring 2005). CDWA includes 381 categories and subcategories. A small subset of categories are considered core in that they represent the minimum information necessary to identify and describe a work.

The core categories and subcategories are those that represent the minimum information necessary to uniquely and unambiguously identify and describe a particular work of art or architecture. Table 13.6 contains an example of how the CDWA elements were used to describe a painting by Van Gogh. The elements are self-explanatory and are not described in detail here (see Baca and Harpring 2005), because the sample application discussed in Section 13.4 adopts the VRA Core elements, described in Section 13.3.3.

CDWA considers the differences between information intended for display and data intended for retrieval. Information for display may reflect all the nuances of language necessary to convey the uncertainty and ambiguity that are common in art information. By contrast, certain key metadata elements must be formatted to facilitate retrieval. Such indexing activity should be the responsibility of expert cataloguers, who consider the retrieval implications of the indexing terms. That is, indexing should not be carried out by an automated method that simply parses every word in a text intended for display into indexes.

In CDWA, display metadata elements are often described as free-text fields, whereas indexing metadata elements are controlled-vocabulary fields. CDWA describes when categories should be controlled by a simple controlled list (e.g., Classification), an authority (e.g., Creator), or by consistent formatting of certain information (e.g., Earliest and Latest Dates) to ensure efficient end-user retrieval. This is marked in the example of Table 13.6 by the text "Authority/Controlled Vocabulary."

Table 13.6 CDWA fielded example: An oil painting by van Gogh.

Classification*	Paintings	*Authority/ Controlled Vocabulary*
Object/Work Type*	paintings	*Authority/ Controlled Vocabulary*
Title or Names*	Irises	
Creation- Creator/Role*	Vincent van Gogh	
	painter: Gogh, Vincent van (Dutch painter, 1853-1890)	*Authority/ Controlled Vocabulary*
Creation-Date*	1889	
	earliest: 1889	latest: 1889
Subject Matter*	irises	regeneration
	Iridaceæ	soil
	nature	*Authority/ Controlled Vocabulary*
Context- Historical/Cultural	exhibited at Salon des Indépendents, September 1889	
Measurements	71 x 93 cm (28 x 36 5/8 in.)	
	height: 71 cm	width: 93 cm
Materials and Techniques	oil on canvas, applied with brush and palette knife	
	oil paint	brush
	canvas	impasto
	palette knife	*Authority/ Controlled Vocabulary*
Descriptive Note	This work was painted when the artist was recuperating from a severe attack of mental illness, and it depicts the garden at the asylum at Saint-Rémy. It is influenced by the work of Gauguin and Hokusai, and is remarkable for the contrasts of color ...	
Current Location- Repository Name*	J. Paul Getty Museum	
Current Location- Repository Location	Los Angeles (California, USA)	
Current Location- Repository Numbers	90.PA.20	

Image Credits: *Irises* (painting), 1889; artist: Vincent van Gogh (1853-1890, active in Holland); oil on canvas, 71 x 93 cm; J. Paul Getty Museum (Los Angeles, California), 90.PA.20. © The J. Paul Getty Trust, 2000. All Rights Reserved.

http://www.getty.edu/research/conducting_research/standards/cdwa/3_cataloging_examples/index.html
© 2000 The J. Paul Getty Trust & College Art Association, Inc.

13.3.2 The ISO 21127 — A Reference Ontology for the Interchange of Cultural Heritage Information

Development of the ISO 21127 began in 1994 under the International Committee for Documentation of the International Council of Museums (ICOM-CIDOC). The resulting metadata schema is known as the CIDOC Conceptual Reference Model or CRM. It was accepted as a working draft by the ISO/TC46/SC4/WG9 in September 2000 and is currently in the final stage of the processing to become a standard, known as the ISO 21127:2006 (ISO 2006). Therefore, the CIDOC CRM and the ISO 21127:2006 are synonymous.

As stated in the ISO document (ISO 2006),

the primary purpose of the ISO 21127 is to offer a conceptual basis for the mediation of information between cultural heritage organizations such as museums, libraries and archives. The standard aims to provide a common reference point against which divergent and incompatible sources of information can be compared and, ultimately, harmonized.

The ISO 21127:2006 defines a domain ontology that covers all concepts relevant to describe cultural heritage collections. The term cultural heritage collection refers to all types of material collected and displayed by museums and related institutions. This includes collections, sites, monuments relating to natural history, ethnography, archaeology, and historic monuments, as well as collections of fine and applied arts.

The ontology has 81 classes and 132 properties. As summarized in the RDF graph of Figure 13.6, the central notions of the ontology are (Crofts et al. 2003; Boeuf 2006):

- The *TemporalEntities* class, whose instances include *events*, defined as "something that happens in space and time and brings about some change in the world." Events are the central notion of the model
- The *Actors* class, whose instances denote persons, groups, and so on, who can play a decisive role in provoking the event or just witness it or undergo it
- The *PhysicalEntities* class, whose instances stand for objects of the physical world
- The *ConceptualObjects* class, whose instances are abstractions or conceptual objects
- The *TimeSpans* class, whose instances define the duration of an event
- The *Places* class, whose instances define the location of an event

The major properties are those depicted in Fig. 13.6. We refer the reader to the ISO document for the details (ISO 2006).

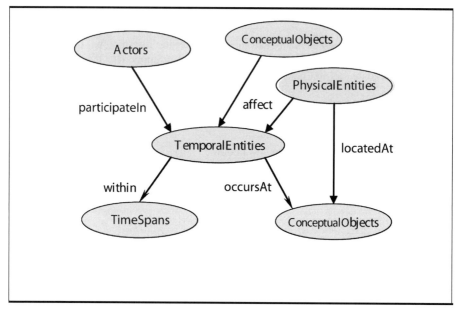

Fig. 13.6 A simplified RDF graph of the major concepts of the ISO 21127
(Crofts et al. 2003).

13.3.3 The Visual Resources Association Core Categories

The *Visual Resources Association* (VRA) is a multidisciplinary organization dedicated to furthering research and education in the field of image management within the educational, cultural heritage, and commercial environments. The *VRA Core Categories, Version 3.0* is a reinterpretation of the Dublin Core metadata schema (see Section 9.2.2) that can be applied as many times as necessary to create metadata records to describe works of visual culture, as well as the images that document them. The VRA Core 3.0 is intended as a point of departure, in the sense that additional fields can be added to fully describe a local collection. Furthermore, every element may be repeated as many times as necessary within a given set to describe the work or image.

The VRA Data Standards Committee recommends the use of controlled vocabularies, particularly the Getty vocabularies described in Section 13.2.1 and other standard authorities, for use with many of the categories. No single authority will suffice for the entire set of the VRA Core or even, in many cases, for a single element in the set. The VRA committee suggests that the organization responsible for a collection should compile a list of vocabularies and authorities that are appropriate for each field in their local applications.

Table 13.7 summarizes the VRA Core categories and their relationship to the Dublin Core elements, and Fig. 13.7 shows two sets of metadata elements that describe an etching in a museum collection and a digital image of the etching.

Table 13.7 VRA Core categories, Version 3.0 (VRA, 2002).

VRA 3.0	Dublin Core	Description
Record Type	TYPE	Identifies the record as being either a Work record, for the physical or created object, or an Image record, for the visual surrogates of such objects. **Data Values (controlled):** Work, Image
Type	TYPE	Identifies the specific type of Work or Image being described in the record. **Data Values (controlled):** recommend AAT
Title	TITLE	The title or identifying phrase given to a Work or an Image.
Measurements	FORMAT	The size, shape, scale, dimensions, format, or storage configuration of the Work or Image.
Material	FORMAT	The substance of which a work or an image is composed. **Data Values (controlled):** AAT
Technique	FORMAT	The production or manufacturing processes, techniques, and methods incorporated in the fabrication or alteration of the work or image. **Data Values (controlled):** AAT
Creator	CREATOR, CONTRIBUTOR	The names, appellations, or other identifiers assigned to an individual, group, corporate body, or other entity that has contributed to the design, creation, production, manufacture, or alteration of the work or image. **Data Values (controlled):** recommend ULAN and AAAF (LC authority files).
Date	DATE, COVERAGE	Date or range of dates associated with the creation, design, production, presentation, performance, construction, or alteration, etc. of the work or image.

Table 13.7 VRA Core categories, Version 3.0 (cont.).

VRA 3.0	Dublin Core	Description
Location	CONTRIBUTOR, COVERAGE	The geographic location or name of the repository, building, or site-specific work or other entity whose boundaries include the Work or Image. **Data Values (controlled):** BHA index, AAAF (LC), Grove's Dictionary of Art Location Appendix
ID Number	IDENTIFIER	The unique identifiers of a Work or an Image.
Style/Period	COVERAGE, SUBJECT	A defined style, historical period, group, school, dynasty, movement, etc. whose characteristics are represented in the Work or Image. **Data Values (controlled):** recommend AAT
Culture	COVERAGE	The name of the culture, people (ethnonym), or adjectival form of a country name from which a Work or Image originates or with which the Work or Image has been associated. **Data Values:** recommend AAT, LCSH
Subject	SUBJECT	Terms or phrases that describe, identify, or interpret the Work or Image and what it depicts or expresses. **Data Values:** recommend AAT, TGM, ICONCLASS, Sears Subject Headings
Relation	RELATION	Terms or phrases describing the identity of the related work and the relationship between the Work being catalogued and the related work.
Description	DESCRIPTION	A free-text note about the Work or Image, including comments, description, or interpretation, that gives additional information not recorded in other categories.
Source	SOURCE	A reference to the source of the information recorded about the work or the image.
Rights	RIGHTS	Information about rights management; may include copyright and other intellectual property statements required for use.

```
Record Type = work
Type = print
Title = This is how it happened
Title.Variant = As Sucedi
Measurements.Dimensions = 24.5 x 35 cm
Material.Medium = ink
Material.Support = paper
Technique = etching
Technique = drypoint
Creator.Personal Name = Francisco Jose de Goya y Lucientes
Creator.Role = printmaker
Date.Creation = ca. 1810-1814
Location.Current Repository = Ann Arbor (MI,USA), University of
Michigan Museum of Art
Location.Creation Site = Madrid (ESP)
ID Number. Current Accession = 1977/2.15
Style/Period = Romanticism
Culture = Spanish
Subject = war
Relation.Part of = Part of Disasters of war
Description = This is how it happened is No. 47 (33) from the
series "The Disasters of War", 4th edition, plates for the series
ca. 1810-14, 1820, 4th edition was published 1906.
Rights = Weber family trust
```

Fig. 13.7a A dataset describing an etching in a museum collection (VRA, 2002).

```
Record Type = image
Type = digital
Title = general view
Measurements.Dimensions = 72 dpi
Measurements.Format = jpeg
Technique = scanning
Creator = Fred Technician
Date.Creation = 1999
Location.Current Repository = Ann Arbor (MI,USA), University of
Michigan Museum of Art
ID Number.Current Repository = PCD5010-1611-1037-27
ID Number.Current Repository = 1977_2.15.jpeg
Description = For more information, see
http://www.si.umich.edu/Art_History/demoarea/details/1977_2.15.html
Source = University of Michigan Museum of Art
Rights = University of Michigan Museum of Art
```

Fig. 13.7b A dataset describing a digital image of the etching (VRA, 2002).

13.4 Semantic Annotation of Art Images

In this section, we describe a tool for the semantic annotation and search of collections of art images, following Hollink et al. (2003). The description concentrates on how the tool combines the VRA Core categories with WordNet and three thesauri to provide semantic annotations for art images, rather than on the design of the interface and other details. The thesauri used are the AAT, ULAN, and IconClass, an iconographic classification system that provides a hierarchically organized set of concepts for describing the content of visual resources (van den Berg 1995).

Fragments of WordNet and the three thesauri were first translated into RDF triples, resulting in over half a million triples, as shown in Table 13.8.

Table 13.8 Number of RDF triples in the combined ontologies.

Source	Triples
WordNet 1.5 (limited to hyponym relations)	280,558
AAT — Art & Architecture Thesaurus	179,410
IconClass (partial)	15,452
ULAN (limited to painters)	100,607
Total	576,027

WordNet and the thesauri were then aligned, with the help of the subClassOf and equivalentClass relationships, as well as domain-specific relationships. These relationships were superimposed onto the ontologies, preserving their original definitions. Such an approach is fully consistent with the Semantic Web guideline that emphasizes ontology reuse.

For example, the *artistic movements* branch of WordNet was linked to the equivalent *styles and periods* subtree of AAT. Similarly, the WordNet concept *wife* was linked to the AAT concept *wives* (the preferred terms in AAT are always in the plural).

When differences in the structure of the thesauri are significant, it is feasible to define equivalence relationships only at the most specific branches of the hierarchies. In this case, the RDFS subClassOf relationship was used to create links at a higher level in the hierarchies. For example, the WordNet concept *artist* and the AAT concept *artist* are not equivalent, because the WordNet concept includes subconcepts such as *musician*. Therefore, the AAT concept *artist* was linked to the WordNet concept *artist* by a subClassOf relationship.

Examples of domain-specific relationships are those linking painting techniques to materials and artists in ULAN and painting styles in AAT. Hence, Picasso is linked to Cubism, Matisse is linked to Fauve, Van Gogh to Impressionism, and so on.

The tool adopted the VRA metadata scheme, grouping the core elements into three sets:

- Production-related descriptors: *Title, Creator, Date, Style/Period, Technique, Culture*, and *Relation*
- Physical descriptors: *Materials.Medium, Materials.Support, Measurements, Type*, and *Record Type*
- Administrative descriptors: *Location, Collection ID, Source* and *Rights*

Following the VRA Data Standards Committee recommendation, each element was bound to one or more subtrees of the thesauri or WordNet. For example:

- *Style/Period* was bound to two subtrees in AAT containing the appropriate style and period concepts
- *Culture, Technique, Style/Period, Type, Record Type, Material.Support,* and *Material.Medium* were bound to parts of AAT
- *Creator* was bound to ULAN

Two VRA data elements, *Description* and *Subject*, which describe the content of the image, received a different and very interesting treatment. The values for these elements are sets of structured statements of the form *"agent / action / object / recipient"* (Tam and Leung 2001). Each statement should have at least an agent or an object. Moreover, each role must use terms selected from specific parts of the ontologies.

For example, the painting in which Chagall kisses his wife, and gets flowers from her, can be described by the following two statements (the source of the term is shown in parentheses):

```
1. Agent:       "Chagall, Marc"    (ULAN)
2. Action:      "kiss"             (WordNet)
3. Recipient:   "wives"            (AAT)

1. Agent:       "woman"            (WordNet)
2. Action:      "give"             (WordNet)
3. Object:      "flower"           (WordNet)
4. Recipient:   "Chagall, Marc"    (ULAN)
```

This strategy avoids the problem of parsing natural language descriptions, while maintaining some of naturalness. It also facilitates image retrieval, as described later in this section.

The tool explores this combination of VRA metadata elements and ontologies to implement both a module to help users create the semantic annotations and a module to search image collections.

For example, consider the following text describing a painting by Marc Chagall:

```
Chagall, Marc
Birthday
1915
Oil on cardboard
31 3/4 x 39 1/4 in.
The Museum of Modern Art, New York
```

The annotation tool may parse the above text and derive, or at least suggest, values for some VRA elements, as follows

- *Title:*   Birthday
- *Creator:*   Chagall, Marc
- *Date:*   1915
- *Measurements:*   31 3/4 x 39 1/4 in
- *Location:*   The Museum of Modern Art, New York
- *Technique:*   Oil painting
- *Style/Period:*   Surrealist
- *Culture:*   Russian

Indeed, the value of *Technique* is deduced by analyzing the phrase "oil on cardboard," and the values of *Style/Period* and *Culture* are deduced from the value of *Creator*.

The application also incorporates a module to help annotators create structured statements to populate the *Description* and *Subject* elements. For example, consider the painting "Portrait of Derain" by Maurice de Vlaminck, whose content can be described by the following statement (the source of the term is again shown in parentheses).

```
1. Agent:    "Derain, Andre"             (ULAN)
2. Action:   "smoke"                     (WordNet)
3. Object:   "pipes(smoking equipment)" (AAT)
```

Because role values are taken from specific parts of the ontologies, the module may help the annotator select the appropriate (and correct) term to fill in each role. Indeed, for annotation purposes, the ontologies help provide the right context for finding an adequate index term. Moreover, the hierarchical organization of the thesauri helps disambiguate terms. For example, in the above example, the word "pipes" is used in the sense of "smoking equipment" and not in the sense, say, of "plumbing system components" (in fact, AAT returns 51 entries when searched for the term 'pipes'). In general, an annotation is most effective if the annotator chooses the concepts as specifically as possible, and focuses on agent and object descriptions.

Hollink et al. (2004b) describe experiments about what users look for in images that might help fine tune image annotations to increase recovery precision.

We conclude with brief remarks about how the search module uses ontologies to increase image recall.

The module offers both unrestricted term search and template-guided search. In the first mode, the module searches for image annotations such that the term occurs anywhere in the annotation. However, the module also uses the ontologies to expand the search by including equivalent terms. For example, suppose that the user wants to search for images associated with "Aphrodite" (as a Greek deity). Because WordNet contains an equivalence relation between "Venus" (as a Roman deity) and "Aphrodite" (as a Greek deity), the module expands the search and also retrieves images such that "Venus" (as a Roman deity) occurs anywhere in the annotation.

In the second mode, the module allows the user to exploit the annotation template for search proposes. For example, the user may restrict her search for images in which the term "Netherlandish" occurs in the value of the *Culture* element. Again, the module uses the ontologies to expand the search. In this case, it also retrieves images of Dutch and Flemish paintings, because these are subconcepts of "Netherlandish."

References

Baca, M.; Harpring, P. (Ed.) (2005) Categories for the Description of Works of Art (CDWA) - List of Categories and Definitions. The J. Paul Getty Trust. Available at: http://www.getty.edu/research/conducting_research/standards/cdwa/8_printing_options/d efinitions.pdf.

Boeuf, P. Le (2006) Using an ontology-driven system to integrate museum information and library information. In: *Proceedings of the Symposium on Digital Semantic Content across Cultures*, Paris, the Louvre, 4–5 May 2006. Available at: http://www.seco.tkk.fi/ events/2006/2006-05-04-websemantique/presentations/articles/LeBoeuf-DigSemAcross Cultures_200605_LeBoeuf.pdf.

CIDOC (2006) CIDOC Conceptual Reference Model. Available at: http://cidoc.ics.forth.gr/.

Crofts, N.; Doerr, M.; Gill, T. (2003) The CIDOC Conceptual Reference Model: A standard for communicating cultural contents. In: Cultivate Interactive [on line], Issue 9. February 2003. Available at: http://www.cultivate-int.org/issue9/chios/

Getty (2006a) Learn about the Getty Vocabularies. The J. Paul Getty Trust. Available at: http://www.getty.edu/research/conducting_research/vocabularies/.

Getty (2006b) Art & Architecture Thesaurus Online. The J. Paul Getty Trust. Available at: http://www.getty.edu/research/conducting_research/vocabularies/aat/aat_about.pdf.

Getty (2006c) Data Standards and Guidelines. The J. Paul Getty Trust. Available at: http://www.getty.edu/research/conducting_research/standards/.

Hollink, L.; Nguyen, G.; Schreiber, G.; Wielemaker, J.; Wielinga, B.; Worring, M. (2004a) Adding spatial semantics to image annotations. In: *Proceedings of the Fourth International Workshop on Knowledge Markup and Semantic Annotation at ISWC'04*.

Hollink, L.; Schreiber, A.Th.; Wielemaker, J.; Wielinga, B. (2003) Semantic annotation of image collections. In: *Proceedings of the KCAP'03 Workshop on Knowledge Capture and Semantic Annotation*, Florida, USA, October 2003.

Hollink, L.; Schreiber, A.Th.; Wielinga, B.; Worring, M. (2004b) Classification of user image descriptions. *International Journal of Human Computer Studies* 61/5, pp. 601–626.

Hollink, L.; Worring, M.; Schreiber, A.Th. (2005) Building a visual ontology for video retrieval. In: *Proceedings of the Thirteenth Annual ACM International Conference on Multimedia*, Hilton, Singapore, pp. 479–482.

Hunter, J. (2001) Adding Multimedia to the Semantic Web - Building an MPEG-7 ontology. In: *Proceedings of the First Semantic Web Working Symposium, SWWS'01.*

Isaac, A. (2005) Accessing cultural heritage collections using Semantic Web techniques. In: *Proceedings of the Digitaal Erfgoed Conferentie*, 9-10 November 2005. Available at: http://www.den.nl/bestanden/Conferentie_2005/A_Isaac.pdf.

ISO (2001) Multimedia Content Description Interface - Part 3: Visual. ISO/IEC 15938-3 FCD Information Technology. March 2001, Singapore.

ISO (2006) Information and Documentation - A reference ontology for the interchange of cultural heritage information. Draft International Standard ISO 21127:2006. International Organization for Standardization. Available at: http://www.niso.org/international/SC4/n500.pdf.

McRae, L.; Lanzi, E.; Baca, M. (2001) Project proposal for guide to good practice: Cataloging standards for describing cultural objects and images. Visual Resources Association Data Standards Committee. January 12, 2001.

Mintzer, F. et. al. (2001) Populating the Hermitage Museum's new Web site. *Communications of the ACM (CACM)*, Vol. 44, N. 8, August 2001, pp. 52–60.

Tam, A.M.; Leung, C. H. C. (2001) Structured natural-language description for semantic content retrieval of visual materials. *Journal of the American Society for Information Science and Technology*, Volume 52, Issue 11, pp. 930–937 (Published online: 10 Aug 2001).

van Assem, M.; Gangemi, A.; Schreiber, G. (2005) RDF/OWL Representation of WordNet. Editor's Draft 17 October 2005. W3C Org.

van den Berg, J. (1995) Subject retrieval in pictorial information systems. In: Electronic Filing, Registration, and Communication of Visual Historical Data. Abstracts for Round Table no 34 of the 18th International Congress of Historical Sciences. Copenhagen, pp. 21–28, 1995. Available at: http://www.iconclass.nl.

VRA (2002) VRA Core Categories, Version 3.0. Visual Resources Association Data Standards Committee. Available at: http://www.vraweb.org/vracore3.htm#core.

14

Geospatial Semantic Web

14.1 Introduction

The large volume of geospatial data available on the Web opens up unprecedented opportunities for data access and data interchange, facilitating the design of new geospatial applications and claiming for the redesign of traditional ones. However, to interoperate, geospatial applications must be able to locate and access the data sources, and agree both on the syntax and on the semantics of the data that flow between them. Achieving interoperability is more difficult in this case simply because geospatial data are much more complex than conventional data, with respect to both syntax and semantics.

A convenient way to provide universal access (over the Web) to geospatial data sources is to implement *geospatial Web services* that encapsulate the data sources, because this strategy obviates the need for traditional means of data distribution. Furthermore, as pointed out in Lieberman et al. (2005), geospatial Web services would benefit from the adoption of Semantic Web technologies, thereby becoming understandable to the applications. This evolution includes the development and encoding of formal geospatial ontologies, which would leverage existing standards. The result is called the *Geospatial Semantic Web*.

A major enabling technology of the Geospatial Semantic Web is the service-oriented architecture, which in turn depends on interoperability standards related to all aspects of geospatial service operations. The geospatial community has already developed a set of specifications through standard-setting bodies, including the *ISO Technical Committee 211* (TC 211), the *Open Geospatial Consortium* (OGC), the European Community initiative *Infrastructure for Spatial Information in Europe* (INSPIRE), and the U.S. *Federal Geospatial Data Committee* (FGDC).

The geomatics standardization activity under the ISO TC 211 is developing a family of international standards that will: (1) support the understanding and usage of geospatial information; (2) increase the availability, access, integration, and sharing of geospatial information, enabling interoperability of geospatial computer systems; and (3) facilitate the establishment of geospatial infrastructures on the local, regional, and global level. The work is divided into over 40 projects that resulted or will result in standard definitions.

The OGC comprises more than 310 companies, government agencies, and universities with the purpose of creating and promoting the development of technologies that facilitate interoperability between systems that process spatial and location data. The OGC working groups publish their results as interface specifications and standards for data interchange.

INSPIRE is an initiative of the European Commission to implement a European Spatial Data Infrastructure, built on the principle that it must be possible to seamlessly combine spatial information from different sources across Europe, and share it between many users and applications.

The FGDC is a U.S. interagency committee that coordinates the sharing of geospatial data through a portal that searches metadata held within the National Spatial Data Infrastructure (NSDI) Clearinghouse Network. The network is a collection of metadata catalogues, known as Clearinghouse Nodes. Each node is hosted by a different organization and contains metadata that describe geospatial data within the area of responsibility of the organization.

This chapter overviews the technologies that facilitate the development of the Geospatial Semantic Web, emphasizing the role of standard proposals. Each technology is first discussed from a broad perspective and then illustrated with implemented applications.

14.2 Basic Geospatial Concepts

In this section, we summarize a minimum set of geospatial concepts required for the understanding of the next sections.

Geospatial data relates to geography, location, addresses, or a place on the Earth's surface. The term is often used in place of other terms such as maps, geographic data, or spatial data, but it also includes digital imagery of the Earth. Examples are property records, elevation, migratory routes, crime scenes, and burned areas.

Geospatial services are applications that process geospatial data. There are many types of geospatial services, such as Web mapping services, spatial analysis services, metadata services, and visualization services. A service may be tightly coupled with a specific dataset or dataset collection, or loosely coupled, otherwise.

A *feature* is an abstraction of a real world phenomenon and a *geospatial feature* is a feature associated with a location relative to the Earth (Percivall 2002). Geospatial features are usually classified into types (or classes), such as bays, rivers, cities, and so on, with well-defined characteristics. Feature types are in turn organized according to specific aspects, such as rivers and creeks are hydrographic feature types, and cities and environmental protection areas are administrative areas.

Note that geospatial datasets typically contain representations of the locations of a set of features, as in a map, or portray a set of features, as in a remote sensing image. We address the problem of classifying geospatial features in Section 14.3.

A *geospatial field* is a function that maps points of a domain region on the Earth's surface into values from a given set, the range of the function. For example, a vegetation map associates each point of the domain region with a specific type of vegetation, whereas a gravimetric map associates each point of the domain region with a real value.

A *coordinate reference system* (CRS) defines how geospatial data relate to real locations on the Earth's surface. The specific details of the CRS used for geospatial data need not concern us here. It suffices to point out that the specification of the location of a geospatial feature or the domain region of a geospatial field must include the CRS used.

A *gazetteer* (Fitzke and Atkinson 2006) defines a vocabulary consisting of identifiers, location descriptions, and attributes for a set of geospatial features, typically from a well-defined region, such as a country. A gazetteer therefore helps applications locate the desired geospatial features by their names or by a limited set of attribute values. We discuss gazetteers in Section 14.4.

A *metadata catalogue* stores descriptions of datasets housed in data sources (Nebert and Whiteside 2005), offering services to query and update metadata, and to request datasets from the data sources. Note that, typically, a catalogue does not store the datasets themselves. We describe two geospatial metadata standards in Section 14.5, and discuss geospatial metadata catalogues in Section 14.6.

As defined in Chapter 7, a *Web service* is a software system designed to support machine-to-machine interaction over a network. It has an interface described in WSDL and interacts with other components using SOAP messages. A *geospatial Web service* is a Web service that manipulates geospatial data. We briefly address geospatial Web services in Section 14.7.

Finally, a *spatial data infrastructure* is an integrated set of services that allow users to identify and access geospatial data from several sources. We provide two examples of spatial data infrastructures in Section 14.8.

14.3 Classifying Geospatial Features

In this section, we address how to define geospatial feature types (or classes). We first discuss how to construct *feature type thesauri*, which is the preferred way to organize geospatial features in a gazetteer. Then, we expand the discussion to consider ontologies that explore more complex relationships than those thesauri offer.

14.3.1 Geospatial Feature Type Thesauri

Recall from Chapter 2, that a *thesaurus* is defined as "the vocabulary of a controlled indexing language, formally organized so that a priori relationships between concepts (for example as 'broader' and 'narrower') are made explicit" (ISO 1986).

Table 14.1 Thesaurus relationships according to the ISO-2788 guidelines.

Relationship	Abbr.	Description
Scope Note	**SN**	a note attached to a term to indicate its meaning within an indexing language.
Use	**USE**	the term that follows the symbol is the preferred term when a choice between synonyms or quasi-synonyms exists.
Use For	**UF**	the term that follows the symbol is a nonpreferred synonym or quasi-synonym.
Top Term	**TT**	the term that follows the symbol is the name of the broadest class to which the specific concept belongs; sometimes used in the alphabetical section of a thesaurus.
Broader Term	**BT**	the term that follows the symbol represents a concept having a wider meaning.
Narrower Term	**NT**	the term that follows the symbol refers to a concept with a more specific meaning.
Related Term	**RT**	the term that follows the symbol is associated, but is not a synonym, a quasi-synonym, a broader term, or a narrower term.

A thesaurus usually provides a binary relationship between terms and annotations (Scope Note) and six binary relationships between terms, as summarized in Table 14.1.

The ADL Gazetteer effort exemplifies the difficulties of constructing a feature type thesaurus (Hill et al. 1999; Hill 2000). The ADL Feature Type Thesaurus (FTT) is the result of amalgamating a number of other gazetteer classifications and geospatial dictionaries. The FTT Version 2.0 of July, 2002 contains nearly 200 top terms and 3000 relationships. The topmost terms are:

```
1.  administrative areas
2.  hydrographic features
3.  land parcels
4.  manmade features
5.  physiographic features
6.  regions
```

Table 14.2 shows the *Narrow Term* hierarchy rooted at regions. Table 14.3 lists the same *Narrow Term* relationships, together with a few entries of the *Used For* and *Related Term* relationships involving such terms, to illustrate how thesauri relationships are used in the FTT.

Table 14.2 The narrow term/broader term hierarchy rooted at `regions`.

```
regions                          regions (cont.)
. agricultural regions           . climatic regions
. biogeographic regions          . coastal zones
. . barren lands                 . economic regions
. . deserts                      . land regions
. . forests                      . . continents
. . . petrified forests          . . islands
. . . rain forests               . . . archipelagos
. . . woods                      . . subcontinents
. . grasslands                   . linguistic regions
. . habitats                     . map regions
. . jungles                      . . chart regions
. . oases                        . . map quadrangle regions
. . shrublands                   . . UTM zones
. . snow regions
. . tundras
. . wetlands
```

Table 14.3 Selected relationships involving terms under region.

Term	Rel.	Term
regions	NT	biogeographic regions
regions	NT	cadastral areas
regions	NT	climatic regions
regions	NT	coastal zones
regions	NT	economic regions
regions	NT	firebreaks
regions	NT	land regions
regions	NT	map regions
regions	NT	research areas
regions	RT	ocean regions
land regions	UF	lake districts
land regions	UF	lake regions
land regions	NT	continents
land regions	NT	islands
land regions	NT	subcontinents
land regions	BT	regions
islands	UF	atolls
islands	UF	cays
islands	UF	island arcs
islands	UF	isles
islands	UF	islets
islands	UF	keys (islands)
islands	UF	land-tied islands
islands	UF	mangrove islands
islands	NT	archipelagos
islands	RT	bars (physiographic)
islands	BT	land regions

---

islands » *A feature type category for places such as the island of Manhattan.*

Used for: » *The category **islands** is used instead of any of the following.*

- atolls
- cays
- island arcs
- isles
- islets
- keys (islands)
- land-tied islands
- mangrove islands

Broader Terms: land regions » *islands is a subtype of "land regions.."*
Related Terms: » *The following is a list of other categories related to **islands** (non-hierarchical relationships)*

- bars (physiographic)

Scope Note: Tracts of land smaller than a continent, surrounded by the water of an ocean, sea, lake or stream. [Glossary of Geology, 4th ed.]. » *Definition of islands .*

Fig. 14.1 Complete thesaurus entry for the term `islands` with explanations.

Figure 14.1 shows the complete FTT entry for the term `islands` with explanations where (sentences after the symbol "»" are treated as comments):

- The *Scope Note (SN)* clause shows the definition adopted for the term `islands`
- The *Used For (UF)* clauses indicate the nonpreferred terms that should be replaced by the term `islands`
- The *Broader Term (BT)* clause indicates that the term `islands` is classified under the term `land regions`
- The *Related Terms (RT)* clause points to other thesauri terms related to `islands`

In the construction of the ADL Feature Type Thesaurus, the choice of the preferred terms took into account their frequency of use in the reference sources. Closely related terms were entered as nonpreferred terms and linked to the preferred term via *Related Term* relationships, as illustrated in Fig. 14.1. The depth of the hierarchy was determined based on the specificity needed by the ADL gazetteer. Terms more specific than needed were entered as nonpreferred terms pointing to the broader term. For example, `atolls` are a specific type of `islands` that the FTT defines as a nonpreferred term related to `islands` by the *Used For* relationship. Therefore, a user searching for features classified as `atolls` will be redirected to `islands`.

14.3.2 Geospatial Feature Ontologies

As summarized at the end of Section 2.2.3, organizing a set of terms as a thesaurus has intrinsic limitations: (1) the set of term relationships is fixed, as shown in Table 14.1; and (2) term definitions are not formalized, in the sense that they are just natural language text linked to terms by Scope Notes.

Such limitations become apparent, for example, when one tries to automatically align two thesauri, even if they refer to the same concepts, for various reasons. The syntax of the terms is not a safe indication that they denote the same concept; the thesauri may in fact be written in different (natural) languages. The *Narrow Term* relationships (i.e., the hierarchy of terms) are likely to be different, reflecting the original purposes of the thesauri. One cannot directly rely on an automatic analysis of term definitions because they are not formalized. Lastly, a simple analysis of the definitions based on the frequency of occurrences of similar words might end up with wrong alignments.

Consider, for example, the definitions for the term `bay` from the ADL gazetteer and for the terms `bay` and `island` from the GEOnet Names Server (GNS) (URL: http://gnswww.nga.mil/geonames/GNS/index.jsp):

1. (ADL) bay: *indentation*s of a *coast*line or shoreline enclosing a part of a body of **water**; bodies of **water** partly **surrounded** by **land.**
2. (GNS) bay: a *coast*al *indentation* between two capes or headlands, larger than a cove but smaller than a gulf.
3. (GNS) island: tracts of **land**, smaller than a continent, **surrounded** by **water** at high **water.**

The reader may verify that the term `bay` from ADL has three words in common with the term `island` from GNS ("**water**", "**surrounded**", and "**land**"), and two with the term `bay` from GNS, even considering just the radix of the words ("*coast*al" "*indentation*s"). Therefore, an automatic alignment tool that compares term definitions based only on word frequency might end up aligning the term `bay` from ADL with the term `island` from GNS.

A strategy to circumvent this problem would be to use a geospatial vocabulary borrowed from an upper-level ontology, such as OpenCYC, as a *pivot vocabulary*. In this strategy, each thesaurus would be manually aligned with the pivot vocabulary. That is, each term from the thesaurus would be linked to a term of the pivot vocabulary, say, by a *Scope Note* relationship. Hence, two terms from different thesauri would be aligned if they were linked to the same term of the pivot vocabulary.

A much more sophisticated approach to create classifications for geospatial features would be to adopt full-fledged ontologies, which provide much more powerful constructs to define and relate classes. By doing so, one would be able to resort to OWL reasoners to analyze the classifications. In the rest of this subsection, we discuss three examples of such ontologies.

#$Island *islands*

A specialization of both #$LandBody and #$IslandOrIslandGroup. Each instance of #$Island is a body of land surrounded by water. #$Islands are typically much smaller in area than (instances of the similarly-defined collection of) #$TrueContinents (q.v.), though it would be rather arbitrary to try to distinguish these types on the basis of size alone. (And note that #$ContinentOfAustralia, e.g., is both an #$IslandOrIslandGroup (q.v.) and a #$TrueContinent.) For groups of #$Islands that form a geographical cluster, see #$Archipelago.

guid: bd58bb39-9c29-11b1-9dad-c379636f7270
direct instance of: #$ConventionalClassificationType #$ExistingObjectType
direct specialization of: #$LandBody #$IslandOrIslandGroup

(Cyc® Knowledge Base Copyright© 1995-2002 Cycorp, Inc., Austin, TX, USA.)

Fig. 14.2 Definition of the term `island` from OpenCYC.

The OpenCYC Selected Vocabulary and Upper Ontology — Geography (OpenCYC 2002) provides an example of a classification for geospatial features, using a proprietary ontology language. For example, Fig. 14.2 shows the definition of the term island.

Originally written in SUO-KIF, the Suggested Upper Merged Ontology (SUMO) (SUMO 2006; Niles and Pease 2001) organizes concept definitions into three levels (with the corresponding namespaces):

- SUMO Top Level: high-level abstractions of SUMO
  (http://reliant.teknowledge.com/DAML/SUMO.owl#)

- MILO (Mid-Level Ontology): a bridge between the abstract content of SUMO and the rich details of the various domain ontologies
  (http://reliant.teknowledge.com/DAML/Mid-level-ontology.owl#)

- Ontology of Geography: contains a number of classes that correspond to geospatial concepts, and instances that represent geospatial features; organized in the parts: (I) the Geography Terms for the CIA World Fact Book; and (II) the General Geography Terms and Background
  (http://reliant.teknowledge.com/DAML/Geography.owl)

Figure 14.3 contains a fragment of SUMO, in OWL, ending on the class Island. This fragment, albeit fairly long, does not come close to illustrating the richness of the definitions that SUMO contains.

```
<rdf:RDF xmlns:rdf="http://www.w3.org/1999/02/22-rdf-syntax-ns#"
         xmlns:rdfs="http://www.w3.org/2000/01/rdf-schema#"
         xmlns:owl="http://www.w3.org/2002/07/owl#"
         xmlns="http://reliant.teknowledge.com/DAML/SUMO.owl#">

<!-- copyright 2003 (c) Teknowledge  -->
...

<rdfs:Class rdf:ID="Region">
  <rdfs:subClassOf rdf:resource="#Object"/>
  <rdfs:comment>A topographic location. Regions encompass surfaces
of Objects, imaginary places, and Geographic Areas. Note that a
Region is the only kind of Object which can be located at itself.
Note too that Region is not a subclass of SelfConnectedObject,
because some Regions, e.g. archipelagos, have parts which are not
connected with one another.
  </rdfs:comment>
</rdfs:Class>
...

<rdfs:Class rdf:ID="GeographicArea">
  <rdfs:subClassOf rdf:resource="#Region"/>
  <rdfs:comment>A geographic location, generally having definite
boundaries. Note that this differs from its immediate superclass
Region in that a GeographicArea is a three-dimensional Region of the
earth. Accordingly, all astronomical objects other than earth and
all one-dimensional and two-dimensional Regions are not classed
under GeographicArea.
  </rdfs:comment>
</rdfs:Class>
...

<rdfs:Class rdf:ID="LandArea">
  <rdfs:subClassOf rdf:resource="#GeographicArea"/>
  <rdfs:comment>An area which is predominantly solid ground, e.g. a
Nation, a mountain, a desert, etc. Note that a LandArea may contain
some relatively small WaterAreas. For example, Australia is a
LandArea even though it contains various rivers and lakes.
  </rdfs:comment>
</rdfs:Class>
...

<rdfs:Class rdf:ID="Island">
  <rdfs:subClassOf rdf:resource="#LandArea"/>
  <rdfs:comment>A LandArea that is completely surrounded by a
WaterArea.</rdfs:comment>
</rdfs:Class>
...
</rdf:RDF>
```

Fig. 14.3 A fragment of SUMO ontology ending on the class `Island`.

The *Semantic Web for Earth and Environmental Terminology* (SWEET) provides an upper-level ontology for the Earth system sciences (SWEET 2006; Raskin 2006). The SWEET ontologies include several thousand terms, grouped into facet ontologies, whose classes are connected by properties. For example, the *EarthRealm* ontology covers physical properties of the planet. It contains classes corresponding to realms, such as Ocean, and subclasses corresponding to the associated subrealms, such as "ocean floor". For comparison, Figures 14.4a, 14.4b, and 14.4c show the definition of the class island.

```xml
<?xml version="1.0" encoding="UTF-8" ?>

<rdf:RDF xmlns:rdf="http://www.w3.org/1999/02/22-rdf-syntax-ns#"
 xmlns:owl="http://www.w3.org/2002/07/owl#"
 xmlns:xsd="http://www.w3.org/2001/XMLSchema#"
 xmlns:rdfs="http://www.w3.org/2000/01/rdf-schema#"
 xmlns:substance="http://sweet.jpl.nasa.gov/ontology/substance.owl#"
 xmlns:space="http://sweet.jpl.nasa.gov/ontology/space.owl#"
 xmlns:numerics="http://sweet.jpl.nasa.gov/ontology/numerics.owl#"
 xmlns:property="http://sweet.jpl.nasa.gov/ontology/property.owl#"
 xmlns="http://sweet.jpl.nasa.gov/ontology/earthrealm.owl#">

<owl:Ontology rdf:about="">
  <dc:title>Earthrealm</dc:title>
  <dc:date>1/27/2004 2:59:58 PM</dc:date>
  <dc:creator>SWEET project</dc:creator>
  <dc:description></dc:description>
  <dc:subject></dc:subject>
  <owl:versionInfo>1.0</owl:versionInfo>
  <owl:imports
   rdf:resource="http://purl.org/dc/elements/1.1/"/>
  <owl:imports
  rdf:resource="http://sweet.jpl.nasa.gov/ontology/substance.owl" />
  <owl:imports
   rdf:resource="http://sweet.jpl.nasa.gov/ontology/space.owl" />
  <owl:imports
   rdf:resource="http://sweet.jpl.nasa.gov/ontology/numerics.owl" />
  <owl:imports
   rdf:resource="http://sweet.jpl.nasa.gov/ontology/property.owl" />
</owl:Ontology>
...
<owl:Class rdf:ID="Ocean">
  <rdfs:subClassOf rdf:resource="#BodyOfWater" />
  <rdfs:subClassOf>
    <owl:Class>
      <owl:complementOf>
        <owl:Class rdf:about="#LandWaterObject" />
      </owl:complementOf>
    </owl:Class>
  </rdfs:subClassOf>
</owl:Class>
```

Fig. 14.4a A fragment of the SWEET Earthrealm Ontology ending on the class Island.

```
<owl:Class rdf:ID="LandRegion">
  <rdfs:subClassOf>
    <owl:Restriction>
      <owl:onProperty rdf:resource=
"http://sweet.jpl.nasa.gov/ontology/space.owl#isPartOf" />
      <owl:allValuesFrom>
        <owl:Class>
          <owl:unionOf rdf:parseType="Collection">
            <owl:Class rdf:about="#LandSurfaceLayer" />
            <owl:Class rdf:about="#LandwaterSurfaceLayer" />
          </owl:unionOf></owl:Class>
      </owl:allValuesFrom>
    </owl:Restriction>
  </rdfs:subClassOf>
  <rdfs:subClassOf>
    <owl:Restriction>
      <owl:onProperty rdf:resource="#hasEcosystemType" />
      <owl:allValuesFrom rdf:resource="#TerrestrialEcosystem" />
    </owl:Restriction>
  </rdfs:subClassOf>
  <rdfs:subClassOf>
    <owl:Class>
      <owl:complementOf>
        <owl:Class rdf:about="#OceanRegion" />
      </owl:complementOf>
    </owl:Class>
  </rdfs:subClassOf>
  <rdfs:subClassOf rdf:resource="#TopographicalRegion" />
</owl:Class>
...
<owl:Class rdf:ID="OceanRegion">
  <rdfs:subClassOf>
    <owl:Restriction>
      <owl:onProperty rdf:resource=
"http://sweet.jpl.nasa.gov/ontology/space.owl#isPartOf" />
      <owl:allValuesFrom rdf:resource="#Ocean" />
    </owl:Restriction>
  </rdfs:subClassOf>
  <rdfs:subClassOf>
    <owl:Restriction>
      <owl:onProperty rdf:resource="#hasEcosystemType" />
      <owl:allValuesFrom rdf:resource="#MarineEcosystem" />
    </owl:Restriction>
  </rdfs:subClassOf>
  <rdfs:subClassOf rdf:resource="#TopographicalRegion" />
</owl:Class>
...
```

Fig. 14.4b A fragment of the SWEET Earthrealm Ontology ending on the class Island.

```
<owl:Class rdf:ID="LandwaterRegion">
  <rdfs:subClassOf>
    <owl:Restriction>
      <owl:onProperty rdf:resource=
"http://sweet.jpl.nasa.gov/ontology/space.owl#isPartOf" />
      <owl:someValuesFrom rdf:resource="#LandwaterSurfaceLayer" />
    </owl:Restriction>
  </rdfs:subClassOf>
  <rdfs:subClassOf rdf:resource="#LandRegion" />
</owl:Class>
...
<owl:Class rdf:ID="Island">
  <rdfs:subClassOf>
    <owl:Restriction>
      <owl:onProperty rdf:resource=
"http://sweet.jpl.nasa.gov/ontology/space.owl#surroundedBy_2D" />
      <owl:allValuesFrom>
        <owl:Class>
          <owl:unionOf rdf:parseType="Collection">
            <owl:Class rdf:about="#OceanRegion" />
            <owl:Class rdf:about="#LandwaterRegion" />
          </owl:unionOf>
        </owl:Class>
      </owl:allValuesFrom>
    </owl:Restriction>
  </rdfs:subClassOf>
  <rdfs:subClassOf rdf:resource="#LandRegion" />
</owl:Class>
...
</rdf:RDF>
```

Fig. 14.4c A fragment of the SWEET Earthrealm Ontology ending on the class `Island`.

To summarize, OpenCYC and SUMO provide little more than a hierarchy of geospatial concepts, just as the ADL Feature Type Thesaurus does. The SWEET ontology goes further and uses OWL class restrictions to capture the semantics of the geospatial concepts. In turn, such class restrictions depend on the SWEET facets that model concepts related to time, space, and numerical extents (Raskin 2006).

In general, the creation of a rich geospatial feature ontology depends on defining specific ontologies to capture the semantics of geospatial metric operators and topological relationships, as already recognized in Egenhofer (2002) and in Hobbs (2005). However, as pointed out in Raskin (2006), a deficiency of RDF and OWL is that these languages provide no direct support for numerical concepts, and must rely on the XML Schema datatypes, which do not include operations or relations over those concepts.

Finally, as a benchmark for geospatial feature ontologies, one may select a small set of GNS (or ADL) definitions and check if they can be formalized in the ontology. For example, consider the GNS definition of "island" as "a tract of land, smaller than a continent, surrounded by water at high water." To formalize this concept, the ontology must capture the notions of "tract", "smaller", "surrounded by", and "high", provided that the concepts of "land", "continent", and "water" are already in the ontology.

14.4 Gazetteers

14.4.1 Examples of Gazetteers

The common-sense geospatial reference system relies on explicitly naming geospatial features. This form of geospatial reference is usually supported by geospatial dictionaries, called *gazetteers*, containing lists of geospatial names, together with their geospatial locations and other descriptive information.

Most atlases have a gazetteer section that can be used to look up a geospatial name and find the pages where the corresponding geospatial feature appears. Digital gazetteers, readily available on the Web, have been developed to support geospatial information systems. They typically store the name, type, a point-based footprint, and a parent administrative area for each geospatial feature. They also provide various services to handle the stored data.

We now briefly describe some well-known digital gazetteers. The Getty Thesaurus of Geospatial Names (TGN 2004) is a structured, world-coverage vocabulary of 1.3 million names, coordinates, and other information for around 892,000 geospatial places. For each place name, the TGN maintains a unique id, a set of place types taken from the Art and Architecture Thesaurus (see Section 12.2.1), alternative versions of the name, a containing administrative region, and a footprint in the form of a point in latitude and longitude.

The U.S. Geological Survey's *Geospatial Names Information System* (GNIS) and the National Imagery and Mapping Agency's *Geospatial Names Processing System* (GNPS) are maintained in cooperation with the U.S. Board of Geospatial Names (BGN). GNIS contains information about almost 2 million physical and cultural geospatial features in the United States and its territories (GNIS 2005). The *GEOnet Names Server* (GNS) provides access to the National Geospatial-Intelligence Agency and the BGN database of foreign geospatial names, containing about 4 million features with 5.5 million names.

The Alexandria Digital Library (ADL) Project (Smith and Frew 1995; Smith 1996; Hill et al. 1999; Frew et al. 2000) is a research project for modeling, educational applications, and software components. The ADL Project also developed HTML clients to access the ADL collections and gazetteer.

The ADL Gazetteer prototype to evaluate digital library architectures, and gazetteer applications, has approximately 5.9 million geospatial names, classified according to the ADL Feature Type Thesaurus, discussed in Section 14.3.1. It combines data from the GNIS (U.S. names) and the GNPS (non-U.S. names). The ADL Catalogue stores the georeferenced holdings of the Map & Imagery Laboratory (UCSB Davidson Library), with more than 2 million items. Metadata for the catalogue holdings combine elements taken from the USMARC standard (USMARC 1976) and from the FGDC metadata scheme, discussed in Section 14.5.1. The complete metadata scheme has about 350 elements.

Finally, we mention Geonames (URL: http://www.geonames.org), which provides free access to a database with over six million entries for geographical names. The data are accessible through a user interface, as well as through Web services that offer geocoding based on geographical names or postal codes.

14.4.2 Standards for Gazetteers

In this section, we briefly discuss standards for gazetteer data and interfaces. The geomatics standardization activity under ISO Technical Committee 211 published a standard for gazetteer data, the ISO 19112:2003 *Spatial Referencing by Geospatial Identifiers* (ISO 2003), which defines a conceptual schema and guidelines for describing indirect spatial (noncoordinate) reference systems. Table 14.4 lists some of the attributes defined for gazetteer entries.

The ADL Gazetteer Content Standard supports rich descriptions of geospatial features that go beyond those of most traditional gazetteers. Table 14.5 contains the major sections of the ADL standard, which may be further divided into subsections for encoding more detailed information. For example, the streetAddressSection is divided into streetAddress, city, stateProvince, postalCode, and country.

Table 14.4 Selected attributes of the ISO 19112 conceptual schema.

Attribute	Comment
geospatial identifier	a unique identifier for the feature taken from a given identifier space
alternative identifiers	one or more alternative identifiers
name	the preferred name for the feature
type	the type of the feature, typically taken from a feature type thesaurus
description	a description of the feature
position	coordinates of a representative point of the feature
temporal extent	a description of the temporal extension of the feature
geospatial extent	a description of the geospatial extension of the feature
administrator	organization responsible for maintaining the feature's name
parent	identifier of the parent feature of which the entry is a subdivision
child	identifiers of the features that the entry is a parent

Table 14.5 Selected attributes of the ADL Gazetteer Content Standard.

Attribute	Comment
featureID	unique identifier for the feature
featureName	the names for the feature
classSection	the primary type of the feature
codeSectionType	the code associated with the feature
spatialLocation	the map location of the feature
streetAddressSection	the street address of the feature
relatedFeature	relationships of the feature with other features
description	a short narrative description of the feature
featureData	data about the feature, such as population or elevation
featureLink	Web site that provides information on the feature
supplementalNote	note explaining unusual circumstance of the feature
entryMetadata	documents about entry and modification dates

The Open GIS Consortium has been developing a Web Gazetteer Service standard (Fitzke and Atkinson 2006) for distributed access to gazetteers. The gazetteer service interface specifies four operations that can be requested by a client and performed by a gazetteer service:

- *GetCapabilities* (required implementation by servers): allows a client to request and receive back service metadata (or *capabilities*), which are documents that describe the abilities of the specific server implementation. This operation also supports negotiation of the specification version being used for client-server interactions.

- *DescribeFeatureType* (mandatory implementation by servers): allows a client to retrieve an XML schema document that describes the structure of any feature type the server can service.

- *GetFeature* (mandatory implementation by servers): allows a client to retrieve feature instances. In addition, the client should be able to specify which feature properties to fetch and should be able to constrain the query spatially and non-spatially.

- *GetGMLObject* (optional implementation by servers): allows a client to retrieve element instances by traversing XLinks that refer to their XML IDs.

14.5 Geospatial Metadata

14.5.1 Geospatial Metadata Standards

Recall from Chapter 9 that the term *metadata* designates "data about other data," that is, metadata describe the data content, historic information about the data, how the data were obtained, and so on. Therefore, metadata facilitate interoperability by describing details about the data, which applications may explore to access the data. In fact, Haas and Carey (2003) point out that the lack of proper metadata is one of the top ten reasons why federated databases may fail.

We consider geospatial metadata schemas specified by two authorities, the U.S. Federal Geospatial Data Committee (FGDC) and the International Organization of Standards (ISO).

The FGDC defined the *Content Standard for Digital Geospatial Metadata* (CSDGM) (FGDC 1998), originally published in 1994 and revised in 1998. The FGDC is currently leading the development of a U.S. profile of the international metadata standard, ISO 19115:2003, discussed next.

The geomatics standardization activity under ISO Technical Committee 211 published, among others, three international metadata specifications:

- ISO 19115:2003 provides metadata elements about the identification, the extent, the quality, the spatial and temporal schema, spatial reference, and distribution of digital geospatial data (ISO 2003)
- ISO 19119:2005 provides metadata elements to describe geospatial information services (ISO 2005)
- ISO 19139 defines a formal encoding and structure of ISO metadata for exchange (ISO 2006)

A catalogue service should therefore support metadata according to the ISO 19115:2003 and ISO 19119:2005, and publish XML encoding consistent with the ISO 19139 or profiles thereof. These and related standards can be found in the form of ontologies in Islam et al. (2004).

In the next three subsections, we briefly outline the CSDGM and the ISO 19115:2003 and ISO 19119:2005 specifications.

14.5.2 The FGDC Metadata Standard

The *Content Standard for Digital Geospatial Metadata* (CSDGM) (FGDC 1998) establishes a common set of terminologies and definitions for the documentation of digital geospatial data, including metadata elements for the following topics (FGDC 2000):

- *Identification*: name, developer, geospatial area covered, information themes included, access restrictions, currentness
- *Data Quality*: positional and attribute accuracy, completeness, consistency, provenance

- *Spatial Data Organization*: spatial data model used to encode the spatial data, number of spatial objects, methods other than coordinates, such as street addresses, used to encode locations
- *Spatial Reference*: encoding of coordinate locations, map projection or grid system used, parameters to convert the data to another coordinate system
- *Entity and Attribute Information*: geospatial information (roads, houses, elevation, temperature, etc.) included, information encoding
- *Distribution*: distribution agency, formats and media available, online availability, price
- *Metadata Reference*: timestamp and agency responsible for the metadata compilation

Table 14.6 lists the CSDGM essential metadata elements and Fig. 14.5 shows a sample XML metadata record with such elements.

Table 14.6 Required CSDGM XML tags*.

XML Tag Metadata Element	Description
Data Originator /metadata/idinfo/citation/citeinfo/origin/	the name of an organization or individual that developed the dataset
Data Title /metadata/idinfo/citation/citeinfo/title/	the name by which the dataset is known
Abstract /metadata/idinfo/descript/abstract/	a brief narrative summary of the dataset
Progress /metadata/idinfo/status/progress	the state of the dataset
West Bounding Coordinate /metadata/idinfo/spdom/bounding/westbc/	westernmost coordinate of the limit of coverage expressed in longitude
East Bounding Coordinate /metadata/idinfo/spdom/bounding/eastbc/	easternmost coordinate of the limit of coverage expressed in longitude
North Bounding Coordinate /metadata/idinfo/spdom/bounding/northbc/	northernmost coordinate of the limit of coverage expressed in latitude
South Bounding Coordinate /metadata/idinfo/spdom/bounding/southbc/	southernmost coordinate of the limit of coverage expressed in latitude
Theme Keyword /metadata/idinfo/keywords/theme/themekey/	common-use word or phrase used to describe the subject of the dataset
Metadata Contact Organization /metadata/metainfo/metc/cntinfo/cntorgp/cntorg/	the name of the organization to which the contact type applies
Metadata Contact Person /metadata/metainfo/metc/cntinfo/cntperp/cntper/	the name of the individual to which the contact type applies
Metadata Contact Address City /metadata/metainfo/metac/cntinfo/cntaddr/city/	the city of the address

*Adapted from (FGDC 2006b).

Table 14.6 Required CSDGM XML tags (cont.)*.

XML Tag Metadata Element	Description
Metadata Contact Address State or Province /metadata/metainfo/metac/cntinfo/cntaddr/state/	the state or province of the address
Metadata Contact Address Postal Code /metadata/metainfo/metac/cntinfo/cntaddr/postal/	the ZIP or other postal code of the address
Publication Date /metadata/idinfo/citation/citeinfo/pubdate/	the date when the dataset is published or otherwise made available for release
Purpose /metadata/idinfo/descript/purpose/	a summary of the intentions with which the dataset was developed
Time Period of Content: Single Date /metadata/idinfo/timeperd/timeinfo/sngdate/caldate Time Period of Content: Range of Dates, Beginning Date /metadata/idinfo/timeperd/timeinfo/rngdates/begdate/ Time Period of Content: Range of Dates, Ending Date /metadata/idinfo/timeperd/timeinfo/rngdates/enddate/	time period(s) for which the dataset corresponds to the currentness reference
Currentness Reference /metadata/idinfo/timeperd/current/	the basis on which the time period of content information is determined
Maintenance and Update Frequency /metadata/idinfo/status/update	the frequency with which changes and additions are made to the dataset after the initial dataset is completed
Theme Keyword Thesaurus /metadata/idinfo/keywords/theme/themekt/	reference to a formally registered thesaurus or a similar authoritative source of theme keywords
Access Constraints /metadata/idinfo/accconst/	restrictions and legal prerequisites for accessing the dataset
Use Constraints /metadata/idinfo/useconst/	restrictions and legal prerequisites for using the dataset after access is granted
Metadata Contact Address Type /metadata/metainfo/metc/cntinfo/cntaddr/addrtype/	the information provided by the address
Metadata Contact Phone number /metadata/metainfo/metc/cntinfo/cntvoice/	the telephone number by which individuals can speak to the organization or individual
Metadata Date /metadata/metainfo/metd	the date that the metadata were created or last updated

*Adapted from (FGDC 2006b).

```
<?xml version="1.0" encoding="ISO-8859-1" ?>
   <metadata>
   <idinfo>
     <citation>
       <citeinfo>
           <origin>   Louisiana State University Coastal
                   Studies Institute
         </origin>
                 <pubdate>20010907</pubdate>
                 <title> Geomorphology and Processes of
                     Land Loss in Coastal Louisiana,
                     1932 - 1990
             </title>
       </citeinfo>
     </citation>
     <descript>
       <abstract>A raster GIS file that identifies the land loss
process and geomorphology associated with each 12.5 meter
pixel of land loss between 1932 and 1990. Land loss processes
are organized into a hierarchical classification system that
includes subclasses for erosion, submergence, direct removal,
and undetermined. Land loss geomorphology is organized into a
hierarchical classification system that includes subclasses
for both shoreline and interior loss.
       </abstract>
       <purpose>The objective of the study was to determine the
land loss geomorphologies associated with specific processes
of land loss in coastal Louisiana.
       </purpose>
     </descript>
     <timeperd>
       <timeinfo>
         <rngdates>
             <begdate>1932</begdate>
             <enddate>1990</enddate>
         </rngdates>
       </timeinfo>
       <current>ground condition</current>
     </timeperd>
     <status>
       <progress>Complete</progress>
       <update>None planned</update>
     </status>
     <spdom>
       <bounding>
          <westbc>-92.000057</westbc>
          <eastbc>-88.81416</eastbc>
          <northbc>30.498417</northbc>
          <southbc>28.914905</southbc>
       </bounding>
     </spdom>
   <keywords>
```

```
      <theme>
         <themekt>ISO 19115 Topic Category</themekt>
         <themekey>biota</themekey>
      </theme>
      <theme>
         <themekt>none</themekt>
         <themekey>land loss</themekey>
         <themekey>wetlands</themekey>
         <themekey>geomorphology</themekey>
         <themekey>landscape ecology</themekey>
      </theme>
   </keywords>
   <accconst>none</accconst>
   <useconst>The metadata should be read completely prior to
use of the dataset.
Data were collected and compiled as 12.5 meter pixels and
should not be extended beyond the reasonable limits of the
resolution. This is not a survey data product and should not
be utilized as such.
   </useconst>
   </idinfo>
   <metainfo>
      <metd>20010907</metd>
      <metc>
        <cntinfo>
          <cntorgp>
            <cntorg> Louisiana State University Coastal
                  Studies Institute
            </cntorg>
          </cntorgp>
          <cntaddr>
            <addrtype>mailing and physical address</addrtype>
            <city>Baton Rouge</city>
            <state>LA</state>
            <postal>70803</postal>
          </cntaddr>
          <cntvoice>(225) 578-2395</cntvoice>
        </cntinfo>
      </metc>
      <metstdn> FGDC Content Standards for Digital
            Geospatial Metadata
      </metstdn>
      <metstdv>FGDC-STD-001-1998</metstdv>
   </metainfo>
</metadata>
```

Fig. 14.5 A sample XML metadata record with CSDGM essential elements (FGDC 2006b).

14.5.3 The ISO 19115:2003 Metadata Standard

The ISO 10115:2003 introduces an extensive set of metadata elements, of which, typically, only a subset is used. It presents metadata as UML packages, containing UML classes, which have attributes that identify the *metadata elements*. That is, a metadata element and a class attribute are synonymous. A data dictionary accompanies the UML description.

Tables 14.7a and 14.7b list the core metadata elements, selected to answer the following questions: "Does a dataset on a specific topic exist ('what')?", "For a specific place ('where')?", "For a specific date or period ('when')?", and "A point of contact to learn more about or order the dataset ('who')?"

The ISO 19115:2003 also defines a set of *topic categories*, shown in Table 14.8, which offer a high-level geospatial data thematic classification to assist in the grouping and search of available geospatial datasets.

Finally, to illustrate the use of the ISO 19115:2003, Fig. 14.6 shows the first few entries of a sample metadata, taken from Annex I of ISO (2003).

Table 14.7a ISO 19115:2003 Mandatory Core metadata elements[1,2].

Metadata Element	Description
Dataset title (Q)	name by which the cited resource is known
Dataset reference date (Q)	reference date for the cited resource
Dataset language	language(s) used within the dataset
Dataset topic category	main theme(s) of the dataset
Abstract describing the dataset (Q)	brief narrative summary of the content of the resource(s)
Metadata point of contact	identification of and means of communicating with person(s) and organization(s) using the resource(s)
Metadata date stamp	date that the metadata was created

Notes:
1. Tables 14.7a and 14.7b are adapted from Annex B — Data dictionary for geospatial metadata of ISO (2003).
2. The indication "Q" after the name of the elements is explained in Section 14.6.

Table 14.7b ISO 19115:2003 Conditional Core metadata elements.

Metadata Element	Description
Geographic location of the dataset (Q) (by 4 coordinates or by geographic id)	geographic area of the dataset
Dataset character set	full name of the character coding standard used for the dataset
Metadata language	language used for documenting metadata
Metadata character set	full name of the character coding standard used for the metadata set
Dataset responsible party	identification of, and means of communication with, persons and organizations associated with the dataset
Spatial resolution of the dataset	level of detail expressed as a scale factor or a ground distance
Distribution format (Q)	provides a description of the format of the data to be distributed
Additional extent information for the dataset (vertical or temporal)	information about horizontal, vertical, and temporal extent
Spatial representation type	digital mechanism used to represent spatial information
Reference system (Q)	description of the spatial and temporal reference systems used in the dataset
Lineage	general explanation of the data producer's knowledge about the lineage of a dataset
Online Resource	information about online sources from which the dataset, specification, or community profile name and extended metadata elements can be obtained
Metadata file identifier	unique identifier for this metadata file
Metadata standard name	name of the metadata standard (including profile name) used
Metadata standard version	version (profile) of the metadata standard used

Table 14.8 ISO 19115:2003 topic categories.

Name	Definition
	Examples
farming	rearing of animals or cultivation of plants
	agriculture, irrigation, aquaculture, plantations, herding, pests/diseases affecting crops and livestock
biota	flora and/or fauna in natural environment
	wildlife, vegetation, biological sciences, ecology, wilderness, sea life, wetlands, habitat
boundaries	legal land descriptions
	political and administrative boundaries
climatologyMeteorologyAtmosphere	processes and phenomena of the atmosphere
	cloud cover, weather, climate, atmospheric conditions, climate change, precipitation
economy	economic activities, conditions and employment
	production, labor, revenue, commerce, industry, tourism and ecotourism, forestry, fisheries, commercial or subsistence hunting, exploration and exploitation of resources such as minerals, oil, and gas
elevation	height above or below sea level
	altitude, bathymetry, digital elevation models, slope, derived products
environment	environmental resources, protection, and conservation
	environmental pollution, waste storage and treatment, environmental impact assessment, monitoring environmental risk, nature reserves, landscape
geoscientificInformation	information pertaining to earth sciences
	geophysical features and processes, geology, minerals, sciences dealing with the composition, structure, and origin of the earth's rocks, risks of earthquakes, volcanic activity, landslides, gravity information, soils, permafrost, hydrogeology, erosion
health	health, health services, human ecology, and safety
	disease and illness, factors affecting health, hygiene, substance abuse, mental and physical health, health services

Table 14.8 ISO 19115:2003 topic categories (cont.).

Name	Definition
	Examples
imageryBaseMapsEarthCover	base maps
	land cover, topographic maps, imagery, unclassified images, annotations
intelligenceMilitary	military bases, structures, activities
	barracks, training grounds, military transportation, information collection
inlandWaters	inland water features, drainage systems, and their characteristics
	rivers and glaciers, salt lakes, water utilization plans, dams, currents, floods, water quality, hydrographic charts
location	positional information and services
	addresses, geodetic networks, control points, postal zones and services, place names
oceans	features and characteristics of salt water bodies (excluding inland waters)
	tides, tidal waves, coastal information, reefs
planningCadastre	information used for appropriate actions for future use of the land
	land use maps, zoning maps, cadastral surveys, land ownership
sociology	characteristics of society and cultures
	settlements, anthropology, archaeology, education, traditional beliefs, manners, and customs, demographic data, recreational areas and activities, social impact assessments, crime and justice, census information
structure	man-made construction
	buildings, museums, churches, factories, housing, monuments, shops, towers
transportation	means and aids for conveying persons and/or goods
	roads, airports/airstrips, shipping routes, tunnels, nautical charts, vehicle or vessel location, aeronautical charts, railways
utilitiesCommunication	energy, water, and waste systems and communications infrastructure and services
	hydroelectricity, geothermal, solar and nuclear sources of energy, water purification and distribution, sewage collection and disposal, electricity and gas distribution, data communication, telecommunication, radio, communication networks

```
MD_Metadata
+identificationInfo
MD_DataIdentification
citation:
. CI_Citation
. title: Exploration Licences for Minerals
. date:
. CI_Date
. dateType: 001
. date: 193001
abstract: Location of all current mineral Exploration Licences issued under the Mining Act, 1971.
Exploration Licences provide exclusive tenure rights to explore for mineral resources for up to a
maximum of 5 years. Comment is sought on applications for Exploration Licences from
numerous sources before granting. Exploration programs are subject to strict environmental
and heritage conditions. Exploitation of identified resources must be made under separate
mineral production leases.
      ...
extent:
.. EX_Extent
........ +geographicElement
........ EX_GeographicBoundingBox
.. .... westBoundLongitude: 129.0
.. .... eastBoundLongitude: 141.0
.. .... southBoundLatitude: -26.0
.. .... northBoundLatitude: -38.5
........ description: South Australia
language: en
      ...
+referenceSystemInfo
MD_ReferenceSystem
referenceSystemIdentifier:
. RS_Identifier
. code: GDA 94
. codeSpace: DIPR
fileIdentifier: ANZSA1000001233
language: en
characterSet: 001
contact:
CI_ResponsibleParty
role: 002
organisationName: Department of Primary Industries and Resources SA
dateStamp: 20000803
metadataStandardName: ISO 19115
metadataStandardVersion: FDIS
dataset: https://info.pir.sa.gov.au/geometa/migs/MIGS_Down_cat.jsp
```

Fig 14.6 Sample metadata following the ISO 19115:2003 standard (Annex I of ISO (2003)).

14.5.4 The ISO 19119:2005 Service Metadata Standard

The ISO 10119:2005 introduces metadata elements that describe services, rather than data (Percivall 2002; ISO 2005). The metadata elements for a service provide sufficient information to allow a client to invoke the service based on the metadata record. If a service instance is tightly coupled with a dataset instance, the service metadata describes both the service and the geospatial dataset, using the ISO 19115 specification for the latter. For the loosely coupled case, dataset metadata need not be provided in the service metadata.

Table 14.9 summarizes the mandatory service metadata elements, and Table 14.10 introduces a geospatial services taxonomy. Table 14.11 indicates how the ISO 19100 series standards relate to the services taxonomy.

Table 14.9 ISO 19119:2005 mandatory service metadata elements*.

Section	Element	Description
Service Identification		provides a general description of the service sufficient to allow a client to invoke the service
	serviceType	a service type name from a registry of services
	containsOperations	provides information about the operations that comprise the service
Operation Metadata		describes the signature of one and only one method provided by the service
	operationName	a unique identifier for this interface
	DCP	distributed computing platforms on which the operation has been implemented
	connectPoint	handle for accessing the service interface
Service Provider		describes an organization that provides services
	providerName	a unique identifier for this organization
	serviceContact	information for contacting the service provider
Data Identification		(data available from a particular service, defined using elements of ISO 19115)
Operation Chain Metadata	name	the name, as used by the service for this chain
Parameter	name	the name, as used by the service for this parameter
	Optionality	indication if the parameter is required
	Repeatability	indication if more than one value of the parameter may be provided

*Adapted from Annex C, data dictionary for geospatial service metadata (ISO 2005).

Table 14.10 Geospatial services taxonomy.

Classification	Selected Examples
Geographic human interaction services	- Catalogue viewer - Geographic viewer - Geographic feature editor - Geographic symbol editor
Geographic model/ information management services	- Feature access service: provides a client access to and management of a feature store - Map access service: provides a client access to pictures of - geographic data - Catalogue service: provides discovery and management services on a store of metadata about instances - Gazetteer service: provides access to a directory of instances of a class or classes of real-world phenomena containing some information regarding position
Geographic workflow/ task management services	- Chain definition service: service to define a chain and to enable it to be executed by the workflow enactment service - Workflow enactment service: interprets a chain and controls the instantiation of services and sequencing of activities
Geographic processing services	- modify feature attributes
spatial	- Coordinate conversion service - Dimension measurement service
thematic	- Thematic classification service - Spatial counting service
temporal	- Temporal reference system transformation service - Temporal proximity analysis service
metadata	- Geographic annotation services
Geographic communication services	- Encoding service - Transfer service
Geographic system management services	(none identified).

Table 14.11 Mapping ISO 19100 series standards to service categories.

Service Category	Relevant ISO 19100 Series Standard
Geographic human interaction services	19117 Geographic information — Portrayal
	19128 Geographic information — Web Map server interface
Geographic model/ Information management services	19107 Geographic information — Spatial schema
	19110 Geographic information — Methodology for feature cataloguing
	19111 Geographic information — Spatial referencing by coordinates
	19112 Geographic information — Spatial referencing by geographic identifiers
	19115 Geographic information — Metadata
	19123 Geographic information — Schema for coverage geometry and functions
	19125-1 Geographic information — Simple feature access — Part 1: Common architecture
	19128 Geographic information — Web Map server interface.
Geographic Workflow/ Task management services	(no relevant ISO 19100 series standards)
Geographic processing service	19107 Geographic information — Spatial schema
	19108 Geographic Information — Temporal schema
	19109 Geographic information — Rules for application schema
	19111 Geographic information — Spatial referencing by coordinates
	19116 Geographic information — Positioning services
	19123 Geographic information — Schema for coverage geometry and functions
	19118 Geographic information — Encoding
Geographic communication services	(no relevant ISO 19100 series standards)
Geographic system management services	(no relevant ISO 19100 series standards)

14.6 The OGC Catalogue Specification

The OGC Catalogue Services Specification Catalogue (OGC)Catalogue (Nebert and Whiteside 2005) is a general model for catalogue services. It defines interfaces to publish and access digital catalogues of metadata for geospatial data, services, and related resource information. The specification is in fact a framework, in the sense that it leaves open, to a certain extent, the specific catalogue scheme, the query language, the format of the result sets, and how the catalogue should be updated. This point is important to accommodate different catalogue implementations and increase the opportunities for interoperability.

In this section, we outline a specialization of the framework for managing metadata resources that comply with ISO 19115:2003 and ISO 19119:2005 (Senkler et al. 2004; Voges and Senkler 2006). The discussion that follows refers to this particular specialization.

The catalogue services support:

- *Publishing* metadata, that is, inserting new metadata into the catalogue, either by the owner of the georesource or by a broker that acts on behalf of the owner.

- *Discovering* metadata, either by browsing the content of the catalogue or querying the catalogue.

- *Harvesting* metadata, that is, uploading new metadata from records located elsewhere.

Figure 14.7 shows the reference architecture for OGC-compliant catalogue services. The architecture is a multitier arrangement of clients and servers. The application client interfaces with the catalogue service using the OGC catalogue interface. The catalogue service may respond to an application request by accessing a local metadata repository, a resource service, or another catalogue service.

The catalogue discovery interface offers the following operations:

- *GetCapabilities:* allows clients to retrieve service metadata from a server.

- *GetRecords:* allows clients to search the catalogue and receive the results of the search.

- *GetRecordById:* retrieves the default representation of catalogue records.

- *DescribeRecord:* allows a client to discover elements of the information model supported by the target catalogue service.

- *GetDomain:* used to obtain runtime information about the range of values of a metadata record element or request parameter.

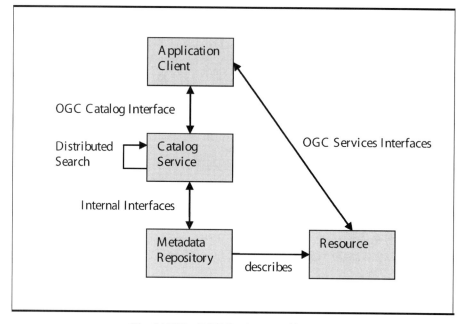

Fig. 14.7 The OGC Catalogue architecture.

The catalogue manager interface offers two operations:

- *Transaction Operation:* this operation allows clients to create, modify, and delete catalogue records (i.e., to "push" metadata into the catalogue).

- *Harvest Operation:* this operation only references the data to be inserted or updated in the catalogue, and it is the job of the catalogue service to resolve the reference, fetch those data, and process them into the catalogue (i.e., to "pull" metadata into the catalogue).

The specification defines a minimum set of *queryable* metadata elements, marked as "Q" in Table 14.7, to which *GetRecords* operations may refer (specific implementations may support additional elements). The specification also defines that the results must be returned as XML documents created using a new group of public metadata elements, expressed using the nomenclature and syntax of Dublin Core metadata. In other words, the metadata repository may have its own organization, as long as the catalogue services that encapsulate the repository accept this minimum set of queryable metadata elements and return results in the appropriate markup. This strategy, therefore, allows for maximum flexibility while guaranteeing minimum interoperability capability.

We leave an example of a catalogue federation to Section 14.8.2, where we discuss the U.S. National Spatial Data Infrastructure (NSDI).

14.7 Geospatial Web Services

In this section, we outline the effort of the Open Geospatial Consortium to define a set of specifications for geospatial Web services. The discussion is meant to instigate the reader to visit the OGC Web site (URL: www.opengeospatial.org) and browse through the documentation. Indeed, several OGC specifications have already become ISO standards, or permeated to SQL:2003, the latest version of the relational query language SQL (Eisenberg et al. 2004).

As an implementation example, we briefly address the *HDF-EOS Web GIS Software Suite (NWGISS) Project* (Di et al. 2001). Again, we refer the reader to the OGC Web site for a comprehensive list of implementations.

14.7.1 The OGC Services Framework

The *Open Geospatial Consortium (OGC)* specifications follow a reference architecture, called the *OpenGIS® Services Framework (OSF)* (Percivall 2002; Buehler 2003), that identifies services, interfaces, and exchange protocols that the applications may use. Briefly, the OpenGIS Services Framework consists of (see Fig. 14.8):

- *Coding Standards:* standards that specify geospatial data interchange and storage formats, including spatial reference systems and geospatial object geometry and topology. They include the *Geography Markup Language (GML)*.

- *Application Services:* components that, on the client side, interact with the users and, on the server side, interact with the application and data servers.

- *Registry Services:* components that offer mechanisms to classify, register, describe, search, maintain, and access data about the resources available. They include the *Web Registry Service (WRS)*.

- *Portrayal Services:* components that offer specific support for the visualization of geospatial data, in the form of maps, 3-D terrain perspectives, annotated images, and so on. They include the *Web Map Service (WMS)*, the *Coverage Portrayal Service (CPS)*, and the *Style Management Service (SMS)*.

- *Data Services:* components that offer basic access services to geospatial data. They include the *Web Object Service* (WOS), the *Web Feature Service* (WFS), the *Sensor Collection Service* (SCS), the *Image Archive Service* (IAS), and the *Web Coverage Service* (WCS).

- *Processing Services:* components that operate on geospatial data and provide value-added services for applications. They include gazetteer and catalogue services.

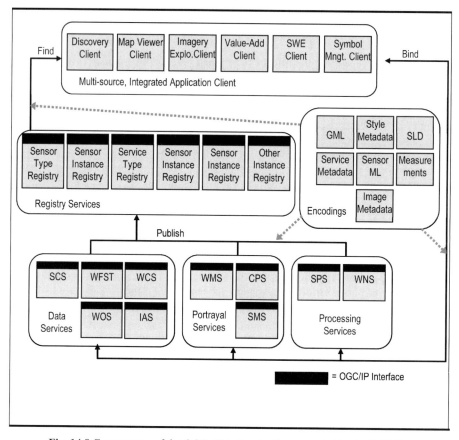

Fig. 14.8 Components of the OGC Web Service Framework (Percivall 2002).

The Geography Markup Language (GML) is an XML markup specification for geospatial data interchange (Cox et al. 2003), defined as an XML schema that contains models for geometries, features, surfaces, and the like. Applications may then define their own XML schemas based on the GML schema types.

The OGC services offer fairly uniform interfaces. For example, the Web Map Service (WMS) defines three interfaces:

- *GetCapabilities* permits a client application to obtain information about the WMS service and about the data stored in the WMS server.

- *GetMap* permits a client application to request a map (sent as an image) that portrays datasets stored in the WMS server.

- *GetFeatureInfo* permits a client application to request data associated with objects portrayed in the current map.

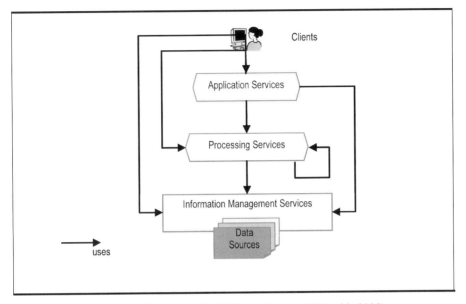

Fig. 14.9 Service tiers in the OWS architecture (Whiteside 2005).

14.7.2 A Geospatial Web Services Architecture

The OSF was developed independently of the W3C protocol architecture for Web services. Only recently, a series of specification proposals, collectively known as the *OpenGIS Web Service 2 Initiative* (Sonnet 2004; Whiteside 2005), defined interfaces that abide by the W3C standards. OGC also started a large-scale experiment to test the concept of a Geospatial Semantic Web (OGC 2005).

The *OGC Web Services (OWS) Architecture* is a service-oriented architecture, with all components providing one or more services to other services or to clients. This service-oriented architecture is based on the fundamental roles of service provider and service consumer within a distributed computing system. It also focuses on interactions among components implementing defined services, in the form of service requests, service responses, and service exceptions.

Following Whiteside (2005), we define:

- A *service* is a distinct part of the functionality that is provided by an entity through interfaces.

- An *interface* is a named set of operations that characterize the behavior of an entity.

- An *operation* is a specification of a transformation or query that an object may be called to execute. It has a name and lists of input and output parameters.

The OGC Web service interfaces use open standards and provide only a few static operations per service. Standard XML-based data encoding formats and languages are used in many server-to-client and client-to-server data transfers. Services are loosely organized into four tiers, as shown in Fig. 14.9.

The information management services tier contains adapters that encapsulate the data sources. The services at this tier usually include some processing of the data retrieved. For example, WMS, WCS, and WFS can perform coordinate transformation and format conversion. The processing services tier contains services designed to process data. The application services tier contains services designed to support clients, especially thin clients, such as Web browsers.

The OWS architecture supports *service chaining*, either *transparently* (defined and controlled by the client), *translucently* (predefined but visible to the client), or *opaquely* (predefined and not visible to client), according to ISO (2005).

14.7.3 Example of an Integrated Collection of Geospatial Web Services

Mission to Planet Earth

The *Mission to Planet Earth* (MTPE) is a NASA project designed to study our planet using data collected by a number of satellites. The *EOS Data and Information System (EOSDIS)* (Kobler et al. 1995) is the component responsible for providing access to the data generated in the context of the MTPE project. It is a distributed system with the following components.

- Distributed Active Archive Centers (DAACs): responsible for processing, archiving, and distributing EOS and related data, and for providing user support.

- Science Data Processing Segment (SDPS): responsible for supporting product generation, data archiving and distribution, and information management.

- Science Investigator-led Processing Systems (SIPSs): process EOS data into standard products.

- Networks, EOS Data and Operations System (EDOS): dedicated resource that supports inter-DAAC data flows for generation of interdependent EOS products.

- Flight Operations Segment (FOS): provides mission planning and scheduling, and monitors health and safety of the spacecraft and instruments.

At present, EOSDIS is managing and distributing data from: EOS missions (Landsat-7, QuikSCAT, Terra and, ACRIMSAT), Pre-EOS missions (UARS, SeaWIFS, TOMS-EP, TOPEX/Poseidon, and TRMM), and all of the Earth Science Enterprise legacy data (e.g., pathfinder datasets). EOSDIS handles extraordinary rates and volumes of scientific data. For example, the Terra spacecraft alone produces 194 GB of data per day, and downlinks data at 150 Mb/s.

Finally, HDF-EOS is the standard file format for storing EOS data.

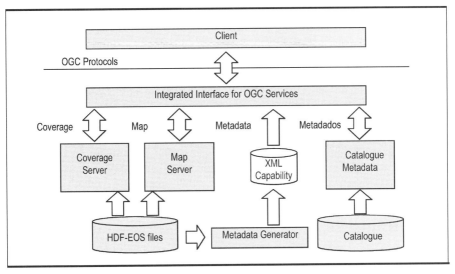

Fig. 14.10 HDF-EOS Web GIS software suite (NWGISS) architecture.

HDF-EOS Web GIS Software Suite (NWGISS) Project

The goal of the *HDF-EOS Web GIS Software Suite (NWGISS) Project* (Di et al. 2001) is to make EOS data available to other applications that follow the OGC specifications. The NWGISS architecture (see Fig. 14.10) consists of three major components: a map server, a coverage server, and a catalogue server. The NWGISS also includes an OGC WCS client.

The map server implements the OGC WMS services for all HDF-EOS data formats. In particular, it generates georeferencing information for a map at runtime, if necessary. The coverage server implements the OGC WCS services for three data formats: HDF-EOS, NITF, and GeoTIFF. The server may resample, cut, and reassemble coverages (geographic fields) in realtime, as well as apply format transformations.

The coverage client implements the OGC WCS specifications. The client acts as a mediator (Gupta et al. 2000) to access coverages in the HDF-EOS, NITF, and GeoTIFF formats, stored at any OGC WCS server (not just those the NWGISS implements). The client supports data access and visualization, among other operations.

The NWGISS client is a limited mediator that allows the user to select coverages from one or more sources, using their metadata, and to visualize them together, among other operations.

14.8 Examples of Spatial Data Infrastructures

A *spatial data infrastructure* (SDI) delivers integrated spatial information services, which should allow users to identify and access spatial or geographical information from a wide range of sources, from the local level to the global level, in an interoperable way for a variety of uses. One of the main elements of these infrastructures is a *geoportal*, which facilitates access to the spatial data and provides complementary services. *Catalogue geoportals* facilitate accessing metadata catalogues, whereas *application portals* provide dynamic geospatial Web services.

This section introduces two initiatives, the European Community INSPIRE, and the U.S. National Spatial Data Infrastructure (NSDI), the latter supported by a catalogue geoportal. Comprehensive surveys of SDI initiatives around the globe can be found in Crompvoets et al. (2005) and Bregt and Crompvoets (2005).

14.8.1 INSPIRE

Overview

The *Infrastructure for Spatial Information in Europe* (INSPIRE) is an initiative of the European Commission to implement a European Spatial Data Infrastructure, built on the basis of the following principles (INSPIRE 2004):

- Data should be collected once and maintained at the level where this can be done most effectively.

- It must be possible to seamlessly combine geospatial data from different sources across Europe and share it among many users and applications.

- It must be possible for data collected at one level to be shared among all the different levels, for example, detailed for detailed investigations, and general for strategic purposes.

- Geospatial data needed for good governance at all levels should be abundant and widely available under conditions that do not restrain its extensive use.

- It must be easy to discover which geospatial data are available, fit the needs for a particular use, and under what conditions they can be acquired and used.

- Geospatial data must become easy to understand and interpret because they can be visualized within the appropriate context and selected in a user-friendly way.

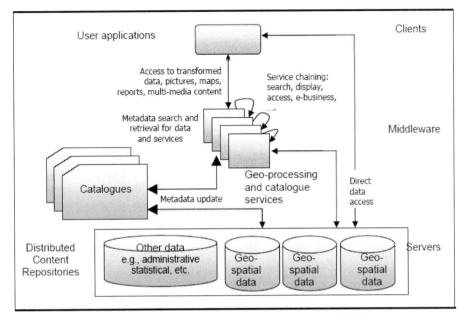

Fig. 14.11 The architecture reference model for INSPIRE.

Architecture

The INSPIRE architecture (Smits 2002) considers a network of SDIs that follow the reference model shown in Fig 14.11. The reference model distinguishes four major groups of components: user applications, geoprocessing and catalogue services, catalogues, and content repositories

User applications include general-purpose interfaces for querying, and viewing, a tool for database administrators, and analytical applications tailored to the information needs of the user. Geoprocessing and catalogue services may process user queries, draw maps from data, regulate access, perform payment operations, and extract and send data to a user application. Content repositories provide data. Finally, catalogues allow clients and services to find out what repositories or services are available and appropriate for their use.

Reference Data and Metadata

The INSPIRE Reference Data and Metadata (RDM) (Rase et al. 2002) describe the necessary geographical reference data and their metadata. The following components form the geographical reference data:

- Geodetic reference data
- Units of administration
- Units of property rights (parcels, buildings)
- Addresses

- Selected topographic themes (hydrography, transport, height)
- Orthoimagery
- Geographical names

The list of the common aspects include: geodetic reference system, quality, maintenance, interoperability, resolution/scale, and implementation priorities, language and culture, and metadata. We refer the reader to Rase et al. (2002) for a complete discussion of all such aspects.

As for metadata, the RDM group recommends that:

- All the reference data should be documented by metadata
- The three aspects of metadata must be considered: discovery, access, and use
- A metadata profile compatible with ISO 19115 must be developed
- Metadata shall be kept up to date
- The member states shall identify a competent authority for coordinating the national producers of data and for managing the metadata information systems
- Priority should be given to create a one-stop geoportal for discovering and accessing geospatial data

14.8.2 NSDI

Overview

The U.S. *National Spatial Data Infrastructure* (NSDI) is a virtual network designed to enable the development and sharing of U.S. digital geographic information resources. The goals of the NSDI are: to reduce duplication of efforts among agencies; to improve quality and reduce costs related to geographic information; to make geographic data more accessible to the public; to increase the benefits of using available data; and to establish key partnerships with states, counties, cities, tribal nations, academia, and the private sector to increase data availability.

The Federal Geographic Data Committee (FGDC) is charged with coordinating the development of the NSDI through three major activities:

- Establishment of a National Geospatial Data Clearinghouse
- Development of standards for data documentation, collection, and exchange
- Development of policies, procedures and partnerships to create a national digital geospatial data framework

NSDI Clearinghouse Network

The National Geospatial Data Clearinghouse Network (FGDC 2006c) is a community of distributed data providers who publish collections of metadata that describe their map and data resources within their areas of responsibility, documenting data quality, characteristics, and accessibility. Each metadata collection, known as a *Clearinghouse Node*, is hosted by an organization to publicize the availability of data within the NSDI. The metadata in these nodes are searched by the geodata.gov portal, discussed next.

The geodata.gov Portal

The geodata.gov is a catalogue of geospatial information containing metadata records and links to maps, features, catalogue services, downloadable datasets, images, clearinghouses, map files, and more. The metadata records are submitted to the portal directly by government agencies, individuals, and companies, or by harvesting the data from geospatial clearinghouses. The portal is operated in support of the *Geospatial One-Stop Initiative* to provide one-stop access to all registered geographic information, and related online access services within the United States.

The Geospatial One-Stop Initiative follows standards intended to establish common requirements to facilitate data exchange for seven themes of geospatial data that are of critical importance to the NSDI. The seven geospatial data themes are: geodetic control, elevation, orthoimagery, hydrography, transportation, cadastral, and governmental unit boundaries. These themes are known as *NSDI framework themes*. The Framework Data Content exchange standard is being processed as an American National Standard through the ANSI-accredited organization, INCITS. It is anticipated to become a formal standard in late 2006. Finally, the portal supports both the FGDC and the ISO metadata standards, discussed earlier in this chapter.

14.9 Example of a Metadata Catalogue for Earth Science Data

In this section, we overview the Global Change Master Directory (GCMD), a metadata catalogue for Earth science data, developed at the NASA Goddard Space Flight Center (Meaux 2005; Olsen 2005). The information in this section was extracted from the GCDM Web site (URL: http://gcmd.gsfc.nasa.gov) with permission (Olsen 2006).

14.9.1 Overview of the GCMD

The *Global Change Master Directory* (GCMD) is a metadata catalogue based on the DIF, Directory Interchange Format (DIF 2006), and the SERF, Services Entry Resources Format (SERF 2006). The DIF is used to create directory entries that describe a group of data. A DIF entry consists of a collection of fields that detail specific information about a group of data. DIF fields are compatible with the ISO 19115. SERF is a *de facto* standard used to create directory entries that describe a group of services. GCMD also supports a set of controlled science keywords.

GCMD allows a user to access subsets by organization (e.g., NOAA metadata records). In general, GCMD supports searches that include spatial and temporal restrictions, as well as restrictions on attributes such as data center, geographical location, science-data platform, topics, and so on. GCMD also offers a metadata authoring tool for adding information to the catalogue, which uses templates that minimize user interaction and contribute to correctness of the metadata.

Fig. 14.12 The Global Change Master Directory (GCMD) Web site.

As illustrated in Fig. 14.12, GCMD supports datasets for the following:

- Agriculture (forest science, soils, etc.)
- Atmosphere (precipitation, air quality, etc.)
- Biosphere (vegetation, zoology, etc.)
- Climate indicators (air temperature, drought conditions, etc.)
- Cryosphere (frozen ground, sea ice, etc.)
- Human dimensions (land use, populations, etc.)
- Hydrosphere (rivers/streams, water quality, etc.)
- Land surface (erosion, topography, etc.)
- Oceans (marine biology, salinity, etc.)
- Paleoclimate (icecores, land records, etc.)
- Solid Earth (geochemistry, seismology, etc.)
- Spectral/engineering (radar, visible imagery, etc.)
- Sun-Earth Interactions (auroras, solar activity, etc.)
- Data centers (locations, instruments, projects, platforms/sources)

The GCMD system supplies data services that can be found by topic, including:

- Data analysis and visualization (GIS, image processing, etc.)
- Data management/handling (archiving, reformatting, sub/supersetting, etc.)
- Education/outreach (interactive programs, etc.)
- Environmental advisories (fire, health, weather, climate, etc.)
- Hazards management (recovery/relief, mitigation, response, etc.)
- Metadata handling (authoring tools, discovery, transformation, conversion, etc.)
- Models (numerical, physical, etc.)
- Reference and information service (bibliographic, subscription services, etc.)

It is worth noting that GCMD is the American Coordinating Node of the Committee on Earth Observation Satellites (CEOS) International Directory Network. CEOS membership encompasses the world's government agencies responsible for civil Earth Observation (EO) satellite programs, along with agencies that receive and process data remotely acquired from space.

GCMD has recognized the importance of customization for partner organizations and is doing so by generating subset views of the GCMD catalogue through portals. Portals have made it easier for organizations to maintain and document their data in one place without duplicating the effort to create another online catalogue.

14.9.2 GCMD and Other Data Sources

GCMD is a mature project. Its value has been recognized both nationally and internationally. In what follows, we briefly discuss GCMD's collaborations with NASA, other U.S. government agencies, and international organizations as an indication of GCMD's maturity and value.

NASA Collaborations

GCMD/NASA collaborations include:

- *NASA Earth Observing System Data Information System (EOSDIS):* GCMD provides dataset descriptions for all of NASA's EOSDIS publicly available data holdings.

- *Federation of Earth Science Information Partners (ESIP):* GCMD collaborates directly with two ESIP and indirectly with others. ESIP include the Distributed Oceanographic Data System (DODS) and the Seasonal and Inter-annual Information Partnership (SIESIP). GCMD has provided a customized ESIP data portal and ESIP services portal to search for ESIP data.

U.S. Government Federal Agency Collaborations

GCMD/Federal Agencies collaborations include:

- *Biological Resources Division (BRD), U.S. Geological Survey:* The BRD provides the scientific understanding and technologies needed to support the sound management and conservation of U.S. biological resources. NASA and the BRD are in a partnership to increase access to ecological data through shared metadata population efforts of the GCMD and the National Biological Information Infrastructure.

- *Geospatial One-Stop (GOS):* Metadata records about NASA's earth science data are being contributed from GCMD to the GOS portal (see Section 14.8.2). GCMD provides access to project-level information as part of NASA's contribution to GOS. A custom portal is available to search NASA projects.

- *National Oceanic and Atmospheric Administration (NOAA):* GCMD continues close collaborations with NOAA through the exchange of metadata information. GCMD is a participant in the NOAA Operational Model Archive and Distribution System (NOMADS) program and has contributed a custom portal for model output datasets.

- *National Spatial Data Infrastructure/Federal Geographic Data Committee (NSDI/FGDC):* GCMD is an NSDI/FGDC participant and a node of the FDGC Clearinghouse (see Chapter 14.8.2). Geospatial data can be searched across many different spatial servers by accessing the clearinghouse gateway.

- *Data Management and Communications (DMAC):* GCMD has contributed to the U.S. Integrated Ocean Observing Program (IOOS) proposed Data Management and Communications (DMAC) system. The GCMD will participate in the search and discovery of IOOS datasets.

- *Marine Metadata Interoperability (MMI):* GCMD is collaborating with the MMI project, a community effort aimed at making marine science datasets easier to find, access, and use. Scientists and data managers can find valuable information about data management and metadata policies on the MMI Web site. GCMD contributes by sharing its extensive list of keywords and metadata expertise with the community.

International Collaborations

GCMD maintains several international collaborations, which include:

- *Committee on Earth Observation Satellites International Directory Network (CEOS IDN):* The CEOS IDN is an international effort to assist researchers in locating information on available datasets. GCMD shares information with other CEOS IDN nodes throughout the world and also provides software, search interfaces, and metadata writing tools.

- *Antarctic Master Directory:* GCMD is collaborating with the Joint Committee on Antarctic Data Management (JCADM), an international effort to make available Antarctic research data holdings. GCMD has developed an Antarctic Master Directory (AMD) to search for Antarctic datasets.

- *United Nations Environmental Programme (UNEP):* GCMD is continuing collaborations with the United Nations Environmental Programme (UNEP) Global Resources Information Database (GRID) to make available dataset descriptions from many nations throughout the world. The UNEP/GRID site in Budapest, Hungary, is a partner in the testing of new GCMD software technologies.

- *The Global Observing Systems Information Center (GOSIC):* GCMD is collaborating with the Global Observing Systems Information Center (GOSIC) to develop a portal to GOSIC data that will be collected by three major observing programs: the Global Climate Observing System (GCOS), the Global Ocean Observing System (GOOS), and the Global Terrestrial Observing System (GTOS). GCMD has contributed a customized Global Observation of Forest Cover (GOFC) portal GOFC, originally a joint program of the Committee on Earth Observation Satellites (CEOS) and GTOS, which now is part of the GTOS program.

- *The International Oceanographic Data and Information Exchange (IODE):* GCMD has collaborated with the International Oceanographic Data and Information Exchange (IODE) by testing the MEDI metadata tool. MEDI is compatible with the Directory Interchange Format (DIF) and IODE has encouraged their data centers to create new MEDI records and send metadata to the GCMD.

Additional examples of international GCMD collaborations are: the Global Ocean Ecosystems Dynamics Project (GLOBEC), the Gulf of Maine Ocean Data Partnership (GoMODP), and the Ocean Biogeographic Information System (OBIS).

Recommended Reading

In this chapter, we covered some of the more stable technologies that will lead to the Geospatial Semantic Web. However, we left out other useful technologies, such as geocoding, defined as "the process of linking words, terms and codes found in a text string to their applicable geospatial features, with known locations" (Margoulies 2001). We have also not touched on the design of search engines that deal with the spatial context implicit in Web documents (Hiramatsu and Reitsma 2004; Souza et al. 2005).

As a starting point for additional reading, we recommend the proceedings of the First International Conference on GeoSpatial Semantics (Rodríguez et al. 2005), especially the keynote address that discusses the development of a common ontology for expressing and reasoning about spatial information for the Semantic Web (Hobbs 2005).

References

ADL (2006) The Alexandria Digital Library Project — Gazetteer. Available at: http://www.alexandria.ucsb.edu/gazetteer/.

ADL (2002) ADL Gazetteer Content Standard. Available at: http://www.alexandria.ucsb.edu/gazetteer/FeatureTypes/ver070302/index.htm.

Bregt, A.; Crompvoets, J. (2005) Spatial data infrastructures: Hype or hit? In: *Proceedings From Pharaohs to Geoinformatics. FIG Working Week 2005 and GSDI-8*. Cairo, Egypt, April 16–21.

Buehler, K. (Ed.) (2003) OpenGIS® Reference Model. Document number OGC 03-040 Version: 0.1.3. Open Geospatial Consortium, Inc.

Cox, S.; Daisey, P.; Lake, R.; Portele, C.; Whitside, A. (Eds.) (2003). OpenGIS® Geography Markup Language (GML) Implementation Specification. Open Geospatial Consortium, Inc.

Crompvoets, J.; Bregt, A.; de Bree, F.; van Oort, P.; Lownen, B.; Rajabifard, A.; Williamson, I. (2005) Worldwide (Status, Development and) Impact Assessment of Geoportals. In: *Proceedings From Pharaohs to Geoinformatics. FIG Working Week 2005 and GSDI-8*. Cairo, Egypt, April 16–21.

Di, L.; Yang, W.; Deng, M.; Deng, M.; McDonald, K. (2001) The prototype NASA HDF-EOS Web GIS Software Suite (NWGISS). In: *Proceedings of the NASA Earth Science Technologies Conference*. Greenbelt, Maryland. August 28-30, (CD-ROM, 4pp). Available at: http://laits.gmu.edu/Papers/NWGISS.htm.

DIF (2006) *Directory Interchange Format (DIF) Writer's Guide*. Global Change Master Directory. National Aeronautics and Space Administration. Available at: http://gcmd.nasa.gov/User/difguide/.

Egenhofer, M.J. (2002) Toward the semantic geospatial Web. In: *Proceedings of the ACM GIS'02*, November 8–9, McLean, Virginia, USA.

Eisenberg, A.; Melton, J.; Kulkarni, K.G.; Michels, J-E..; Zemke, F. (2004) SQL: 2003 has been published. *ACM SIGMOD Record*, Vol. 33, No. 1, pp. 119–126.

FGDC (1998) Content Standard for Digital Geospatial Metadata. Metadata Ad Hoc Working Group, Federal Geographic Data Committee. FGDC-STD-001-1998. Available at: http://www.fgdc.gov/standards/projects/FGDC-standards-projects/metadata/base-metadata/v2_0698.pdf.

FGDC (2000) Content Standard for Digital Geospatial Metadata Workbook. Federal Geographic Data Committee. Available at: http://www.fgdc.gov/metadata/documents/workbook_0501_bmk.pdf.

FGDC (2005) Towards A National Geospatial Strategy & Implementation Plan. Federal Geographic Data Committee. Available at: http://www.fgdc.goc/futuredirections/.

FGDC (2006a) Geospatial Metadata Standards. Federal Geographic Data Committee. Available at: http://www.fgdc.gov/metadata/geospatial-metadata-standards.

FGDC (2006b) Creating and Publishing Metadata in Support of Geospatial One-Stop and the NSDI. Federal Geographic Data Committee. Available at: http://www.fgdc.gov/dataandservices/pub_guidance.

FGDC (2006c) NSDI Framework Introduction and Guide (Handbook). Federal Geographic Data Committee. Available at: http://www.fgdc.gov/framework/handbook/index_html.

Fitzke, J.; Atkinson, R. (2006) Gazetteer Service Profile of the Web Feature Service Implementation Specification, Version 0.9.1. OGC® Implementation Specification, OGC 05-035r1. Open Geospatial Consortium Inc.

Frew, J.; Freeston, M.; Freitas, N.; Hill, L.; Janée, G.; Lovette, K.; Nideffer, R.; Smith, T.; Zheng, Q. (2000) The Alexandria Digital Library architecture. *International Journal on Digital Libraries*, Vol. 2, No.4, pp. 259–268.

Fu, G.; Abdelmoty, A.; Jones, C. (2003) Design of a Geographical Ontology. SPIRIT - Spatially-Aware Information Retrieval on the Internet, EU IST Programme, D5 3101.

Gardels, K. (1996) The Open GIS approach to distributed geodata and geoprocessing. In: *Proceedings of the Third International Conference/Workshop on Integrating GIS and Environmental Modeling.* Santa Fe, NM, USA, pp. 21–25.

GNIS (2005) Geographic Names Information System. U.S. Department of the Interior, U.S. Geological Survey, Reston, USA. Available at: http://geonames.usgs.gov/index.html.

Gupta, A.; Zaslavsky, I.; Marciano, R. (2000) Generating query evaluation plans within a spatial mediation framework. In: *Proceedings of the Ninth International Symposium on Spatial Data Handling.* Beijing, China, pp. 8a18–8a31.

Haas, L.; Carey, M. (2003) Will federated databases ever go anywhere? In: *Lowell Database Research Self-Assessment Meeting.* Lowell, Massachusetts, USA.

Hill, L.L. (2000) Core elements of digital gazetteers: Placenames, categories, and footprints. In: J. Borbinha and T. Baker (Eds.) *Research and Advanced Technology for Digital Libraries*, pp. 280–290.

Hill, L.L.; Frew, J.; Zheng, Q. (1999) Geographic names: The implementation of a gazetteer in a georeferenced digital library. *D-Lib*, January 1999.

Hiramatsu, K.; Reitsma, F. (2004) GeoReferencing the Semantic Web: Ontology-based markup of geographically referenced information. In: *Proceedings of the Joint EuroSDR /EuroGeographics Workshop on Ontologies and Schema Translation Services.* Paris, France.

Hobbs, J. (2005) Interoperability among geospatial ontologies (Keynote Address). In: Rodríguez, M.A.; Cruz, I.F.; Levashkin, S.; Egenhofer, M.J. (Eds.) (2005) *Proceedings of the First International Conference on GeoSpatial Semantics - GeoS 2005*, Mexico City, Mexico, November 29–30, 2005. Available at: http://colab.cim3.net/file/work/SICoP/2006-06-20/JHobbs06202006.ppt.

Hobbs, J.; Pan, F. (2006) Time Ontology in OWL. Ontology Engineering Patterns Task Force of the Semantic Web Best Practices and Deployment Working Group, World Wide Web Consortium (W3C) notes, Editor's Draft.

INSPIRE (2004) INSPIRE: INfrastructure for SPatial InfoRmation in Europe. Commission of the European Communities. Brussels, Belgium. Available at: http://inspire.jrc.it/proposal/EN.pdf.

ISO (1986) Documentation - Guidelines for the development of monolingual thesauri. International Standard ISO-2788, Second edition.

ISO (2003) Geographic information – Metadata. Draft International Standard ISO/FDIS 19115:2003(E). International Organization for Standardization.

ISO (2003b) Geographic information – Spatial Referencing by Geographic Identifiers. ISO International Standard 19112:2003.

ISO (2005) Geographic Information - Services. ISO 19119:2005. International Organization for Standardization.

ISO (2006) Geographic information – Metadata – Implementation specification. ISO 19139 (2006, v1.0).

Islam, A.S.; Bermudez, L.; Beran, B.; Fellah, S.; Piasecki, M. (2004) Ontologies for ISO Geographic Information Standards. Available at: http://loki.cae.drexel.edu/~wbs/ontology/2004/09/bug/iso-19115/index.htm.

Kobler, B.; Berbert, J.; Caulk, P.; Hariharan, P.C. (1995) Architecture and design of storage and data management for the NASA earth observing system data and information system (EOSDIS). In: *Proceedings of the Fourteenth IEEE Symposium on Mass Storage Systems.* Monterey, California, USA, p. 65.

Lieberman, J.; Pehle, T.; Dean, M. (2005) Semantic evolution of geospatial Web services. In: *Proceedings of the Workshop on Frameworks for Semantics in Web Services, DERI,* Innsbruck, Austria. June 9–10.

Maguire, D.J.; Longley, P.A. (2005) The emergence of geoportals and their role in spatial data infrastructures. *Computers, Environment and Urban Systems,* Vol. 29, pp. 3–14.

Margoulies, S. (Ed.) (2001) Geocoder Service Specification. Version 0.7.6. OGC-IP Draft Candidate Implementation Specification OGC-01-026r1, Discussion Paper. Open Geospatial Consortium. Available at: http://feature.opengis.org/members/archive/arch01/01-026r1.pdf.

Meaux, M. (2005) Online metadata directories: A way of preserving, sharing and discovering scientific information. In: *Proceedings of the Gulf of Maine Ocean Data Partnership (GoMODP) Metadata Training Workshop,* Gulf of Maine Research Institute, Portland, ME, 19–20 October.

Mena, E.; Illarramendi, A.; Kashyap, V.; Sheth, A. (2000) OBSERVER: An approach for query processing in global information systems based on interoperation across pre-existing ontologies. *International Journal on Distributed and Parallel Databases (DAPD),* Vol. 8, No. 2, pp. 223–272.

Nebert, D.; Whiteside, A. (Eds.) (2005) OpenGIS® Catalogue Services Specification, Version 2.0.0 with Corrigendum, OpenGIS® Implementation Specification OGC 04-021r3, Open Geospatial Consortium.

Niles, I.; Pease, A. (2001) Towards a standard upper ontology. In: C. Welty and B. Smith (Eds.). *Proceedings of the Second International Conference on Formal Ontology in Information Systems (FOIS-2001),* Ogunquit, Maine, October 17–19, 2001.

Nogueras-Iso, J. (2005) Web ontology service, a key component of a spatial data infrastructure. In: *Proceedings of the Eleventh EC-GI & GIS Workshop, ESDI: Setting the Framework.* Alghero, Sardinia, 29th June – 1st July.

Nogueras-Iso, J.; Zarazaga-Soria, F.; Muro-Medrano, P. (2005) *Geographic Information Metadata for Spatial Data Infrastructures Resources, Interoperability and Information Retrieval.* New York, Springer-Verlag.

NSDI (2006) National Spatial Data Infrastructure. Available at: http://www.fgdc.gov/nsdi /nsdi.html.

OGC (2005) OGC to Begin Geospatial Semantic Web Interoperability Experiment. Press Release, 12/04/2005. Available at: http://www.opengeospatial.org/press/?page= pressrelease&year=0&prid=222.

Olsen, L. (2005) Data discovery worldwide using the Global Change Master Directory. In: *Proceedings of the Computing in Atmospheric Sciences Conference (CAS2K5)*, Annecy, France, 11–15 September.

Olsen, L. (2006) Private communication.

OpenCYC (2002) OpenCyc Selected Vocabulary and Upper Ontology - Geography. Cycorp. http://www.cyc.com/cycdoc/vocab/geography-vocab.html.

Percivall, G. (Ed.) (2002) The OpenGIS® Abstract Specification - Topic 12: OpenGIS® Service Architecture Version 4.3. OpenGIS® Project Document Number 02-112. Open GIS Consortium.

Rase, D.; Björnsson, A.; Probert, M.; Haupt, M-F. (Eds.) (2002) Reference Data and Metadata Position Paper. INSPIRE RDM PP v4-3 en. European Commission, Joint Research Centre. Available at: http://inspire.jrc.it/reports/position_papers/inspire_rdm_pp_v4_3_ en.pdf.

Raskin, R. (2006) Guide to SWEET Ontologies. NASA/Jet Propulsion Lab, Pasadena, CA, USA. Available at: http://sweet.jpl.nasa.gov/guide.doc.

Rodríguez, M.A.; Cruz, I.F.; Levashkin, S.; Egenhofer, M.J. (Eds.) (2005) *Proceedings of the First International Conference on GeoSpatial Semantics - GeoS 2005*, Mexico City, Mexico, November 29–30, 2005. Lecture Notes in Computer Science, Volume 3799, 2005, Berlin / Heidelberg, Springer.

Senkler, K.; Voges, U.; Remke, A. (2004) An ISO 19115/19119 Profile for the OGC Catalogue Services CSW 2.0. In: *Proceedings of the tenth EC GI & GIS Workshop, ESDI State of the Art*, Warsaw, Poland, 23–25 June.

SERF (2006) Service Entry Resource Format (SERF) Writer's Guide. Global Change Master Directory. National Aeronautics and Space Administration. Available at: http://gcmd.nasa.gov/serfguide/.

Smith, T.R. (1996) A digital library for geographically referenced materials. *IEEE Computer*, Vol. 29, No. 5, pp. 54–60.

Smith, T.R.; Frew, J. (1995) Alexandria Digital Library. *Communications of the ACM*, Vol. 38, No. 4, pp. 61–62.

Smits, P (Ed) (2002) INSPIRE Architecture and Standards Position Paper. INSPIRE AST PP v4-3 en. European Commission, Joint Research Centre. Available at: http://inspire.jrc.it/ reports/position_papers/inspire_ast_pp_v4_3_en.pdf.

Sonnet, J. (Ed) (2004) OWS 2 Common Architecture: WSDL SOAP UDDI, Version: 1.0.0. Discussion Paper OGC 04-060r1. Open Geospatial Consortium, Inc.

Souza, L.A. et al. (2005) The role of gazetteers in geographic knowledge discovery on the Web. In: *Proceedings of the Third Latin American Web Congress*. Buenos Aires, Argentina.

Stubkjær, E. (2001) Integrating ontologies: Assessing the use of the Cyc ontology for cadastral applications. In: *Proceedings of the Eighth Scandinavian Research Conference on Geographical Information Science - ScanGIS'2001.* Ås, Norway, 25th–27th June.

SUMO (2006) Suggested Upper Merged Ontology (SUMO). Available at: http://www.ontologyportal.org/.

SWEET (2006) The Semantic Web for Earth and Environmental Terminology (SWEET). Jet Propulsion Laboratory, California Institute of Technology. Available at: http://sweet.jpl.nasa.gov/index.html.

TGN (2004) Thesaurus of Geographical Names. The Getty Foundation. Available at: http://www.getty.edu/research/tools/vocabulary/tgn.

USMARC (1976) A MARC Format, in OFFICE, L. O. C. M. D., ed., Washington, D.C., Library of Congress Information Systems Office.

Voges, U.; Senkler, K. (2006) OpenGIS® Catalogue Services Specification 2.0.1 (with Corrigendum) - ISO Metadata Application Profile. OpenGIS® Application Profile OGC 04-038r4, Version: 1.0. Open Geospatial Consortium Inc.

Whiteside, A. (Ed) (2005) OpenGIS® Web services architecture description, Version: 0.1.0. OpenGIS® Best Practices, OGC 05-042r2. Open Geospatial Consortium Inc.

Wordnet (2005). Wordnet - A lexical database for the English language. Cognitive Science Laboratory, Princeton University, Princeton, NJ, USA. Available at: http://wordnet.princeton.edu.

Index